American Soccer

American Soccer

History, Culture, Class

Gregory G. Reck *and*
Bruce Allen Dick

McFarland & Company, Inc., Publishers
Jefferson, North Carolina

LIBRARY OF CONGRESS CATALOGUING-IN-PUBLICATION DATA

Reck, Gregory G., 1945–
American soccer : history, culture, class / Gregory G. Reck and Bruce Allen Dick.
p. cm.
Includes bibliographical references and index.

ISBN 978-0-7864-9628-0 (softcover : acid free paper) ♾
ISBN 978-1-4766-1756-5 (ebook)

1. Soccer—United States—History. 2. Soccer—Social aspects—United States. 3. Social structure—United States. I. Dick, Bruce, 1953– II. Title.

GV944.U6R44 2015
796.3340973—dc23 2014046591

BRITISH LIBRARY CATALOGUING DATA ARE AVAILABLE

Printed in the United States of America

McFarland & Company, Inc., Publishers
Box 611, Jefferson, North Carolina 28640
www.mcfarlandpub.com

For Gabriella, Melanie, Julien,
Ahana, Annie, Ava, and Beau

Table of Contents

Acknowledgments

First and foremost, we want to thank our good friend and colleague, Andrés Fisher, for helping us coach our daughters' soccer team for three years and for teaching us the intricacies of the game of soccer. His knowledge and passion for the sport are contagious. We hope this book reflects his friendship and valuable insights.

We also want to thank V. Kemp Jones from Athens, Georgia, who provided an original soundtrack for our documentary video on youth soccer, *Offside(s): Soccer in Small-Town America.* Kemp also read chapters of this book and provided valuable suggestions on how to improve the manuscript.

The contributions of other authors made this book possible. In particular, we'd like to thank Roger Allaway, Colin Jose, David Litterer, and David Wangerin for their dedication to keeping soccer history alive. We'd also like to thank author Paul Cuadros for his support over the years and for the information he provides in his writings about Latino soccer in North Carolina.

Appalachian State University supported this project in numerous ways. We want to thank ASU's past and present soccer coaching staff for both providing archival material and granting interviews for our chapter on Appalachian soccer. In particular, we'd like to thank Vaughn Christian, Hank Steinbrecher, Art Rex, Paul Stahlschmidt, Ben Popoola, and Matthew Nelson for their support. Steve DeGroat also supplied biographical material for his father, Eric DeGroat, ASU's first varsity men's soccer coach. Jim Jones, retired athletic director, likewise provided valuable information on the early years of ASU soccer. And we never could have written the ASU chapter without the information provided by Emmanuel "Ike" Udogu and Thompson Usiyan, Appalachian stars from the 1970s.

The technical assistance we received from Appalachian was invaluable. Jeremy Wright formatted our documentary and parts of this book. A former

North Carolina soccer player, he also gave us insight into the club soccer experience. Tom McDonnell, computer technologist in ASU's College of Arts and Sciences, provided support from the very beginning. Gabrielle Motta-Passajou also lent her technical skills for both the documentary and the book, as did Edison Midgett from the Department of Art. Working with two technological dinosaurs, these faculty and staff members taught us the difference between "My Documents" and "My Computer."

We also need to thank ASU's library staff, especially John Boyd and Beth Cramer, for their continuous support. Other colleagues in the university and friends in the larger soccer community provided assistance and encouragement. We'd especially like to thank Jeff Boyer, Tom Whyte, Diane Mines, Leon Lewis, Tom McLaughlin, Mark Vogel, Jim Fogelquist, Carl Eby, Leslie Cook, Alfredo Alvarez, Gabriel Raeburn, Don Porterfield, Lucas Clary, and our brothers. In addition, the College of Arts and Sciences and ASU's Hubbard Center provided financial assistance along the way. Conversations with numerous other faculty, staff, students and friends likewise should not go unnoticed.

Finally, we thank our children—Melanie, Julien, Ahana, Annie and Ava (and Lucia, Andrés's daughter)—whose years of playing soccer inspired us to write this book. They were especially gracious for tolerating their fathers as coaches. Thanks also go to the other girls (and their parents) whom we coached over the years. They added humor and humanity to that chapter of our lives.

Preface

American Soccer: History, Culture, Class offers a unique critical and historical overview of American soccer from its working-class origins in the 1880s to the present. It also provides a participatory perspective on the sport, including a chapter on our own three-year involvement as coaches of youth soccer in the Appalachian community of Boone, North Carolina, where we live, as well as local case studies of university and Latino soccer.

While there are books on particular historical soccer moments and a number of treatises written by soccer enthusiasts on esoteric soccer subjects, as well as websites with soccer statistics and minutia, there are no other books that we know of that conflate all of this material inside a single cover, especially one that brings a critical cultural studies perspective to the sport. Our book is not just a historical summary of the past and present U.S. soccer landscape but also a narrative with an accessible viewpoint that addresses the central issue of the socioeconomic space occupied by U.S. soccer. The history of soccer in the United States is informative in itself, but its real purpose in this book is to demonstrate a stark contrast with the socioeconomic space occupied by soccer in the United States today. The sections on contemporary soccer cover that landscape—from its beginnings in relatively informal Parks and Recreation leagues through more formal club soccer programs, university soccer, professional soccer, and U.S. national teams.

We became interested in the cultural landscape of American soccer after we coached our daughters in a county Parks and Recreation youth soccer league. That experience led to a documentary video titled *Offside(s): Soccer in Small-Town America,* which examines five local soccer venues in our small, mountainous community. The feedback we received after screening the video at film festivals and professional conferences convinced us that our own story as coaches and related soccer experiences were tied to multiple threads of soccer on other levels around the country. This book explores those links.

Because our book is a comprehensive overview of both the past and present cultural landscape of U.S. soccer, the most important similar texts in print include two books by David Wangerin: *Soccer in a Football World: The Story of America's Forgotten Game* (2006) and *Distant Corners: American Soccer's History of Missed Opportunities and Lost Causes* (2011). Our book differs from those of Wangerin in several ways, however. Wangerin's texts focus almost exclusively on the history of male national teams and professional leagues. While our book overlaps in some of the history of U.S. soccer Wangerin outlines in his work, it adopts a much broader examination of the total past and present landscape of U.S. soccer and includes material on the relatively recent development of women's soccer, the origins and development of youth soccer, the alternative narrative of Hispanic soccer leagues in the United States, and historical and contemporary material on national and professional soccer. Our book does not present itself as a history of the highest levels of soccer in the United States, but rather as a broad overview of soccer's past and present that includes material not present in Wangerin's work.

Equally important, this book contains an accessible theoretical perspective that is both critical and prescriptive. It includes an analysis of class and immigration that is metaphorically embedded in Jürgen Klinsmann's observation of "the upside down pyramid" associated with American soccer, whereby a pay-to-play system of development discriminates against prospective youth players across the country. Although we cover a significant amount of soccer history in our book, we emphasize the difference between the social class space occupied by U.S. soccer in the past and the space it occupies today. Viewing the cultural space of soccer through this critical lens allows one to see the stark contrast between U.S. soccer of the past and the present, as well as the obvious differences between American soccer and that in the rest of the world. Using this theoretical lens, this book serves as both a critique of U.S. soccer based on social analysis and a prescription for reconfiguring that space to make soccer in the United States more competitive and broadly appealing.

Introduction

Why write another book on soccer?

This is a question we've asked ourselves numerous times over the last three years. After all, in addition to the almost limitless number of "how-to" books on playing and coaching soccer, the market is flooded with soccer minutia—from treatises on hooliganism, pitch strategies, and international gender discrimination to detailed analyses of players, teams, leagues, and World Cup matches. Fiction writers, memoirists, journalists, essayists, poets, biographers, and scholars have all joined the fray, churning out countless titles on just as many subjects related to soccer. Of course, for dedicated soccer fans whose appetites cannot be satiated by detail, enough is never enough. Others may scratch their heads and wonder what the fuss is all about.

The issue is not so much the sheer volume of books as it is the curious diversity of angles taken. It's almost as if soccer has transcended its own mundane existence as a sport to acquire the larger-than-life qualities of mythology—a body of stories full of heroes, metaphors of panhuman struggles, and the ongoing search for the meaning of existence.

The seemingly unending list includes memoirs of well-known soccer players like Pelé (*My Life and the Beautiful Game*) and lesser-known soccer players, including former Southampton forward Matthew Le Tissier (*Taking Le Tiss*), which reveal the flaws, foibles, and victories that define true heroes. There are also dramatic histories of U.S. soccer, English soccer, Italian soccer, and Brazilian soccer. And there are heartwarming and often gut-wrenching stories of soccer in different social contexts, among them Mexican and African immigrant kids defying the odds while competing against wealthy, predominantly white high school teams (*The Boys of Little Mexico; Home on the Field; Outcast United*), or soccer in violence-torn settings (*This Love Is Not for Cowards: Salvation and Soccer in Ciudad Juarez*).

As if these were not enough, there is a book applying economic theory to successes and failures in the world of international professional soccer (*Soccernomics*), which argues that statistics and cost-benefit analysis can explain why England loses, why Scotland allegedly "sucks," and why the United States and Japan are destined to be soccer superpowers. There is a book on the philosophy of soccer (*Soccer and Philosophy*) that compares Cristiano Ronaldo's artful feet to the genius of Picasso and the masterful, intuitive moves of Pelé to Plato. The book also answers the question that plagues soccer fans everywhere: What team would Nietzsche have supported? There is yet another book on the scientific side of the sport (*The Science of Soccer*) that examines such "critical" issues as the physics of a soccer ball in flight contrasted with the physics of a soccer ball bouncing, something that, perhaps, players like Pelé, Beckham, and Messi intuitively understand, just as Einstein apparently intuited his famous formula, $E = mc^2$. There is even a book (*How Soccer Explains the World*) that persuasively views soccer as a central analytic category for explaining the positive and negative complexities of globalization.

For the soccer fan uninterested in science, philosophy, economics, and globalization theory (and perhaps seeking more lurid topics), there is a book claiming that world soccer is endangered by corruption and the murky world of organized Asian crime (*The Fix: Soccer and Organized Crime*), or books that promise tabloid-like excursions into the secret sexual lives of soccer celebrities, losers, boozers, and abusers (*Playing Away: The A–Z of Soccer Sex Scandals* and *Hampden Babylon: Sex and Scandal in Scottish Football*). One can almost imagine the next big reality TV show—*The Wives of Manchester United.*

And these are just the tip of the iceberg, or, in soccer jargon, a meter of the pitch. Even in a soccer-suspect nation like the United States, there is certainly enough writing on soccer to go around.

The most obvious answer to the question of writing another book about soccer is: Why not? After all, soccer is the only truly international sport actively played in almost every country in the world. It's as universal as marriage, kinship, religion, sex, and war. Just because sports enthusiasts in the United States often classify soccer, along with water ballet and curling, as marginal to the world of *real* sports, or because media pundits like Glenn Beck, Rush Limbaugh, and G. Gordon Liddy vilify soccer as a foreign sport systematically crammed down the throats of *real* Americans by the liberal media in order to "feminize" the American male and establish European socialism, doesn't mean that soccer is without global significance.

The Fédération Internationale de Football Association (FIFA) ranks 207 national men's teams in the world. No other sport comes close to that mark. With new nations emerging around the globe almost every year, this number might not cover all of them, but at least the national teams of Tahiti, American Samoa, and Papua New Guinea make the list. Not surprisingly, Spain, the winner of the 2010 World Cup, is ranked number one based on World Cup performance and international friendlies over the past four years. But who would guess which country is ranked at the bottom of the heap? As of December 2013, Turks and Caicos Islands, San Marino, and Bhutan were all tied at 207th. The fact that most people have never heard of these countries, and that even fewer can identify their geographic locations on a world map, surely attests to the global reach of the sport. Otherwise invisible countries—invisible at least to those who do not live or vacation there—nevertheless field national soccer teams. They are also members of FIFA, the governing branch of international soccer and arguably the most inclusive athletic organization in the world.

On the women's side, FIFA ranks 176 national teams, a number that is particularly impressive since the first FIFA women's World Cup wasn't held until 1991. The United States is currently ranked number one in the world, a position it has maintained for five straight years. Comoros is ranked at the bottom. International women's teams fielded not only by predictable countries in Europe, North and South America, Africa and Asia but also by those countries least expected, from Bhutan to Qatar (host of the 2022 men's World Cup), Comoros to Fiji, the Solomon Islands to Kyrgyzstan.

Journalist John Doyle writes in *The World Is a Ball* (2010) that in Brazil children are taught that the soccer ball is a symbol for Mother Earth, and that when they stroke, caress, and propel the ball with their feet, the children are like gods rotating Mother Earth through space, creatively and respectfully. Although this imagery and its impact on the style of what Brazilians call *futebol de arte*, an official national treasure, cannot be measured (nor, perhaps, even understood by anyone other than Brazilians), the metaphor is not a far stretch. In the global sports world, the earth and the soccer ball actually seem to be one and the same.

Even in the United States, a country notable for its complacency, if not outright hostility, toward soccer, the game is gaining unprecedented popularity. According to youth programs across the country, more children play organized soccer today than any other sport, including the "big three" of baseball, basketball, and football. The U.S. Men's National Team (USMNT) has qualified for seven consecutive World Cups, while the women's national team has won two of the six women's World Cups and placed either second or third in the other four. A reasonably viable professional league for men—Major League

Soccer—is operating in 17 U.S. cities and two Canadian cities. After two earlier failed attempts, a professional women's league, the National Women's Soccer League, was revived in 2013.

To the chagrin of naysayer commentators, U.S. TV ratings for the 2010 World Cup increased by 22 percent from the 2006 World Cup. While the numbers might pale in comparison to the 106.5 million people in the United States who watched the 2010 Super Bowl, almost 20 million Americans watched the United States lose its final soccer match that same year to Ghana. A record 24 million people in the United States watched Spain defeat the Netherlands in the 2010 World Cup final.

While this obviously global reach of soccer and the even more remarkable growth of the sport in the United States might be reason enough to write yet another book on soccer, we were motivated by different concerns. For us it all started rather innocently, in the mountains of Boone, North Carolina, during the summer of 2005.

* * * *

As friends and colleagues who had three daughters roughly the same age, we joined the thousands of other parent volunteers who support the youth soccer movement in this country, primarily through coaching. It mattered little that we'd grown up in the 1950s and 1960s playing baseball, basketball, and football, and that we had never set foot on a soccer field before. We took comfort in the fact that most parents who volunteered at this recreational level had never played soccer either. We convinced a third friend and colleague, Andrés Fisher, who grew up in Chile playing both soccer and rugby, to give us a hand. We reasoned that sharing responsibilities between coaching and carpooling was a functional plan.

To our surprise, we had a successful team and lots of fun. Over dinner one evening we decided we'd continue coaching our daughters as they progressed through subsequent levels of play. We also had other children participating in recreational and club soccer, so jockeying our time became a primary concern. While we finished two additional seasons coaching our daughters' team, our focus shifted in unexpected ways. In the academic world we call this transformation *serendipity*. Most people outside the university call it dumb luck.

As academics teaching and researching in different disciplines aligned with cultural studies, we began exploring the landscape of youth soccer through the lens of our direct experience. We also started to straddle that precarious fence between participation and observation. While we continued to pursue our role of parents-turned-soccer-coaches, our mutual curiosity about the cultural space occupied by soccer began to create a kind of psychic dissonance, an alienation from that role. Our soccer discussions shifted from questions about the next match or simple field strategies to issues regarding the relationship of youth soccer to class, ethnicity, and cultural symbols. It wasn't long before these interests started to trump our interest in coaching.

Our ongoing questions eventually led to the decision to shoot a documentary video, using our experience as coaches and fathers and the local soccer landscape as a case study to examine larger issues that were beginning to take shape. We looked closely at our own team and the local soccer surroundings. And we asked more questions. Why were the kids we coached even at this recreational level so uniformly white and middle to upper middle class? Where were the Latino kids who were moving into the area in increasing numbers? Why did so many parents seem to know or care so little about the larger world of soccer? How did parents manage to pay so much in time and money to allow their kids to play more competitive club soccer?

As we researched, filmed, and edited, we realized that the story of soccer on our local level was tied to the multiple and complex threads of soccer on other levels. The more we pulled on the thread of local soccer, the longer it became, and we soon began exploring the connections between the various spaces occupied by soccer in the United States—from recreational, club, high school, and university soccer to Latino, national, and international soccer. We talked with parents whose kids played in different competitive venues. We interviewed current and past players, as well as coaches of youth and university teams. We spoke to friends and colleagues who had grown up playing soccer in Iran, Costa Rica, Mexico, Germany, Nigeria, England, and Chile. We conversed with players and organizers of local Latino league teams. We documented a successful high school team comprised primarily of Hispanic kids, none of whom had played club soccer. We crisscrossed back and forth between the local and the global. Our experience was often dizzying.

After three years of filming, we edited the hours of footage into a 56-minute documentary. We called it *Offside(s): Soccer in Small-Town America.* The documentary screened at two national film festivals, an international film festival, and a professional academic meeting.

While shooting the documentary, we simultaneously immersed ourselves in the popular culture world of soccer. We read numerous books of fiction and nonfiction and watched almost as many documentary and feature films. Such immersion made us realize that the global reach of soccer was much more intricately implicit than could be measured by the sports empire of FIFA or the increase in player participation in the United States.

We also studied the history of soccer in the United States and discovered that while most Americans lack historical memory, in the case of soccer it's pure amnesia. Few but the most ardent fans know that soccer has been played in the United States for more than 125 years; that soccer was the second major sport, after baseball, to organize professionally; that the U.S. soccer establishment joined FIFA in the same year as that icon of the beautiful game, Brazil; and that the U.S. Men's National Team placed third in the first FIFA World Cup in 1930. We also discovered the rollercoaster ride that U.S. soccer has traveled, and how the cultural landscape of soccer in this country has shifted dramatically over the past four decades.

It was this immersion into the past and present cultural landscape of soccer in the United States that convinced us we had something unique to say. While the history of U.S. soccer can be found in various bits and pieces, that history, just like the U.S. or world history taught in junior high school, tends to focus on dates, names, and data. Little is said about the cultural landscape of the past, and even less is said about the contrasts with the present scene. This book attempts to weave together those bits and pieces in order to paint contrasting and informative portraits of the past and present.

However, our book is not just a description; it's also a prescription for needed transformations in the present cultural landscape of U.S. soccer. Many people who are more intimately involved in the world of soccer, from the youth to the national team level, are critically examining the deficiencies of soccer in the United States, and there are signs that a restructuring of the organizational characteristics of the sport is on the horizon. To our knowledge, there is no single, lengthy source that examines this organizational restructuring within the context of soccer's cultural origins and the past and present landscape. This book is designed to do just that.

In Section One, we analyze U.S. soccer as a pyramid turned upside down—a metaphor first proposed by Jürgen Klinsmann, the former German striker and recently hired head coach of the USMNT. Klinsmann claimed that because parents have to pay considerable sums of money and invest demanding blocks of time for their children to play more competitive soccer, U.S. soccer excludes potential athletes who could very well raise the competitive bar of the sport. We also contrast the pay-to-play youth development structure so prevalent in this country with the successful development structures that exist in Germany and Japan, the former rich in soccer tradition and the latter a relative newcomer. Section Two examines the history of U.S. soccer from the late 1800s to recent times. This historical overview not only demonstrates that soccer in the United States has long been present in the sports landscape but also illustrates that for several decades the United States had the pyramid right side up, populated by immigrant, working-class, and international players. The final section examines the multifaceted present landscape of U.S. soccer: from grassroots Parks and Recreation programs and organized youth club systems to university soccer, and from Hispanic leagues to professional and international soccer. It also includes selected case studies of soccer found in our local community. The Conclusion summarizes the major ideas of the book and describes how making the documentary film *Offside(s)* led to a more thorough examination of the larger landscape of U.S. soccer. Finally, the Afterword includes a brief statement on the 2014 World Cup, held in Brazil.

Throughout each section we've tried to maintain a critical eye that both paints a comprehensive portrait of U.S. soccer and suggests deficiencies in the American system. We don't examine these deficiencies in terms of technique or strategy, coaching staffs, or specific personnel. Our focus is instead on the cultural space that soccer occupies in the United States yesterday and today. In addition, we have tried to balance our critical approach with a personal touch. We believe that combining the analytical and the anecdotal provides a more thorough picture of the soccer landscape, and that a book from the point of view of both an observer of and a participant in the sport presents a fresh perspective.

While soccer in the United States is showing signs of carving out a viable space within the cultural landscape of sports and entertainment, intractable issues that stunt the growth of this organic game still remain. As others have pointed out, these issues include the multifaceted competitive environment of sports entertainment in the United States; the critical financial component of television and the subsequent conflict of balancing the 45-minute, nonstop action of soccer halves with frequent television commercials; the various business realities of major sports; and the sense among too many Americans that soccer is a "foreign" sport. No one can discount the importance of these issues, but many soccer fans sense that something deeper explains the continuing marginality of soccer in the U.S. sports landscape.

This latter realization highlights another paradox. Even though significant numbers of youth and adults have played organized soccer at some point in their lives, this participation has not translated into a permanent fan base. In the United States, soccer is a sport played by millions but embraced by only a few, particularly over a lifetime. For the supportive parents or young players, once those often arduous days of participating in youth soccer are finished, interest in the sport evaporates like dew. When we polled students in our classes, we found that almost half of them had played organized soccer when younger—yet almost none of them had attended a university soccer match. Even fewer students followed professional U.S. or international soccer. In our contact with parents of kids who played either recreational or club soccer, we found that very few of them truly understood the sport or were interested in the larger arena of soccer beyond their children's immediate experience. They might spend dozens of hours each week taking their children to soccer practice and weekend matches over multiple years as well as thousands of dollars for their kids' club soccer experiences, but neither the experience nor the investment of time or money translated into a genuine passion for the game.

Analyzing this paradox is the ultimate thread that links this book. Such an analysis provides the key to unraveling the present social and cultural context of soccer in the United States. It also presents a way of understanding why soccer has failed to become a larger part of the popular imagination of most Americans, and of comprehending why U.S. soccer lacks the organic passion that melds together the Brazilian *futebol de arte* with *futebol de resultados.*

We should clarify that this book focuses primarily on male soccer leagues, teams, and players instead of their female counterparts. This focus is an editorial decision based on our personal contact and familiarity with Appalachian State University's men's soccer program, our local Latino league, the U.S. Men's National Team, and the realization that competitive women's soccer is relatively new. We do examine various leagues, teams, and individual players who have made an impact on the international soccer scene, however. We also believe that detailing our three-year experience of coaching our daughters in a local Parks and Recreation youth soccer league helps balance the seemingly disproportionate attention paid to men's soccer.

Finally, when analyzing various Latino/Hispanic leagues and teams in North Carolina and the rest of the country, we use the terms "Latino" and "Hispanic" interchangeably throughout the book.

We hope that the perspectives presented here encapsulate our unexpected journey and contribute to the ongoing discussion about how the beauty, art, and physical skills ingrained in soccer might become more deeply embedded in the U.S. fan base and players of the one and only truly global sport.

Section One: A Theoretical Perspective

1

The Pyramid Upside Down

With smoke from a nearby grass fire hovering over the Royal Bafokeng Stadium in Rustenburg, South Africa, the U.S. Men's National Team (USMNT) prepared to meet Ghana in the round of sixteen at the 2010 World Cup. Just three days earlier, after a dramatic last-second goal gave the United States a 1–0 victory over Algeria and propelled them into the knockout round, a surprise clubhouse visit from former president Bill Clinton had raised the U.S. team's spirits seemingly even more than the victory. Clinton was in South Africa not just as a loyal fan but also as the honorary chairman of the U.S. effort to host either the 2018 or the 2022 World Cup. He had planned to deliver a few congratulatory remarks, but he ended up drinking beer and celebrating with the team for 45 minutes. "Imagine," one player remarked after Clinton left, "the ex–President of the United States said that *we* made *him* proud to be an American."[1] One would have thought that the team, like David, had just conquered Goliath. The reality was that Algeria, with a pre-tournament FIFA ranking of thirtieth in the world, was more like the mouse that almost roared against the fourteenth-ranked U.S. squad.

The U.S. team had staggered through the group stage. After initial draws with a stronger England and a much weaker Slovenia, the team needed a victory against Algeria, a less impressive team on paper, to advance. They escaped by the skin of their teeth when Landon Donovan scored the lone goal in stoppage time seconds before the final whistle that would've sent the match into an unpredictable overtime. Although the victory enabled the team to move into the round of sixteen, something they had failed to accomplish in 2006, their play had been less than inspiring.

Now they faced Ghana. In 2006, the United States had been eliminated in the group stage when they lost to Ghana 2–1 in their final match. Ghana returned with most of the players from that 2006 team, including the talented center forward, Asamoah Gyan, who in 2003, at the age of 17, became the youngest Ghanaian national team player to score a goal in a World Cup qualifier. For the 2010 World Cup match, bookies marked the United States a 6–4 favorite, partly because Ghana had struggled offensively in its previous three matches—the team's only two goals had come on penalty shots by Gyan—and partly because pre-tournament standings ranked Ghana thirty-second in the world, far below the United States.

After the victory against Algeria, Clinton rearranged his schedule so that he could attend the Ghana match. He was joined in the FIFA VIP box by rock icon Mick Jagger, Los Angeles Lakers golden boy Kobe Bryant, Sarah Palin destroyer Katie Couric, and FIFA bigwigs. Like previous matches in the Rustenburg stadium, the crowd was far from capacity, with only 34,976 fans in the newly expanded, 42,000-seat stadium. Days earlier, a match between New Zealand and Slovakia in the same venue had actually drawn a larger crowd, a curiosity given that this match pitted the only surviving African team against a favored U.S. team.

As the match began, no one in the stands or on the field knew that the United States was about to solidify its reputation as a team whose defense seemed to sleepwalk through the first minutes of play. The team had struggled from behind in their two 2010 World Cup draws, allowing a goal to England in the fourth minute and to Slovenia in the thirteenth minute. This tendency to give up early goals was particularly dangerous because the United States had never won a World Cup match in which they allowed the opposition to score first. Almost before the crowd had settled into their seats, in the fifth minute of play, Ghanaian midfielder Kevin-Prince Boateng and the sleeping U.S. defense reaffirmed the American reputation, putting Ghana up 1–0. Ghana stole the ball at midfield and Boateng, streaking downfield as if it was tethered to his feet, seemed to catch the U.S. defenders by surprise for the goal from 15 yards out. The quick score by the only remaining African team in the first World Cup to be played on the African continent sent the crowd into a frenzy of *vuvuzela* blasts. The U.S. players now wondered if they could come back and accomplish a feat they'd never managed before.

In the sixty-second minute of play, the U.S. team struck to equalize. Midfielder Bennie Feilhaber sent a hard pass to Landon Donovan, who made a difficult back heel touch to Clint Dempsey. In turn, Dempsey flicked the ball neatly between an advancing defender's legs and broke out toward the goal. As Dempsey raced into the box straight toward the goalie, defender Jonathan Mensah tried to reach the ball before Dempsey could get the shot off. Instead, he took Dempsey to the ground for an in-the-box foul. Donovan's ensuing penalty kick ricocheted off the right post for the tying goal, his third of the 2010 World Cup. Both teams had chances during the final minutes, but the match ended in a 1–1 draw after regulation time.

Just three minutes into non-regulation play, Ghanaian midfielder Andre Ayew sent a long, arching pass downfield from his own defensive half. In the middle of the U.S. side, Gyan controlled the pass with a slight chest touch, and then sprinted downfield. Absorbing a hard bump from defender Carlos Bocanegra, Gyan maintained his balance and split two defenders. Like a muscled, slippery eel, he squeezed through the opening. As the ball bounced erratically forward, he caught it with his left foot after a high bounce and sent it over the leaping goalie, Tim Howard, for the go-ahead goal. Once again, the United States gave up a fast goal. Over the final 17 minutes, the Ghanaian defense thwarted the U.S. offense time and again. When the final whistle sounded, just as it had four years earlier, Ghana defeated the United States by a score of 2–1.

While Ghana and the entire African continent celebrated, and the largest television crowd in the United States to ever watch the men's national team play a World Cup match mourned yet another disappointment, ESPN, which had covered the match live in the United States, prepared for its post-game wrap-up.

The ESPN commentators included former German national team striker Jürgen Klinsmann, who had been approached four years earlier as a possible replacement for USMNT coach Bruce Arena, after his team's disappointment at the 2006 World Cup. At that time, as a condition for hire, Klinsmann had asked that the U.S. Soccer Federation give him full control over restructuring the country's player development system. Unable to reach an agreement, league officials overlooked Klinsmann and named Bob Bradley coach for the 2010 World Cup.

Since its surprise victory over England in 1950, the United States had not performed consistently in World Cup play. From 1954 to 1986, the team failed to qualify for the tournament nine consecutive times. Although they've qualified for all seven World Cups since 1990, they reached the round of sixteen only three times—in 1994, 2002, and 2010. They advanced to the quarterfinals once, in 2002. Since 1990, their overall World Cup record posted a paltry four wins, five draws, and 13 defeats. In 22 matches, they had been outscored 35–20 goals.[2]

With this mediocre history and the recent loss to Ghana as a backdrop, an ESPN commentator asked Klinsmann during the post-match broadcast to assess the current state of U.S. soccer. Klinsmann observed quite confidently that the United States is "the only country in the world that has the pyramid upside down." He hinted that after the earlier last-minute victory over Algeria, the U.S. players seemed more interested in rubbing elbows with Clinton than in concentrating on the upcoming match with Ghana. The team "failed to live up to expectations," he proclaimed.[3]

Klinsmann stressed the need for the United States to "lay out a philosophy" and to ask itself "where [it wanted] to go." He advocated overhauling player development, but he also admitted the difficulty of discussing "that topic" because so much was invested in the current system. He likewise elaborated on why the United States suffered during international competition: "You [the United States] pay for your kid to play soccer. Because your goal is not to have your kid become a professional soccer player; your goal is [to get your kid] a scholarship [to] high school or college, which is the complete opposite of the rest of the world."[4]

Klinsmann maintained that the rest of the world's players who progress to national levels come from "moderate families" and "f[i]ght [their] way through." Such a modest path provides a "hunger" for the game that lasts "throughout life." He concluded that the United States needed to find ways to connect "with everybody in the soccer environment." Klinsmann recommended weaving "really hungry" players, especially Hispanic players, into the fabric of American soccer. Only then would the United States produce quality teams capable of competing at the international level.[5]

Klinsmann's remarks didn't go unnoticed. Fellow ESPN anchor Alexi Lalas, who had played soccer at Rutgers University and against Klinsmann internationally in the 1990s, sat bewilderedly during Klinsmann's critique. One can only imagine what the former collegiate standout and national team striker was thinking. Within the hour, more than a handful of pundits dismissed his comments as off-the-cuff sound bites lacking substantive insight. Some die-hard fans and apologists called them elitist, unfounded, and even traitorous. One U.S. blogger who was playing professionally on a second-tier German professional team accused Klinsmann of trying to impose a German model over a perfectly viable and productive American one, and wanting to substitute players of questionable U.S. citizenship for "real" citizens. Such concerns seemed to echo the insulated, defensive exceptionalism that at times has infected the U.S. sports landscape. Who was this *German* criticizing the U.S. system anyway? And what did a *European* know about American sports?

Despite these reactions, others supported Klinsmann's candid stand, recognizing that the former German striker-turned-coach, businessman, and consultant had leveled similar charges four years earlier when being considered for the coaching position of the USMNT. Klinsmann certainly had the credentials for dissecting how soccer was played in the United States and elsewhere. His professional career as a player had spanned more than two decades with top-tier teams in Germany, Italy, France, and England. From the Bundesliga in Germany to the Premier League in England, Klinsmann had played against some of the very best teams in the world. He had started for Germany's national team in three World Cups, including the West German team that won the 1990 World Cup. He was named an outstanding German footballer in 1988 and again in 1992. His coaching career had been short, but he led the German national squad to a third place finish in the 2006 World Cup and had coached one of his old German teams, Bayern Munich, to a record of 25–9–9 in the Bundesliga and inter–European competition in 2008–2009. During his stint with the German national team, he had become an integral part of restructuring the German youth development program that began in 1999. Nor was he a stranger to U.S. soccer. He had lived in the United States for over 12 years, married an American wife, and was once rumored to be in line for the head coach job with Major League Soccer's L.A. Galaxy.

After the disappointing performance in the 2010 World Cup, Klinsmann was in line once again for the USMNT coaching position. However, the U.S. Soccer Federation signed Coach Bob Bradley instead, after negotiations with Klinsmann fell through a second time. The following year the USMNT competed against Central American and Caribbean national teams in the CONCACAF Gold Cup series. The United States had experienced recent success in this competition, winning the Cup four times since 1991, including Bradley's first year as coach in 2007; the team had finished second three times. But during the finals of the 2009 Gold Cup, Bradley's squad suffered a humiliating 5–0 shutout to Mexico. To add insult to injury, after making it to the same final against Mexico in 2011, the U.S. team suffered another lopsided, 4–2 trouncing. The loss was Bradley's death knell. Some 30 days later, almost 13 months after the World Cup defeat by Ghana, the U.S. Soccer Federation appointed Klinsmann head coach of the USMNT. The Federation gave him more control over player development and a chance to turn the team around.

Since his appointment and subsequent charge, Klinsmann's confrontational ESPN assessment takes on added significance. As head coach, he might very well restructure the U.S. soccer landscape in ways that properly address the problems to which he alluded. As he suggested in his post-game review, however, dislodging such a culturally embedded system of player development is no easy task. Overhauling the current structure is even more daunting when considering the astronomical sum of money involved in American soccer today. While Klinsmann's remarks certainly suggest comprehension of the problem, the answers are much more complex than even he might imagine. Only a more detailed exposition of American soccer both past and present will lead to a fuller awareness of the difficult challenges that lie ahead. At the same time, Klinsmann's disjointed pyramid provides an appropriate starting point for such an analysis.

* * * *

Picture an upside-down pyramid—a strange, geometric figure resting precariously on its point and spreading uniformly upward and outward to a top-heavy, base-turned peak. Three conclusions come to mind. First, the point of entry to such a structure is narrow compared to that of a right-side-up pyramid. Second, the base, which is now the point, is insufficient to support the redesigned structure and dangerously close to collapse. Finally, the structural aesthetic is no longer a sleek form reaching majestically to the sky. It is now a clumsy, unstable, unappealing form that communicates little of the functional grandeur of a right-side-up pyramid.

Imagine if the early civilizations of Egypt and Mesoamerica, the architects *par excellence* of pyramid design, had constructed such edifices. Rather than prime examples of early monumental architecture and civilization, they would have been the laughingstock of ancient history. Cultural tourists seeking to walk like Egyptians, Aztecs, and Mayans would have no place to go.

What does this inverted architectural design say about soccer in the United States today? First and foremost is its inextricable link to a place most Americans fear to tread: socioeconomic class.

From the pioneering studies in the 1930s by W. Lloyd Warner to the television sound bites of today, a unique feature of the U.S. class system is the consistent denial of social class in public discourse. Politicians who rationally try to discuss the negative impact of class on social opportunities such as education, health, and employment are invariably accused of instigating "class warfare." Successful politicians try to hide their often privileged class backgrounds by rewriting personal histories in the guise of "log cabin chic"—contemporary versions of growing up barefoot, reading by candlelight, and walking miles to school, guided by the "traditional" virtues of hard work, honesty, and sacrifice.

In everyday discourse even a superficial analysis of class invokes accusations of "Marxist" or "communist." A discussion of class just won't hold in "polite" conversation. Paradoxically, Americans often feel more comfortable talking about equally contentious issues like race, sex, gender, and crime as opposed to class. We love historical narratives of success in the face of seemingly overwhelming odds, from Horatio Alger, Abraham Lincoln, and Steve Jobs to entertainers and professional athletes—all of whom reinforce the mythology of a classless society in which individual effort, strong values, and dreams help one rise to the top. When push comes to shove, an overwhelming number of Americans consider themselves "middle class," a kind of ideological norm that flattens reality into perceived equality. A 2010 ABC World News survey found that not only did almost all Americans with family incomes between $35,000–$100,000 a year consider themselves "middle class," but 41 percent of those families with incomes below $25,000 also considered themselves "middle class," as did 38 percent of those whose incomes topped $100,000 a year.[6] An analysis of the General Social Survey given to Americans between 2000 and 2004 found that almost 75 percent of those with incomes over $100,000 defined themselves as "middle class" and 12 percent more defined themselves as "working class."[7] Almost 25 percent of Americans earning $20,000 or less considered themselves "middle class." This scheme identifies more than 95 percent of Americans in an inflated "middle class." With the official government poverty rate for a family of four at $22,800 a year, and with less than 10 percent of Americans making more than $100,000 a year, these claims obviously skew the actual numbers. Such a distortion of accurately identifying social class is a triumph of cultural ideals over economic realities, a symptom of the difficulties of admitting the power of class in a country that imagines itself to be a land of unfettered equal opportunity.

The Siamese twin of this ideological denial of class is the illusion of individual choice, or the belief that one unconditionally chooses the life that one leads. In this worldview, just as an individual chooses a Chevy over a Ford, Cheerios over Corn Flakes, soccer over basketball, and a Dell over an Apple, that same person chooses to continue an education or to quit school, to be unemployed or to find work. Like many stereotypes, there is an obvious modicum of truth in these claims, but there is also a deep self-deception that ignores the complicated social structures that create barriers, detours, dead ends, and vacuous bridges leading to the multiple paths of individual choice.

The twin illusions of a classless society and unfettered individual choice not only prevent understanding of oneself and others but also produce superficial reforms that fail to sufficiently address the structural problems stemming from class-based realities. In the end, both the understanding of and the solution to the problems remain stunted.

Although Klinsmann never used the term "class" in his ESPN commentary, his reference to the "pay-to-play system," the obsessive goal of achieving a college scholarship, and the need to open the soccer door to previously excluded populations inevitably lead to exploration of the forbidden terrain of the nature of class and its relationship to the social space occupied by soccer in the U.S. sports landscape today. Unless this issue is honestly broached, U.S. soccer will remain marginal, a sport played by millions but embraced for a lifetime by very few.

* * * *

The key to understanding the relationship of class to soccer is an exploration of the club soccer system that dominates youth development. Unknown to all but a relatively few soccer aficianados in this country, modern soccer has been played in the United States since the late nineteenth century. Anchored in immigrant working-class populations from England, Ireland, and Scotland, the sport was firmly established by the 1890s in ethnic enclaves in northeastern, industrialized cities and other urbanizing centers, including St. Louis. Immigrants developed a passion for the sport and requisite skills in their homelands. The children of these immigrants continued the tradition by playing pick-up games in streets and vacant fields, just as in the rest of the world. This social space continued into the next century, through the so-called "Golden Years" of professional soccer in the 1920s until the sport's subsequent decline during the Depression and Second World War.

During the first postwar World Cup in 1950, the U.S. team was still composed primarily of urban immigrants who'd acquired their skills informally. The U.S. national team all but disappeared over the next four decades, but soccer developed a modest foothold in the collegiate realm as well as a professional league in the late 1960s, the first substantial attempt to professionalize the sport since its decline in the 1930s. These modest changes provided an impetus for a youth development system that would feed the small but growing demand for collegiate players aspiring to join the professional ranks.

Although regional ventures like the American Youth Soccer Organization (AYSO) in California organized incipient programs in the 1960s, the first truly national youth program was the U.S. Youth Soccer Association (USYSA), founded in 1974. For decades, USYSA was the only umbrella youth club system officially affiliated with the U.S. Soccer Federation, the nation's organizational link to FIFA. This system of individual clubs, associated with state organizations and a national office, became the primary youth development program in the United States. Today the typical pipeline for player development starts in the various club levels of USYSA, and then progresses to universities, professional soccer, and national teams. Informal player development in urban, ethnic, working-class enclaves gradually faded, replaced by a highly organized, exclusive, and expensive bureaucracy.

Because there was no strong community, business, or government infrastructure to support player development, organizations like USYSA relied on nonprofit business models. The USYSA needed to create a demand for its services sufficient to support a rapidly growing bureaucracy of state and national offices as well as the services that accompanied those offices. In other words, it needed to generate substantial income to support the system. In the early years USYSA struggled to register 100,000 players aged 5 through 18. Today the organization, renamed U.S. Youth Soccer, boasts more than three million registered players. A number of additional youth development businesses have emerged over the years as USYS competitors.

Such a complex network takes lots of money to run. Ultimately the brunt of financing falls on players' families. From the outset, this new model of player development advocates a pay-to-play system. The families of individual players must pay a club fee per season—typically $500 or more in today's standard—a portion of which goes to the state organization. Each club must pay an initial membership fee to the state office, as well as annual fees. In addition, there are uniform costs and fees for individual tournaments. Travel expenses are borne by individual families. Costs to finance a beginning player for a two-season year can easily reach several thousand dollars. As a player progresses up the ladder of the club system, expenses escalate considerably. While a number of factors influence the precise cost for individual players, a family must provide sufficient financial resources for a youth player to develop through the system over multiple years.

The significant implication of this pay-to-play system is that participation is financially prohibitive for a large number of potential players. A family with an income of $40,000 a year, even though they might consider themselves middle class, would have to struggle to finance the development of even one child, much less several children, through years of club participation.

In the absence of a mass soccer culture in which kids pick up rudimentary skills informally, this club system successfully grabbed the player development market in the 1970s before soccer had become a significant sport supported by county schools and public funds. The big three U.S. sports—baseball, football, and basketball—have enjoyed a long history of support through the public school system, making them accessible to a much more heterogeneous population. While modified club programs have developed for these sports in recent times, recruitment into the university and professional ranks still occurs primarily through high school teams. Soccer recruitment, however, depends almost exclusively on the club system, making high school soccer virtually irrelevant when it comes to fielding university players. University programs recruit primarily through major club tournaments and camps. By the time most prospective university players are 17–18 years of age, they have played club soccer for many years. Their parents' financial investment is significant.

Club soccer and high school soccer are not mutually exclusive, however. Most serious youth players manage to play both. Unlike the big three sports, playing high school soccer exclusively is an unlikely pathway to success. In fact, it can be argued that the incredible growth in the number of high school soccer teams and players since the 1970s is due to the development of a younger player base through the club system. Similarly, club soccer participation has grown exponentially over the decades. According to the American Soccer History Archives, for example, approximately 10,000 females played high school soccer in 1976. By 1990 that number had grown to 122,000, a sign, no doubt, of the club system's success in recruiting and developing younger players who then progress through the club ranks and high school soccer.[8]

To satisfy this commitment to player development, the club system demands not only a significant financial investment but also a substantial investment of time. Even at beginning levels, most club teams practice three times a week and play matches on weekends. Depending upon the locale, weekend matches often involve travel. As one progresses through the club system, practice and travel time become even greater.

While time is not a direct economic resource, it certainly is an indirect consequence of economic capital. At least since Thorsten Veblen's classic work, *Theory of the Leisure Class* (1934), the availability of "time" has been recognized as a significant way to conspicuously display one's class status. If someone has the time to take multiple children to soccer practice and to weekend matches and tournaments, the expenditure of that time becomes yet another commodity to be consumed in order to create class distinctions. In this sense, time is an element of symbolic or cultural capital intricately meshed with economic capital in a web of mutual production. The class distinctions produced by economic capital generate the symbolic distinctions of culture, including time unconnected to the demands of economic necessity, which in turn reproduce and legitimize the class structure. The existence of time to engage in non-economic activities is itself a visible symbol of class position. One has time—literally "owns" time, the way one owns a five-bedroom house in a gated community, with a property owners' association that governs everything from landscaping to the color of houses. One has time to spend countless hours a week transporting children to soccer, dance, music, art, and martial arts classes. Of course, underlying this symbolic consumption is economic capital, but this display of the ownership of time is yet another way that upper-middle- and upper-class families often distinguish themselves from many middle- and working-class families.

In a society of mass consumer culture, class distinctions are often obscured. While there are obvious monetary differences in the ability to purchase a 2012 Cadillac Escalade Premium Edition SUV ($82,000) and a 2012 Kia Sorento SUV ($23,000), the fact that families with radically different amounts of economic capital can nevertheless afford SUVs whose external body parts are highly similar tends to flatten visible class differences. The same can be said about wearing "designer" clothes purchased at reduced prices from outlet and discount retail stores. One can even live in real gated communities with names like Huntington Pointe, Belle Vie Estates, and Thunderbird Harbour, comprising moderately priced, prefabricated, cookie-cutter houses that are overshadowed by cut-stone pillars, ceramic gargoyles, and copper lanterns.

The financial and popular successes of the big three sports in the United States are testimony that each sport has navigated its way into the arena of mass consumer culture, blurring class distinctions in the sports landscape. For example, whether one is a fan of collegiate or professional football does not reveal one's class position. Picture President George W. Bush chomping on a pretzel while watching a football game on television. Or picture the Kennedy clan gathering to play touch football on the manicured lawn of a mansion at Hyannis Port. Now picture the local neighborhood sports bar during Monday Night Football. You get the big picture. Football fans come from every economic class. The same is true for baseball and basketball. Picture the millionaire celebrities in courtside seats at professional basketball games, or presidents throwing out the first pitch in professional baseball's opening game. Then picture the tens of millions who annually watch the World Series or NBA finals. As the primary promoter of mass culture, television has provided equal access to a heterogeneous fan base that is just as rabid sitting in the comfort of their own dens or bars as in prime seats at the 50-yard line, mid-court, or home plate boxes.

While participation in mass consumer culture, from automobiles to sports, diminishes much of the visible symbolic capital that distinguished classes in the pre–mass culture era, some aspects of symbolic capital remain as important spaces of class distinction. U.S. soccer is a case in point.

While the economic realities of long-term participation in the club system are increasingly recognized as impediments to player development access, as evidenced by Klinsmann's observations, there is another essential class ingredient to the youth soccer recipe that is toxic to the final product. The soccer landscape is deeply embedded not only in the realities of economic capital and class but also in the arena of symbolic capital and class.

David Andrews links this use of symbolic capital to the upper-middle-class suburban "lifestyle" that emerged after World War II.[9] The suburban population grew from 27 percent of the total U.S. population in 1950 to over 50 percent of the population by the 1990s, a period that (not coincidentally) also saw the emergence and tremendous growth of youth club soccer. Franklin Foer argues that youth soccer began its migration from urban, working-class, ethnic communities into white suburbia as part of a class-based parenting shift away from football (which was seen as inherently violent), baseball (in which in-the-limelight batters faced "too many stressful, ego-deflating encounters"), and basketball (which to upper-middle-class suburban whites "still had the taint of the ghetto").[10]

While Foer's observations might be construed as glossing over a complex cultural landscape, the critical point is that the development of the pay-to-play youth model fit perfectly with an emerging middle- and upper-middle-class, suburban space of competitive lifestyle consumption geared toward building résumés of both parents and kids with distinctive markers of class position. The stereotype of the "soccer mom" that emerged in the late 1990s developed from a shallow understanding of this phenomenon. This supercharged, competitive lifestyle, designed to both display and develop a competitive advantage that is based in economic capital, embodies signifiers that distinguish class position: parents scurrying through a landscape filled with excessive malls, extravagant country clubs, and treeless, gated communities in order to get their kids to exclusive soccer fields paid for by private family fees and organizations. Within this cultural milieu—certainly not the only one in which soccer exists in the United States, but nevertheless the predominant one—club soccer often becomes a site for the public display of symbolic capital.

This reality explains why soccer hovers at the top of youth sports participation but still does not have a large fan base. Of course, there are also historical, media, and financial factors involved in soccer's relatively marginal position in the U.S. sports landscape, but its position as a site of class distinction cannot be ignored. Why do millions of children play soccer and their parents spend tens of thousands of dollars and countless, precious hours of time in the world of club soccer while rarely becoming dedicated fans of the sport? A logical reason is that by the time players and parents stop participating in the club system, soccer has served its purpose. In the same way that art lessons rarely produce a lifelong passion for art, or that trumpet lessons rarely produce a lifelong interest in music, participation in the club soccer system fails to produce a passion for the sport for the vast majority of players and parents. Typically their participation is of symbolic value rather than substantive value. Playing soccer is a means to an end rather than an end in itself. That end is the résumé building that comes from the financially and logistically grueling, parent-dominated scheduling of extracurricular activities that often serve as sites of class display. For the vast majority of club soccer players and their parents, the soccer experience is an age-specific product that is conspicuously consumed with no long-lasting affinity or passion for the sport itself. As Zwick and Andrews point out, "Within the predominantly European American spaces of suburban affluence, the game has been conclusively appropriated into everyday regimes of privilege."[11]

Occupying this space of both economic and symbolic capital, soccer has an uphill struggle to become a significant part of the mass culture of the U.S. sports landscape. The hope for U.S. soccer lies in two basic directions. The first is revamping the youth development system so that the pyramid is turned right side up, broadening the socioeconomic base of access to authentic player development opportunities. Although this won't be easy, it's still possible. The change would require, however, new ways of financing the system that would break the gridlock produced by the pay-to-play regime, a central point Klinsmann makes. An examination of the systems that exist in other countries might serve as models that could be adapted to the peculiarities of the U.S. system. There are recent signs that the U.S. Soccer Federation is attempting to modify the system through the creation of academy programs, which emphasize year-round player development activities rather than club-level league and tournament competition. Presently, various youth soccer programs are busy creating these academies, but the success of the programs really depends on the creation of alternative financing regimens that ameliorate the entrenched pay-to-play system. If the academy programs continue to rely significantly on parental financing, they may improve the skill level of individual players, and perhaps the performance of the USMNT, but they will not overcome the limitations of the socioeconomic space currently occupied by soccer in the U.S. sports landscape. That can only happen with alternative routes for financing youth development that turn the pyramid right side up.

The second direction of hope lies in the changing demographics of the United States, something that is beyond the direct control of Klinsmann or the larger arena of U.S. soccer. Over the past two decades, the United States has experienced a dramatic increase in immigration from countries where the soccer experience runs deep and wide, primarily from Mexico and Central American countries. Since 1970, the population of both documented and undocumented immigrants born in Mexico and Central America living within the United States has increased by a factor of 20. Immigrants from Mexico and Central America now constitute 37 percent of all foreign-born naturalized citizens of the United States and non-citizens, regardless of immigration status. Adding immigrants from South America and the Caribbean, this total reaches 53 percent of all foreign-born individuals living in the United States.[12]

These immigrants come from countries where soccer is deeply embedded in mass culture, and their expanding numbers present opportunities to both expand the pool of potential players and build a more significant fan base. A glimpse of the untapped fan base located in these immigrant populations can be seen in the buildup to the 2010 World Cup, when the Mexican National Men's Team toured the United States, playing friendlies against a host of relatively obscure national teams from Angola, Bolivia, Ecuador, Iceland, New Zealand, and Senegal.

Ordinarily, international friendlies played by any national team against relatively unheralded rivals draw modest crowds. National teams are still experimenting with their lineups, so that fans never really know whether the players they see in a match will actually make the final rosters. Major rivals, like England–France, Italy–Germany, Brazil–Argentina, or Mexico–United States, rarely compete against each other in these events. Despite these limitations, the Mexican national team drew huge crowds of enthusiastic fans. From their initial match on February 24, 2010, against Honduras in San Francisco to their final match against Angola on May 13 in Houston, raucous crowds of primarily Mexican immigrants cheered the red, green, and white of *El Tri,* as the Mexican national team is affectionately known. In Charlotte, North Carolina, on March 24, the relatively lackluster performance of Mexico against an undermanned Iceland didn't seem to matter to the enthusiastic crowd of 63,227 who partied before the match at a *Futbol Fiesta* outside of the Bank of America Stadium and continued in the stadium throughout the match, despite a 0–0 draw. In total, *El Tri* won four of its U.S.-based matches, drawing the other two, and outscored its opponents nine goals to zero. In the six matches, average attendance was 66,035, topped by the more than 90,000 who saw Mexico beat New Zealand in the Rose Bowl on March 3. In stark contrast, the USMNT during the same time period played four friendlies on U.S. turf, drawing an average attendance of only 32,996, less than half of what Mexico averaged. As a result, the *New York Times* declared the Mexican national team to be "the most popular soccer team in the United States."[13] Can one imagine this happening in England, France, Germany, Brazil, or almost any other major soccer country in the world?

The message is clear: there is a very large and growing segment of the U.S. population that has the potential to develop into a significant fan base for professional and national soccer. The challenge is how to transfer that passion from the teams of their native countries to the teams of their adopted land. Part of the answer may lie in the simple fact of generational assimilation. Like areas of linguistic and cultural assimilation, the transfer of soccer passion to U.S. teams may be just a matter of time. Data do demonstrate that second and third generations of immigrants assimilate more linguistically, culturally, and economically than their parents and grandparents. If the Mexican and Central American segment of the U.S. population continues to expand at anticipated rates, the number of citizens who potentially possess a passion for soccer will increase proportionately. This demographic shift could move the fan base for soccer in the direction of a greater slice of the sport's mass culture landscape.

The other problem is that of access to the pay-to-play system. Of course, as future generations of immigrants move up the socioeconomic ladder, some of them will acquire the economic and symbolic capital to participate in the existing club system. This may impact the ethnic makeup of the elite player pool, but it will not change the socioeconomic space occupied by soccer. The barriers of the pay-to-play system are primarily class-based, although they intersect in complex ways with race and ethnicity since disproportionate numbers of ethnic minorities are poor and working class. Approximately a quarter of Mexican and Central American immigrants live below the official poverty line, as do a quarter of African Americans, and relatively few of these minorities occupy upper-middle-class and upper-class strata.

There have been attempts to break down these class barriers that impact minorities to a greater extent than the white majority. The primary goal of the United States Soccer Foundation, the charitable arm of the U.S. Soccer Federation, is to "enhance, assist and grow the sport of soccer in the United States with a special emphasis on underserved communities." The USSF funds several programs designed to meet this goal, among them the "Soccer for Success Program" that operates in all 50 states and the "Urban Soccer Collaborative" that currently has 64 community-based organizations in 24 states and the District of Columbia. However, both of these programs seem to be primarily directed at encouraging exposure to soccer as a means of reducing social problems in economically disadvantaged communities rather than transforming the system of limited access—certainly a noble goal, but not one that realistically expands access to the player development system.

In 2007, Major League Soccer started an initiative called "Sueño MLS" (Dream MLS), a program with a reality TV format that in its initial year drew more than 2,000 entries from young male soccer players. Allstate Insurance joined with the MLS to sponsor the program. Each year since, regional competitions have been held in different cities across the United States, eventually selecting handful of competitors for the final round. The finalists then receive technical training from MLS staff, perform drills, and play competitive matches against MLS youth development teams. A team of MLS players serves as judges who whittle the finalists down to a single Sueño MLS winner. That individual receives an offer to join one of the youth development programs of an MLS team.

Although the competition is not restricted to players from "underserved communities" or from any particular ethnic group, the competition mainly attracts Latino players, most of whom have not come up through the club system. Without a doubt, the pitch of the program, from its Spanish-language name to the fact that it's televised through Univision on the most popular Spanish-language sports show, *República Deportiva*, taps into the talent of Latino teenagers who typically are invisible to the elite club system. The initial winner in 2007 was Jorge Flores, who was born in California before moving with his family back to Guanajuato, Mexico, and then back to Anaheim, where he was the MVP on his high school soccer team. After winning the competition, Flores was signed by the MLS club Chivas USA, where he played on their U-19 team. A year later he moved to the regular squad, where he ended up starting half the games. The same year he was named to the U.S. U-20 team. Today he is still playing as a professional with Chivas USA, earning a salary of over $70,000 a year. In 2011, he officially changed his name to Jorge Villafaña, taking his mother's last name.

Subsequent years produced similar winners who have gone on to various kinds of soccer success. These individual success stories probably would not have happened were it not for the Sueño MLS program. Like so many other talented Latino players who play on pitches that are largely invisible to the dominant club system, these winners probably would have ended up playing in the various Hispanic leagues that occupy another section of the U.S. soccer landscape. As we point out in Chapter 10, these nonprofessional leagues have emerged over the past 20 years in urban centers and small towns alike, wherever vibrant communities of Hispanic immigrants have settled. They serve as avenues both for the expression of soccer fever and for the creation of spaces of cultural identity and solidarity.

The Sueño MLS program opens the door to a select few individuals without making a substantive dent in the pay-to-play system of youth development. U.S. soccer will continue to languish in a relatively minor corner of the sports landscape unless it is able to break down the barriers to mass culture. This will happen only when the pyramid is turned right side up and development opportunities are more broadly accessible to players from diverse socioeconomic backgrounds. In this way, youth soccer will be freed from the class space where it is chained to its role as symbolic capital, providing it with the opportunity to be diffused into mass culture and appreciated and played with the skills, passion, and excitement that the game deserves.

How is this to be accomplished? With difficulty, to be sure, but an examination of the structure of youth development in other countries may provide direction.

2

Models of the Pyramid Right Side Up

Germany

On March 27, 1990, West German Chancellor Helmut Kohl arrived in Dresden, more than 200 kilometers inside East Germany. His destination was the Dynamo Soccer Stadium, site of the first Old-Timers Match between the East and West German men's national soccer teams. Parking their luxury limousines on the other side of the Elbe River, Kohl and his entourage greeted curious onlookers as they made their way to the stadium. A late winter rain lingered, but the West German politicians seemed undeterred. Like others attending the match, they knew they were witnessing a historic event.

Less than five months earlier, on November 9, 1989, the Berlin Wall had fallen. Dust from its dismantling still hung in the air, as did Pink Floyd's mantra "We don't need no education/We don't need no thought control," which had played repeatedly during the wall's famous demise. Now residents of a divided city could stroll leisurely, albeit hesitatingly, on terrain that had been sealed off for over 20 years. For residents of both Berlins, it must have seemed like an old friend resurrected from the dead—familiar yet strange, dream-like but real. Uncertainty still prevailed, and hope was muted by the sense of an unpredictable future. But on this day, in a city two hours south of Berlin, the once somber mood that permeated the country had changed. Festivity filled the air.

As Chancellor Kohl moved onto the field, an enthusiastic crowd greeted him with a standing ovation. Banned in East Germany only months before, red, black, and yellow West German flags filled the stands, blending with flags of Saxony and the United Germany of 1919. Not a single East German flag could be seen. Despite a delay in the match's start, a formally dressed Kohl kicked a soccer ball with a handful of players. He would later remark, "A great day for football, and for all Germany."[1]

Leaders from the former East German soccer association and their West German counterparts had organized this March match of veterans who had played for their respective teams in the 1974 World Cup, the only time East and West national teams met in a World Cup venue. That year, in a politically charged atmosphere, both teams had landed in the same group. Chile and Australia rounded out the foursome. The draw guaranteed at least one match between the two Cold War German rivals. West Germany won its first two matches without giving up a goal; East Germany easily handled Australia, and managed a 1–1 draw with Chile. With both teams assured of moving to the next stage, East and West met in Hamburg before a sold-out crowd of 60,350. Since the East German association's official recognition by FIFA in 1952, its national team had never qualified for a World Cup. West Germany, however, had emerged from the devastation of World War II as an international soccer power. In 1954, the first postwar World Cup in which they played, West Germany won its first championship. In the next four World Cups they failed to make the semi-finals only once—in 1962, when Yugoslavia upset them in the knockout round. They finished second to England in 1966, third behind Brazil and Italy in 1970, and fourth in 1958, trailing Brazil, Sweden, and France. Captained by Franz Beckenbauer, who as European Footballer of the Year in 1972 had already achieved a trophy case full of awards, the West German squad was the heavy favorite in 1974's match-up.

The political electricity of the match outweighed what most enthusiasts dismissed as a lackluster performance, however. Both teams seemed to be governed by fear and caution. In the end the East Germans miraculously prevailed, shutting out their West German rivals 1–0. The match undoubtedly went down as the high point in East German soccer history. Jürgen Sparwasser's seventy-seventh-minute goal might not have made him an international soccer legend, but he became a hero in East Germany. "Even if they just put 'Hamburg 1974' on my gravestone," Sparwasser reminisced, "everyone will know who is there."[2]

Ironically, the victory against the heavily favored West Germans sealed the East Germans' fate. In the next round they were grouped with three of the best soccer teams in the world—Argentina, Brazil, and the Netherlands. The West Germans drew an easier group against Poland, Sweden, and Yugoslavia. The East Germans were eliminated from the Cup, while the West Germans marched undefeated into the finals against a Johan Cruyff–led Netherlands team known for its brand of "total football" (a euphemism for football anarchy, in which players were encouraged to switch positions as the flow of the match dictated). Compared to the more orderly strategy of most world-class teams, the Dutch Orange looked more like Whirling Dervishes than a disciplined soccer squad. Cruyff preferred to call this unusual strategy "simple football." "Simple football is the most beautiful [type of football]," he explained, "but playing simple football is the hardest thing [to perform]."[3] In reality, total football is intricate, organic, and collaborative, and it depends on a fluid architecture of space constructed intuitively on the pitch. What appears to be anarchy is actually a choreographed dance of ball and players. Using this strategy, the Dutch team, Ajax, had won the European championship three straight years, 1971–1973.

The Dutch received the ball first, and after 13 passes they transformed the pitch into a pinball machine. The ball went to Cruyff, who broke through the German defense. A West German player brought him down in the box for a foul. Cruyff's teammate, Johan Neeskens, took the penalty kick. Eighty seconds into the match, before the Germans had even touched the ball, the Netherlands was on top, 1–0. Total football looked to be in total command. Surprisingly, the West Germans scored a comeback goal, and then a second goal before halftime. They managed to play total defense in the second half, pulling out a 2–1 victory. It was West Germany's second World Cup title in just six post–World War II attempts. Although the loss to East Germany was devastating in terms of soccer and Cold War politics, the championship eased the pain.

Sixteen years later, with reunification of the two Germanys imminent, players from the 1974 West and East German teams joined in their own symbolically reunified soccer team. They played a match against a team comprised of ex-international players from around the globe. Billed as "Reunited Germany vs. the Rest of the World," the match was the first television simulcast to both Germanys. Although the game had obvious political overtones, the 40- and 50-year-olds who came to play had soccer on their minds. Bobby Charlton, age 52, known in his day as the "English Master," noted in the true spirit of a soccer fanatic, "I'll go anywhere for a game of football."[4] Putting his money where his mouth was, he delivered two second-half assists to South Korean star Cha Bum Kun, clinching the victory for the World by a score of 3–1. After the match, Charlton observed, "I guess it would have been very diplomatic to let the Germans win the game. But I've never been very diplomatic."[5] As if to emphasize the reunification of the two countries, 42-year-old Hans-Jürgen Kreische, perhaps the best East German to ever play the game, scored Germany's lone goal. In the end the loss mattered little, as something bigger and more important had happened. This old-timers match represented the first time since the 1938 World Cup that players for a soon-to-be reunified Germany had played together on the same side of the pitch. It seemed fitting that soccer led the way.

The decision to use the estimated $1.2 million profit from the match toward the reconstruction of the Dresden Castle, a victim of the controversial Allied carpet bombing of Dresden in February 1945, added to the powerful symbolic nature of the match. Construction of the castle began in 1533, and for almost 400 years it had served as the residence of the electors and kings of Saxony. Before the bombing, most of the contents of the castle had been removed to safety, but the historical treasure whose architecture ranged from Baroque to Neo-Renaissance was transformed into a roofless shell in one fateful night. For 45 years, it had stood as a reminder of the tragedies of World War II. Both the match and the use of the profits helped to solidify the drive for reunification, and to ensure a peaceful transition with as little animosity as possible following the decades of the contentious Cold War. Today the reconstructed castle serves as a museum, art library, and management center for the Dresden State Art Collections. It is a national treasure, restored with the help of a soccer match and a commitment to reunite a country.

Official national reunification of the two Germanys occurred October 3, 1990. The two respective soccer associations joined forces a month later. The World Cup played that summer in Italy, however, overshadowed the growing excitement over any type of reunification. Qualifying rounds for the Cup had begun two years earlier, and 24 teams, including West Germany, advanced to the final competition. Coached by Franz Beckenbauer, the West German squad was a powerhouse and apparently stronger than the previous two World Cup teams, which had finished second to Italy in 1982 and to Argentina in 1986. Captained by Lothar Matthäus, the West Germans marched undefeated to the finals, where their nemesis from 1986 awaited them. Argentina, the reigning World Cup champs, had stumbled through the group stage, losing to Cameroon, tying Romania, and defeating the Soviet Union. They made it to the elimination stage primarily because they were one of four third-place teams selected to advance. Yet they battled to the finals by beating Brazil (1–0) and both Yugoslavia and Italy in penalty shootouts. In a rough and defensive struggle, which saw two Argentinians ejected, the West Germans finally prevailed, with an eighty-fifth-minute penalty shot the only goal of the match. The win put the West German team on the top of the soccer world, boasting three World Cup championships (1954, 1974, 1990) and three second-place finishes (1966, 1982, 1986).

With a world championship under his belt and national reunification on the horizon, Coach Beckenbauer gazed into the future. He envisioned a team that combined the best of the West and East German national teams. Beckenbauer triumphantly proclaimed, "We are number one in the world, and now we will also have players from East Germany. In the future the German team will be unbeatable."[6] He visualized the 1990s and beyond as years of German dominance, an unparalleled span of consecutive victories stretching seamlessly to the soccer horizon. Much of the rest of the soccer world agreed. Just as England, France, and Israel shared political and economic reservations about the power of a unified Germany, the world of soccer wondered whether the unified German team should be feared as well. The first match for the German unified team, which included former East German national stars Matthias Sammer and Ulf Kirsten, seemed to confirm Beckenbauer's assertion. On December 19, 1990, the Germans destroyed Switzerland 4–0 in an international friendly.

Beckenbaurer's prediction, however, soon faltered. In Euro 1992, the German team reached the final but lost to a surprisingly resilient Denmark team. As defending 1990 champions, they lost 2–1 to a much weaker Bulgaria in the 1994 World Cup quarter-finals. In Euro 1996, the team regained its composure, going undefeated and beating the Czech Republic 2–1 in the final, thus emerging with their first European championship since reunification. But in the 1998 World Cup they floundered once again, losing in the quarter-finals to Croatia by a lopsided 3–0 score. By Euro 2000, Beckenbauer's boastful prediction looked like a Brooklyn palm reader's prognostications of true love and wealth. The Germans lost all three of their matches, exiting in the first round.

By this time, it was clear that Germany's post-unification dominance had failed to materialize. Loyal fans wondered out loud: What in the world had happened?

To understand, one must first examine the boom years of the Bundesliga, the elite German professional soccer league. Paradoxically, the league's success coincided with the declining fortunes of the national German team. In Germany, the 1990s saw an incredible growth in professional soccer. This growth was spearheaded by television revenue from Kirch TV, a conglomerate that had bankrolled the Bundesliga boom. Awash in Kirch money, professional teams increasingly recruited international talent, enticing stars with fat salary packages. In 1992, only 17 percent of Bundesliga players were non–German; by 1997, the figure had doubled to 34 percent; in 2000, it hit 50 percent. Surprisingly, by 2002 non–German players outnumbered their German counterparts 3–2. While improving professional teams, this significant shift toward international players with inflated salaries led to a corresponding decline in developing young, homegrown German talent. It also stifled opportunities for talented German players to receive early professional experience.[7]

In May 1999, Beckenbauer, now president of the German soccer association, recognized the naïve optimism of his 1990 pronouncement. A conversation involving the national association and professional teams about the restructuring of the youth development program in Germany got under way. At the same time, the collapse of the Kirch TV empire led to a corresponding collapse in its financial support for the Bundesliga. Faced with increasingly huge salaries, professional teams had little choice but to release high-paid foreign players and to sign younger (and much cheaper) players from their youth squad. These two events—one planned and the other a fortuitous tragedy—led to the total revamping of the German youth soccer system.

Germany, a country a little more than half the size of Texas, embarked on building 121 national talent centers where 10- to 17-year-old youths could receive technical training and pitch experience under the guidance of association-sanctioned coaches. In addition, the German soccer association required the 18 professional teams in the Bundesliga and a similar number in Bundesliga 2, the second-tier professional league, to develop and operate youth academies. While Bundesliga teams like Bayer 04 Leverkusan had operated youth development centers since the early 2000s, the governing association mandated that all 36 teams operate academies as a condition for receiving a license to compete in the professional leagues. This agreement required close cooperation between the national German football association and the professional teams, based on the shared conviction that a structured program of youth development would benefit everyone involved. Finally, the association built over 1,000 mini-pitches in communities throughout the country, where even younger kids could play informally without adult supervision. The latter initiative operated on the assumption that street soccer was on the decline, and that the positive components of unsupervised youth soccer needed to be preserved.

While the national talent centers and the academy programs of professional teams are indispensable parts of German soccer restructuring, the informal mini-pitches are just as important. The smaller fields encourage matches with fewer players, which in turn give each player more contact with the ball. The compressed space requires the development of greater ball control and passing skills, since defenders are always close at hand. More importantly, the free play of unsupervised soccer strengthens internal motivations that are fundamentally different from adult-supervised sessions, where motivation is more likely determined by external factors. The young player who traipses freely and frequently to these mini-pitches, where he spends more time with the ball at his feet, will develop greater technical skills independently of any coaching he receives. As Jürgen Klinsmann recalls, "I grew up ... coming home from school and eating [and] doing my homework, and then it was four or five hours playing soccer ... wherever there was a little piece of grass or ... in the backyard."[8] Today there are mini-pitches scattered across the German landscape, where kids experience the same free play on more appropriate fields.

The beginning of formal play starts at local sports clubs, which charge minimal membership fees. These clubs feed the most competent players into the more formal talent centers and youth academies. As Klinsmann explains, "So, in Germany, youth soccer is very inexpensive and that way everybody can play. And ... the more you play the better you get ... the more inner drive you have ... the further you will make it in your career."[9]

All systems cost money, and the German youth academies are no exception. At the end of the day, someone has to pay the bills. This role falls to the professional teams that operate the academies. Over the past ten years, the 36 professional teams in the first and second tiers have invested a staggering half billion euros in their youth academies. Beginning with an initial investment of 47 million euros in 2002–2003 and growing to 85 million Euros in 2009–2010, the philosophy follows the old dictum that "to make money you have to spend money." As Thomas Albeck, VfB Stuttgart's head of youth development, states, "More and more clubs woke up to the fact that they could create real assets by spending money on the kids."[10] This realization panned out not only in terms of developing player talent but also because fans flocked to local stadiums to watch more homegrown players with whom they could identify.

The academy system benefits the level of play both in the Bundesliga and on the national team. As Christian Seifert, chief executive of the German professional football league, recently asserted, "A crucial reason for [the Bundesliga's] most recent success is surely the outstanding work of the ... academies ... [an] investment which will prove worthwhile in the future.... Without the work and support of the league, the successes of the national team would be inconceivable.... The national team ... has a real chance of winning titles again."[11] This symbiotic relationship between professional soccer and the national team is one of the keys to the success of the new German development system.

During 2010–2011 the academy system organized 5,445 players into eight age levels, from U-12 to U-23. This system, coupled with the national talent centers feeding the academies with the best players, has dramatically affected the growth of homegrown talent. In 2011, over 52 percent of the professionals playing in the Bundesliga came out of the academy system, and the percentage of Germans overall in the top two tiers once again hovers around 60 percent.[12]

The 2010 World Cup team displayed the first real evidence of the positive impact this development system has had on the men's national team. Germany represented one of only three nations that fielded a team of players drafted solely from its own professional leagues. (England and Italy were the other two.) The 23 members of the German squad averaged 24 years of age, matched with Ghana and North Korea as the youngest teams. Nineteen of these German players had advanced through the Bundesliga academies; the other four came through the Bundesliga 2 academies. Germany won all three of its matches in the group stage, outscoring opponents 6–0. They then demolished England 4–1 in the round of sixteen, and Argentina 4–0 in the quarter-finals. Having won all six matches and outscoring its opponents 14–1, the young squad looked poised to win Germany's fourth World Cup, and its first since 1990. In the semi-finals, however, they were outmaneuvered by the eventual champions, Spain, with a final score of 2–1. In one of the most entertaining matches of the tournament, Germany beat Uruguay for third place by a score of 3–2. At the Cup's conclusion, the overall performance of the young German squad received accolades from around the world.

The individual awards reflected obvious success as well. Thomas Müller received the Golden Boot award, an honor bestowed on the top scorer of the tournament. At 20 he was the youngest player to ever receive this award. Müller scored five goals and added three assists in Germany's seven tournament matches. Müller also received the Best Young Player of the Tournament award, reserved for players 21 years of age or younger. In addition, two Germans made the All-World Cup team—Phillipe Lahon, a defender who, at age 26, was the youngest team captain in the tournament, and Bastian Schweinsteiger, a 25-year-old midfielder who was one of 10 finalists for the Golden Ball award for the top all-around player in the tournament.

Many attributed this 2010 performance to the new system of youth development and the investment of time, energy, and money, and developments over the next two years confirmed this conclusion. In 2010 and 2011, Germany won the European championships at the U-17, U-19, and U-21 levels. These players will be joining the now-seasoned players from the 2010 national team to populate the roster for the 2014 World Cup in Brazil, as well as those that follow. As Franz Beckenbauer should know, it's always difficult to predict the future, particularly that of soccer, but there is hope within the German system and some corresponding anxiety in other prominent soccer nations. The

United European Football Association (UEFA) recently cited the German model as the best in Europe, and there are signs that soccer-rich countries like England are trying to emulate it.[13]

The effect on the German women's national team was equally visible. After a fourth-place finish in the first FIFA women's World Cup in 1991, the women's national team lost to Norway in the finals of the 1995 competition. In 2003 and 2007, when the first effects of the revamped youth development system started to show, Germany marched through the tournaments unscathed to win its first two women's World Cups. In the group stage in the 2003 tournament, the German players dispatched Canada, Japan, and Argentina, outscoring their opponents 13–2. They then proceeded through the knockout stage by beating Russia (7–1) and the United States (3–0). They subsequently beat Sweden 2–1 for the championship. Overall they scored 25 goals to their opponents' four goals, in just six matches. Their performance in 2007 was even more impressive, as they went undefeated a second time, outscoring opponents by a mind-boggling 21–0 in six matches. The 2011 World Cup expected a repeat performance. Germany once again marched through the group stage, defeating Canada, Nigeria, and France, but Japan, the eventual winner, surprised them in the quarter-finals with a 1–0 score.

In 2003, forward Birgit Prinz won both the Golden Shoe award for her tournament- leading seven goals and the Golden Ball award as the World Cup's most valuable player. Germany placed five players on the 11-member all-star squad. In 2007, it repeated this same impressive feat.

Japan

If you haven't heard of Tsubasa Ozora, one of Japan's greatest soccer heroes, you aren't alone. Few soccer nuts around the world have heard of Tsubasa, unless they happen to be twenty-something Japanese who grew up in the 1980s. For those who do know him, Tsubasa is affectionately called *Socca no Moshigo,* roughly translated as the "heaven-sent child of soccer." He is also known as Captain Tsubasa. When he was barely a year old, he was almost killed by a speeding bus when he rushed into the street to retrieve a soccer ball. Miraculously, the ball saved his life, literally bouncing him from beneath the bus and giving substance to what became his life-long motto: "The ball is my friend." Because of the near-fatal accident, his mother believed little Tsubasa was destined to devote his life to soccer. At an early age the small boy astounded anyone who witnessed his extraordinary speed, dexterity, skill, and power on the soccer field.

In the city of Nankatsu, Tsubasa became a star on his elementary and high school soccer teams. He eventually played for the national U-17 squad, which won the FIFA U-17 World Championships. Influenced by an ex–Brazilian national player named Roberto Hungo, who served as his mentor and coach, Tsubasa left Japan to play for São Paulo in Brazil's premiere professional league, Campeonato Brasileiro Série A. He also continued to play for Japan's national teams. Many believe that his successful athletic exploits inspired an entire generation of Japanese youth to play soccer.

Because his accomplishments began in the 1980s, prior to the first Japanese professional soccer league and before Japan's emergence as the dominant force in Asian soccer, Captain Tsubasa is a little-known figure among soccer aficionados. The main reason his name and story may not be familiar to followers of soccer outside Japan, however, is that Captain Tsubasa Ozora (a.k.a. *Socca no Moshigo*) is a tried-and-true, full-fledged fictional cartoon character.

The heaven-sent child of soccer first appeared in 1981 in a comic book called *Weekly Shonen Jump.* The magazine was serialized through 1988. An immediate hit, the comic series soon evolved into a TV animation, or *anime*, series that ran on TV Tokyo network from 1983 to 1986, for 128 episodes. Four 1985–1986 *anime* movies, ranging in length from 35 to 60 minutes, continued the frenzied story of this miraculous player. Subsequent serialized versions both on TV and in comic format continued the story through the 1990s into the 2000s. As with other serialized comics (or *manga*, as they are known in Japan), the comics appeared in book form and were published as popular compilations that could be purchased as complete sets. More recently, Tsubasa and the litany of supporting soccer characters have entered the world of video games, adapted into several Nintendo Super Famicom versions that topped the sales charts in Japan upon release.

While it is impossible to accurately gauge the impact of the *manga* stories and the *anime* movies and TV serials of *Captain Tsubasa* on the growth of Japanese soccer, it seems significant that the popularity of these soccer adventures coincided with the unprecedented development of the sport in Japan. Although there are no data to suggest how many people actually read the series, the *Weekly Shonen Jump* magazine in which the *Captain Tsubasa* installments first appeared had a weekly readership of approximately six million during its heyday in the 1980s. Today the magazine attracts almost three million weekly readers.

To fully appreciate the possible impact of the *manga* phenomenon on a social practice like soccer, one has to understand the importance of Japanese comics and animation. As the *Journal of Japanese Trade and Industry* pointed out in 2002, Japan is a *manga* superpower.[14] *Manga* publications constitute almost 40 percent of yearly publications in Japan and more than 22 percent of all print sales. By the mid–1990s, the *manga* industry published 12 magazines with circulations of over one million and 50 more with circulations topping 125,000. Although the sales of *manga* books and magazines peaked in 1995, the industry boasted a $5 billion profit as late as 2006. *Manga* publications appeal equally to adult and adolescent audiences. They also cross gender lines and social classes. *Manga kissa* (or cafes) operate in every urban center in Japan. For a small fee, readers can relax over a cup of coffee or tea and read from a wide selection of *manga* magazines and books. There are an estimated 50,000 *manga* clubs or circles throughout the country that celebrate specific series and characters. Children and teenagers produce so-called fanzines, or creative versions of their own *manga*, which they exchange and sell. At the 1999 Tokyo Comic Market, an estimated 22,000 booths displayed as many as 100,000 fanzines. If one includes the television shows, movies, computer games, and other product offshoots that span globally, the audience for this mass art form is astronomical.

The genre represents more than a source of diversion and entertainment, however. *Manga* are also a powerful form of mass literature that, according to Paul Gravett, is as culturally influential as the media superpowers of television and film.[15] Frederick L. Schodt, author of *Dreamland Japan: Writings on Modern Manga*, claims that the genre's magazines and books are "like the constant chatter of the [Japanese] collective unconscious."[16] Mark McWilliams, in the introduction to a collection of readings on *manga* and *anime* in Japan, writes, "Rather than just serving up fantasy escapes from the real world, [*manga*] are potentially a source for political, ethical, or existential self-reflection."[17] *Manga* may offer escape, but they do so in a way that generates new resources and possibilities for the construction of the self and a staging ground for action that might result in positive change. It is clear that Japanese consumers and producers of *manga* view this art form as culturally transformative, both a reflection of Japanese culture and a lens for individual and social change.

To highlight this duality, in the early years of the U.S.-led occupation of Iraq the Japanese actually arranged to televise the 2001–2002 season of *Captain Tsubasa* on Iraqi television. The motivation may have been tied up with financial and public relations concerns, but it also reflected the Japanese view that this art form presents positive, transformative potential even across cultural boundaries. In the Iraqi version, "Captain Tsubasa" became "Captain Majed," and a Japanese Foreign Ministry official explained that "we believe children, who will be the future of Iraq, will be filled with dreams and hopes by watching this show."[18] Obviously this *anime* series spoke the universal language of soccer, but it also spoke the universal language of youthful dreams and hopes for the future.

Manga are so embedded in Japanese culture that the art of preschool Japanese children reveals both the style and the content of *manga*. Brent Wilson, a researcher who has studied children's art in different cultural contexts, argues that Japanese children appropriate this adult art form at a very early age, and it serves as a cultural tool of conformity and creativity—as a way of learning what it means to be Japanese at the same time opening up new individual and social possibilities.[19]

So is there a possible relationship between the popularity of *Captain Tsubasa* and the mercurial rise of soccer fever in Japan? What was actually happening in Japanese soccer when the *Captain Tsubasa* series first reached the *manga* audience in the 1980s?

Of course, Japanese soccer didn't begin in the 1980s. British military personnel who used soccer as a recreational and training activity at the naval academy in Tokyo in the early 1870s first introduced soccer to Japan. The sport soon spread to the Japanese school and university systems, along with baseball, which Horace Wilson, an American professor teaching in the capital, inaugurated around the same time. The 1870s were a time of dramatic change in Japan, as leaders of the Meiji period (1868–1912) looked to the West for fresh forms of cultural inspiration. Like baseball, soccer remained a sport played predominantly by high school and university teams. Newly created athletic clubs did sponsor soccer teams, however. The first competitive match in 1888 supposedly pitted the Kobe Regatta and Athletic Club against the Yokohama Country and Athletic Club, exclusive membership groups modeled after elite British organizations. The Japanese Football Association formed in 1921, but soccer remained an amateur sport played primarily by high school, university, club, and industry-sponsored teams. Japan did enter a national team in the 1936 Olympics in Berlin; even though they didn't win a medal, they managed a surprising 3–2 victory over the eventual gold medalist, Sweden.

In post–World War II Japan, corporate sport grew alongside the reconstruction of Japanese industry. Companies embraced soccer as a means of enhancing employee fitness and morale and promoting identification with and commitment to the company. This investment in amateur soccer moved the sport out of its more limited public space in schools, universities, and exclusive clubs into the broader social space of the working class.

In 1965, the Japan Soccer League was formed, comprising eight amateur industry clubs. At the 1968 Olympics in Mexico City, a team consisting of top players from the JSL won a bronze medal. Along the way, Japan beat Nigeria and France and tied Brazil and Spain. They lost in the quarter-finals to the eventual gold medal winner, Hungary. Japan beat Mexico 2–0 in the third-place match. The Olympics at this time were still restricted to amateur athletes and East European teams with rosters of state-supported players often dominating competitions. In fact, from 1952 to 1980, prior to the International Olympic Committee's decision to allow professionals to compete in soccer, the only non–Soviet bloc nations to win medals in soccer included Denmark (silver medalist in 1960), Sweden (bronze in 1952), and Japan (bronze in 1968).

Japan's Olympic success in 1968 created momentum for the amateur JSL, and teams recruited a limited number of foreign players who became the first professionals to play in Japan. Japanese players remained amateurs, having to work day jobs for the companies that sponsored the teams or in other occupations. Although it met the need of corporations to promote identification and commitment of employees to the company as well as serving company public relations efforts, the system did little to promote high-quality soccer. The few exceptional Japanese players who developed during this period had to seek professional opportunities abroad. The first Japanese player to sign with a European professional team was Yasuhiko Okudera, who started his soccer career in 1970 at the age of 18 with Furukawa Electric in the JSL. In 1977, a Bundesliga first division team, FC Koln, recruited him, and he finished his German career with Werder Breman in 1986.[20] A few other Japanese players made this transition to world-class soccer at the same time, but most remained amateurs.

This modest growth in the popularity of soccer continued through much of the 1980s, when the *manga* and *anime* stories of *Captain Tsubasa* were beginning to influence a generation of Japanese youth. In 1989, the Japan Football Association formed an action committee that included four major advertising companies, in order to discuss ways to both move Japanese soccer toward a fully professional league and enact a program of player development. The committee recognized the need to mount a public relations effort to market soccer and to anchor a professional league in local communities. The Japan Professional Football League, known as the J League, was formed in 1991. It began play two years later with an initial 10 teams. In May 1993, over 50,000 fans attended the inaugural ceremony of the J League held at the National Stadium in Yoyogi, Japan. Attendance increased almost immediately. The last games of the old JSL played in 1992 drew an average of 6,000 spectators, but by 1994 popular J League teams like Verdy Kawasaki, now known as Tokyo Verdy 1969, enjoyed an average attendance of over 30,000 fans. In 1999, the J League introduced a two-tiered system like those in other major soccer nations.[21] Currently the J1 League has 18 teams, and the J2 League 20.

A critical change in the J League charter that broke with the old JSL system de-emphasized corporate sponsorship in favor of community-based professional clubs. Professional sports in Japan, most notably baseball, have traditionally been sponsored by corporations. One of the most successful teams in the Nippon Professional Baseball League is the Yomiuri Giants, who take their name from their sponsor, the largest media corporation in Japan. The name does not include the hometown of the Giants—Tokyo—and until recently this pattern characterized all professional baseball teams. As in baseball, previous amateur/semi-pro teams in the JSL bore the names of their sponsors—Nissan Motors, Hitachi, Mitsubishi Motors, Nippon Steel, Furukawa Electric, Toyo Industries—so that teams and their corporate sponsors were undifferentiated. The trick facing the Japan Football Association (JFA) was to convince corporations to continue supporting teams financially while giving up much of the public face that they had enjoyed under the old JSL system. It would be like trying to convince Minute Maid, which gave $170 million to the Houston Astros in 2002 for the rights to call the Astros' stadium "Minute Maid Park" for 28 years, to provide funds without the corporate name attached to the stadium. Although negotiations were difficult, they ultimately succeeded.

The Japan Football Association worked diligently to create partnerships between existing corporate owners, city and prefectural (county) governments, and local business communities to cooperate in building a new, viable professional soccer infrastructure. Local governments agreed to fund the construction or renovation of existing stadiums, and the public and private stakeholders financed community sports centers linked to the new professional soccer teams. Based loosely on the German model, these sports centers provide open access to soccer competition, experience, and coaching in exchange for modest membership fees. Japan Football Association chairman Saburō Kawabuchi, who was part of the reorganization initiative, recalled how he was so moved by seeing German youth playing soccer on grass fields wherever he went in Germany that he became determined to see the same fields built in Japan. Although the sports centers offer a variety of fitness and sports activities, they clearly promote soccer and encourage establishing contact with professional teams. The official J League mission uses the slogan "J League Sports Community for All," which articulates its aim to develop accessible avenues to soccer through community-based sports clubs. In addition, every top-flight J League team must operate U-18, U-15, and U-12 youth development teams. The partnerships are not only ideological but also financial, as each J League team is registered as a corporation, and the public and private stakeholders in many cases own shares in the team-based corporation.[22]

The new system depended on linking teams with specific locales, which required a significant shift in supporter identity: from corporate institution to community location; from support based on a social space of production to support based on a social space of consumption; from allegiance and identity with an employer and business enterprise to allegiance and identity based on location. Given the success of corporate sponsorship of professional baseball, and the fact that most Japanese identify closely with their place of employment rather than the city or town in which they live, the different vision the JFA created was risky. Corporations, local businesses, and town and prefectural governments had to be convinced that the emphasis on community-based teams ultimately would result in economic and social benefits for them. Ultimately, both the J League's financial success and the success of building a culture of soccer in Japan has been absolutely dependent upon connecting with and stimulating a sense of local identification with teams.

Many J League teams were initiated in communities outside major urban areas in order to draw on this strategy of local identity. An example is the Kashima Antlers, located in a city with a population of 60,000 people. The only sizeable industry in Kashima was Sumitomo Steel, a company that had sponsored an amateur team in the past. Kashima and its prefectural government funded the construction of a new stadium, and, although initially reluctant to drop its name from the new J League team, Sumitomo Steel eventually acquiesced to the new J League strategy of naming teams after cities in order to build a local identity. Since the inaugural season in 1993, the Kashima Antlers have won the league championship three times and finished second in three additional seasons. Attendance has flourished and now averages 18,000 fans per match, a sufficient number for the team to profit financially. More importantly, the team has become a focal point for the local community, sponsoring a variety of sports and cultural events ranging from free soccer clinics to community welfare events. From 1997 to 1999, the overall economic impact of the Antlers on the city of Kashima was 3.5 billion yen, or approximately 42 million U.S. dollars.[23]

Because this soccer reorganization began in the 1990s, when professional and national soccer teams for women were gaining momentum worldwide, the new system has had a dramatic impact on women's soccer in Japan.

Although some Japanese universities and corporations had fielded women's teams as early as the 1970s, female participation in the sport was not extensive. The first women's national team was organized in 1986. When the men's J League formed three years later, women's soccer joined the fray. The amateur Japan Women's Football League, nicknamed the L (for Lady) League, was soon formed with an initial six teams. Although the league attracted widespread media attention, with foreign players signing on as professionals, it suffered financially. The national team qualified for its first Women's World Cup in 2003, however, and the following year the league expanded to eight first division teams and eight second division teams. With its newfound success, the L League dropped its initial moniker for the more favorable Nadeshiko League. The *nadeshiko,* or dianthus flower, in Japanese tradition represents the "ideal" woman.

As most soccer fans know, the Japanese women's team defeated the U.S. women's team to win the 2011 Women's World Cup. Making it through the group stage with victories over New Zealand and Mexico and a 2–0 loss to England, the Japanese women beat the reigning champions from 2003 and 2007, Germany (1–0) and Sweden (3–1), to set up a meeting with the powerhouse U.S. team. The latter had won the World Cup in 1991—the first FIFA Women's World Cup—and 1999; it had placed third in the other three Cup tournaments. In the first few minutes of the match, the United States dominated play, with three narrowly missed shots on goal, followed by a ninth-minute goal made by Alex Morgan. The 1–0 lead for the United States held until the eighty-first minute, when diminutive 5'2" Aya Miyama, in the right spot to catch the ball bouncing off a U.S. defender, flicked it into the net for the tying goal. The United States scored first in overtime when Abby Wambach headed a goal in the one hundred fourth minute. With only three minutes left in overtime, a corner kick for Japan sailed to the left of goal. Moving away from the goal, Homare Sawa caught the ball in mid-air, making an almost impossible shot over the U.S. goalie to tie the score once again. Japan won the match and the title on a penalty shootout. The victory seemed particularly fitting given that it came four months after the 2011 earthquake and tsunami that devastated the island nation.

Homare Sawa received the Golden Shoe award for her tournament-leading five goals, as well as the Golden Ball award as the tournament's outstanding player. The Nadeshiko League also placed four women on the 21-member All-Tournament team, the same number as the United States. Clearly, Japanese women's soccer had arrived on the world soccer scene, and it had done so almost overnight.

Although Japan's national men's team has yet to achieve the status of traditionally strong soccer nations in Europe and South America, they have moved steadily up the ladder of FIFA national team rankings. Their highest ranking was thirteenth in the world in March 2011, and they spent the rest of 2011 consistently in the top 20. The women's national team cracked the top ten in the FIFA rankings in December 2007, and they, too, have gradually moved up the ladder to their current third-place spot behind the United States and Germany. (Despite their victory over the United States in the 2011 World Cup, the loss to England on the way to the championship prevented them from moving past these latter two teams.)

This rapid rise in world soccer depended on the development system that feeds the higher levels of Japanese soccer. According to a 2006 survey of 2,500 Japanese boys and girls between the ages of 10 and 19, soccer was the number one sport regularly played by boys, and the Japanese national men's team was the sports team kids most wanted to see live. Between 1980 and 1995, the number of soccer players registered with the Japan Football Association increased by 186 percent.[24]

The extensive cooperation between private and public capital has been one of the primary keys in building Japan's soccer culture. The focus on local identity with specific teams has also contributed to this success. But let's not forget the role of the heaven-sent child of soccer, Tsubasa Ozora. Is it merely a coincidence that this popular series blanketed Japanese mass culture in the 1980s and that the Japan Football Association immediately initiated its massive campaign to broaden and strengthen participation in soccer throughout the country? Is it sheer happenstance that a generation of boys and girls who lifted Japan out of soccer obscurity in the 1990s and beyond grew up reading and watching the exploits of *Captain Tsubasa?* Or is it possible that the synergy of mass culture, local identity building, and public and private financing is responsible for the rapid success of Japanese soccer? These questions are difficult to answer.

We do know the story of one of the greatest Japanese soccer players to ever grace a pitch, however. His name is Hidetoshi Nakata. Born in 1977, Nakata was four years old and learning to read when the *Captain Tsubasa* series first hit the pages of the *manga* world. Nakata started playing organized soccer at the age of nine, the same year the first *Captain Tsubasa* TV series concluded its initial three-year run and the first four *anime* films were released. He went on to star on the national U-15 and U-17 teams as well as the 1995 U-20 team that made it to the quarter-finals of the FIFA World Youth Championships. Nakata also played for the national men's team in three World Cups and two

Olympics. From the age of 21, he played professionally in the Italian Serie A League with A.C. Perugia, Roma, and Parma, and finished out his 10-year professional career with Bolton Wanderers of the English Premier League. In 2004, Pelé, the Brazilian soccer legend, named Nakata in his *FIFA 100,* Pelé's personal ranking of the top 100 living soccer players in the world.

Nakata attributed his passion for soccer and the choice to pursue a professional career to the *Captain Tsubasa manga* and *anime* series. As he explained in a 2005 interview with CNN's Asia Talks after signing with the Bolton Wanderers, "When I first started playing football, baseball was a lot more popular.... But there was also a very popular football *manga,* or comic, at that time. I read that *manga* and was inspired to play football."[25] How many other Japanese soccer players were inspired by the exploits of Tsubasa Ozora is anyone's guess. One thing is certain, however: the fortuitous appearance of this popular soccer *manga,* followed by an innovative plan to extend the reach of soccer into communities through the cooperation of both public and private financing, certainly reshaped the soccer landscape of Japan and put the country on a trajectory toward greater world soccer prominence.

* * * *

Of course, Germany and Japan are not the United States. Because of the unique histories of soccer in different nations and their radically different cultural settings, including the social space occupied by sports, a system that works in one country might not work in another. We can't extract one element of a culture and plant it into another, and then expect it to look, sound, smell, or taste the same. Yoga in the United States will always be slightly different from yoga in Nepal or India, and *mole poblano* served in a Mexican restaurant in North Carolina will never taste the same as *mole poblano* in Puebla. Similarly, the structure of the soccer landscape in the United States will never be the same as that in Japan or Germany. Nevertheless, what would the world be like if we didn't learn, borrow, and creatively modify what other cultures have to offer?

In other words, what can we learn about the social space occupied by soccer in countries like Germany and Japan that might in some way apply to U.S. soccer? Several things are easily discernible. First, both Japan and Germany have created player access systems that are not shaped by socioeconomic class. Because the systems are not pay-to-play systems (or at least not pay-as-much-to-play systems), individuals from a greater diversity of socioeconomic classes have equal access. The by-product of this greater equal access is that soccer is not symbolically identifiable with a limited segment of class hierarchies, as it is in the United States.

Second, both Germany and Japan have successfully financed their systems through creative structures in both public and private spheres. This financing requires greater cooperation between the state and private sectors and all other levels of the soccer landscape—from youth to professional to national teams. Through the club structure the U.S. youth system follows a business model in which the development of high-quality soccer skills is often a secondary consideration. Because of our cultural aversion to what we often label "socialism," Americans may be more reluctant to embrace solutions that require a greater public financial commitment.

Finally, both Germany and Japan, for different reasons, have successfully built a mass culture of soccer. In Germany, soccer is the *only* sport with such a broad-based appeal. Thus the recent changes in the player development system in that country are more an intensification than the construction of a soccer culture. Conventional wisdom dictates that a major problem with soccer in the United States is that it must compete with otherwise entrenched sports like U.S. football, basketball, and baseball. There's simply no more acreage left in the landscape of U.S. sports, or so the argument goes. But there may be a lesson for us in the case of Japan, where soccer had to confront the entrenched sport of baseball. Granted, the landscape was less occupied than that in the United States, but before 1989 soccer in Japan was more like a squatter settlement on the feudal estate owned by baseball. Now more Japanese boys play organized soccer than baseball. What happened? Of course, the reorganization that began in 1989 had a huge impact, but the spread of the soccer ideal through the mass entertainment and educational venues of *manga* and *anime* preceded, and then accompanied, that reorganization. To be successful on a large scale, a sport has to capture the popular imagination of a nation, something that has apparently happened in Japan. The popular imagination of a culture is not just a response to external circumstances, but it can also serve as a stimulus for change. While comics and animated films obviously would not satisfy the U.S. case, something else might. What that is remains to be seen.

Section Two: Retrospective of U.S. Soccer

3

History of U.S. Soccer: Beginnings

Like any other history that attempts to establish a starting point, a history of U.S. soccer must decide where to begin. History is not filled with stops and starts, with dead ends and brand-new highways and byways, just as it is not characterized by innovative ideas emerging out of nowhere, or by brilliant discoveries made independent of similar discoveries preceding them. History is a continuous path—one full of detours, side streets, and twists and turns, but a road nevertheless, complete with interconnections and antecedents where the present is always tied to the past, and the past always viewed through the lens of the present. Perhaps because we are human—animals with a distinct consciousness of our own beginning (birth) and our own eventual end (death)—we have a strong need to impose beginnings and ends on the flow and free-fall of history. But unless we start all histories with the Big Bang—and even then a Big Bang might have forgone *this* Big Bang—the choice of where to begin is always arbitrary.

It may seem unorthodox to locate the beginnings of U.S. soccer in the Napoleonic Wars. Those wars have their own antecedents, and to connect the origins of soccer to such hostile conflicts is a mighty long stretch. Surprisingly, however, a closer look at the events of that time and the introduction of soccer in the United States during the 1870s reveals a series of plausible connections. When Napoleon attempted to extend his power over the European continent in the early 1800s, his armies marched eastward through present-day Germany. In 1806, his forces took the city of Hamburg, a strategic port in northern Germany located at the intersection of the Elbe, Alster, and Bille Rivers. For centuries, cities like Hamburg, Augsburg, Cologne, and Nuremburg functioned as major European trade centers. Hamburg identified itself with silk, and weavers from England and Scotland imported its products to make heddle-thread for looms.

During Napoleon's invasion of Hamburg, the supply of silk diminished significantly, placing an economic strain on early industrial development. For years, small businesses across England and Scotland had turned imported silk threads from Hamburg into twine. The thread supported the larger weaving businesses across Great Britain. Peter Clark and his brother, George, from Paisley, Scotland, ran one such silk-heddle operation. Faced with the declining availability of their essential ingredient, the Clarks began experimenting with a cotton-based thread. Their venture proved successful, leading to an improved thread used in weaving. Like a number of other technological innovations, the Clarks' adapted product helped propel Great Britain to the forefront of an expanding textile industry. Although Napoleon could not have cared less about improving England and Scotland's textile trade, this unintended consequence helped solidify Great Britain's position in the new Industrial Age.

The innovation provided valuable capital for the Clark brothers as well. Soon their firm stopped manufacturing heddle-twine and started making cotton spool-thread, basically using the same design as the colorful spools still used today. When the sewing machine was invented in 1847, the market for cotton spool-thread exploded. Because of the pressure caused by the rapid movement of the machine's needle, the standard thread for the sewing machine often broke. Once again, the Clarks developed a solution. They invented a soft, six-cord cotton thread able to withstand the demands of a machine and be used simultaneously for hand sewing. They called their innovation "Our New Thread," known by the acronym ONT.

In 1856, 50 years after Napoleon and his army marched into Hamburg, George Clark immigrated to the United States as part of the firm's expansion into larger markets. He successfully managed the firm's import business in New York City, and in 1864 he drew up plans to build a huge factory in Newark, New Jersey. The Clark Thread Company began operations in 1866 in Kearney (now East Newark), New Jersey, along the shores of the Passaic River. Within a few decades the financially successful plant expanded to 13 acres and consisted of 35 buildings spread across both sides of the river, employing thousands of workers. The operation in the United States and abroad supplied thread to a large portion of the industrialized world. It also set the stage for the company's next move: soccer.[1]

* * * *

Ball games have characterized human culture for millennia. During the Han Dynasty (206 BC–AD 240) the Chinese played a game called *Tsu Chu,* or *cuju.* Images of women playing with a ball appeared on Egyptian tombs as early as 2000 BC. The Japanese engaged in *kemari,* while ancient Greeks participated in *episkyros.* Early Mexican and Central American civilizations enjoyed similar activities. Although historians refer to these various games as *football,* similarities to modern soccer are inconclusive. Pinpointing the origins of a game remotely akin to soccer is like finding the missing link between early primates and humans. Pinpointing a direct ancestor is as misguided as identifying a million-year-old stone chopper as the designated antecedent of the computer chip. Evolution isn't linear, resembling as it does the branches of a very large tree.

The origins of the modern game of soccer, however, are better known and claim a distinctly English footprint. By the Middle Ages people in Europe and the British Isles played a number of games bearing a general resemblance to soccer. Most of them involved hordes of participants kicking and running after a large ball, lacking any formal rules. Apparently hooliganism helped characterize the sport long before its official emergence. In 1314, the Lord Mayor of London banned the game after identifying "a great noise in the city caused by hustling over large foot balls ... from which many evils might arise."[2] Local citizens received prison terms if caught playing this popular version of the game. As the power of the monarchy declined, puritanical Parliamentarians listed football as one of several proscribed sporting pastimes. Despite these restrictions, enthusiasts continued to play. Over the centuries historical anecdotes refer to a variety of participants, from common laborers to court nobility.

By the beginning of the nineteenth century and the dawning of industrialization, British schools, universities, the military, and other identifiable communities played a variety of football games. Each institution and locale followed its own guidelines, dictating the number of players on each side, the size of the field, how the ball could be moved, what constituted goals, and the ramifications of tackling. In the beginning the absence of standardized play limited competition, and if one community wanted to play another, each side had to renegotiate the rules.

The increasing rationalization of life that characterized the social and economic transformations of industrialization helped eliminate the relative chaos of the football landscape. The 1840s and 1850s saw various attempts to codify rules. These attempts distinguished between the so-called "handling game" (which roughly resembled rugby) and the contrary "kicking or dribbling game" (more akin to soccer). The first football club, the Sheffield FC, started in the 1850s, and 11 teams operated in the Sheffield area by 1862. These teams perfected the "kicking game," and their success helped create standard rules and parameters that allowed teams from different regions to compete on an equal playing field.

In the fall of 1863, individuals who represented variations of the kicking game met in London and hammered out a series of rules that would form the foundations of modern soccer, as well as the establishment of the London Football Association (LFA). These new guidelines marked a clear division between the two most popular forms of football—rugby and soccer. In 1867 Sheffield accepted the new rules, which led to the Rugby Football Union, thus solidifying the overt separation between the two sports. By 1871, the LFA consisted of 50 teams. Soccer officials adopted the title "Association Football" to distinguish it from "Rugby Football," and the following year the London FA held its first FA Cup competition. The Wanderers beat the Royal Engineers 1–0 before a paltry 2,000 spectators.[3] Later that year the first international competition was held between a conglomerate of English FA club players and Queen's Park, the top Scottish team. The match ended in a 0–0 draw. From these somewhat humble beginnings, association football, soon to be known in England by the slang term "soccer," would spread throughout Great Britain and the world.

* * * *

Association football spread rapidly in popularity throughout the British Isles. Within a decade it had reached the working class, particularly those employed in the textile industry in England and Scotland. The codification and rapid spread of the sport also coincided with the dynamic growth of the Clark Thread Company, which had comfortably settled overseas. The company in the United States brought in many skilled workers from two main textile dominions in Great Britain: the Lancashire region of England and the Paisley region near Glasgow, known as the Valley of Clyde. A number of push-and-pull variables characterized this immigration pattern. For example, until 1825 Great Britain prohibited skilled textile workers from leaving the Isles, fearing an exodus would contribute to foreign competition. But England and Scotland relaxed their policies that year. Increasing disputes between mill owners and organized labor actually encouraged union organizers to immigrate; in addition, mechanization in the mills had slowed down the demand for new labor and forced citizens to look elsewhere for economic security. In the United States, the American Civil War had reduced its own labor force. Lax immigration policies through the mid–1880s helped fill the demand for male labor in the new country. By 1890, an unprecedented 15 percent of the U.S. population was foreign born.[4]

The English and Scottish workers hired by the Clark Thread Company found a familiar setting, working for a company run by fellow British immigrants. The town of Kearney, like other mill towns in New England, also felt familiar and soon gained the appellation of "Little Scotland." As historian Maldwyn Jones writes in *Destination America*, "These towns to which British textile workers flocked in the 1860s were not unlike those they had left.... It must have been difficult to believe they were not still in England."[5]

In addition to the necessary skills and experience, laborers from the Valley of Clyde and Lancashire possessed an equally valuable commodity. Both areas were among the first regions to experience the growth of soccer among working-class laborers, including those immigrating to the United States.[6] The Scottish Football Association was founded in 1873. The following year St. Mirren Football Club formed in Paisley (and St. Mirren's plays in the Scottish first division to this day). In 1878, Lancashire gave rise to the Newton Heath Football Club, which evolved into one of England's most famous and enduring clubs—Manchester United.

The new Scottish and English arrivals also settled in immigrant neighborhoods outside Kearney and its Clark Thread employer. They moved to similar small-town mill centers like Fall River and New Bedford, Massachusetts; Pawtucket, Rhode Island; and Paterson, New Jersey. With this convergence, it was only a matter of time before soccer appeared in New England as well. The relationship between immigration and soccer was not a simple one, however. Soccer from Great Britain had not yet spread to Continental Europe and South America, so immigrants from those regions coming to the United States knew very little about the sport. Moreover, soccer in Scotland and England trickled slowly into the working class, and then only in specific regions. The connections between those regions and towns like Kearney were coincidental and depended on companies like Clark Thread located in specific American communities. Thus, while New England represents the first significant region in the world to import soccer from the British Isles, it also reflects a matter of being in the right place at the right time.

The first move to organize soccer in the United States occurred in the summer of 1884. The Clark Thread Company led the way. Representatives from Kearney, Newark, New York, and Paterson met at the Clark Thread Company and agreed to form the American Football Association, only the third "national" football association of its kind. (England had established its own association 20 years earlier, while Scotland had done so in 1873). The newly formed members also agreed to hold an annual competition, originally called the American Football Association Challenge Cup. The winner received a silver trophy.[7]

Thirteen clubs from six towns and cities entered the first competition held the following year. The teams from Newark included the Almas, Domestics, Riversides, Thistles, and Tiffany Rovers. The New York FC and the New York Thistles represented New York City. Fall River, Massachusetts, entered the Fall River Rovers and the Fall River East Ends. The Paterson FC represented Paterson and the Ansonia FC came from Ansonia, Connecticut. Finally, Kearney entered the Kearney Rangers and ONT (All New Thread), the team sponsored by the Clark Thread Company. On April 25, 1885, two finalists met to claim the first U.S. soccer championship. In a hotly contested match, ONT defeated the New York FC 2–1 and received the first Challenge Cup.[8]

Actually, the ONT team had formed in 1883 prior to the start of the AFA. Their first formal, albeit intramural, match on December 2, 1883, pitted the ONT *married* men against the ONT *single* men. Marriage came out on top 4–2. No one has ever determined what secret talents the married players held over their single rivals.

A few months after winning the Challenge Cup, the Western Canadian Football Association, which had formed almost simultaneously with its AFA counterpart, invited the ONT champions to participate in an 11-match tour in southern Ontario. The ONT team won nine matches, tied one, and lost one. The 1–1 tie came against the Canadian champs, the Berlin Rangers.[9] The following November, the Clark Thread Company hosted the first U.S. International on the ONT Athletic Association field. The U.S. team consisted of players from four different AFA teams, and the Canadian team members were all-stars from the Western Association. A crowd of 2,000, "some 60 of whom were ladies," according to the *New York Times*, watched the Canadians win by a score of 1–0.[10]

The ONT chalked up successive championships by winning the AFA Cup in 1886 and 1887. Similarly, in 1886 a more talented U.S. all-star team defeated the Canadian all-star team by a score of 3–2. The Clark Thread Company continued to host the AFA cup, but for the next five years teams from Fall River dominated play, winning successive finals. The Fall River Rovers won the Cup in 1888 and 1889, the Fall River Olympics in 1890, and the Fall River East Ends in 1891 and 1892. The little town of Fall River, whose first mill was built in 1811 along the cascading falls of the Quequechan River, gained the reputation of being the King of U.S. Soccer. Between 1865 and

1885 Fall River's population more than tripled, from 17,000 citizens to 56,000.[11] The number of textile spindles increased fivefold. The rapid growth consisted of textile workers from Lancashire, who had arrived with trunks of clothes and personal belongings, as well as their newly incubated English soccer fever.

In this limited New England geographic space, soccer made a modest effort to compete with other sports for the country's popular imagination. In 1891, the fourth year of the Fall River teams' dominance, eight U.S. players from the Fall River Rovers, Fall River Olympics, and Pawtucket toured England with a group of Canadian players. The joint Canadian-U.S. team played 58 matches in 135 days against some of the strongest English teams, many of them professional. The team returned home with 13 victories, 13 ties, and 32 defeats, but the experience of playing against the best soccer teams in the world gave individual players confidence and the U.S. soccer movement as a whole a tremendous boost.[12]

While the teams from Kearney and Fall River dominated initial AFA Cup competitions, soccer began emerging in other regions of the country. One of the most important new cities included St. Louis, half a continent away. With a population of over 450,000 by 1890, St. Louis was the fourth largest city in the country—only New York, Chicago, and Philadelphia had more citizens. The city of St. Louis had come into its own, and with it came a popular interest in soccer. In fact, close to the turn of the century St. Louis claimed to be America's first "soccer city"—a title with some legitimacy, since soccer centers like Kearney and its New England neighbors still resembled small to medium-size towns. Also, unlike in the New England soccer cradle, the relationship between immigrants and St. Louis soccer did not depend on being in the right place at the right time.

From the 1830s to the 1850s, St. Louis experienced a significant influx of Irish and German immigrants. As early as 1824, a German writer named Gottfried Duden immigrated to the United States and settled 50 miles west of St. Louis. Five years later he published a book in Germany extolling the beauty and bounty of Missouri. He wrote, "People in Europe will not and cannot believe how easy and how pleasant it can be to live in this country. It sounds too strange, too fabulous. Believing in similar places on this earth has too long been consigned to the fairy-tale world."[13] Duden's book met with popular success and helped influence a wave of German immigration to St. Louis and the surrounding territory.

Similarly, the Irish potato famine of 1845–1846 and a failed political uprising two years later influenced significant Irish migrations to the United States. Although a number of these immigrants settled in the northeast, many followed Horace Greeley's admonition to "go west." Thousands of Irish immigrants settled in St. Louis, lured there by the strong Catholic presence established during the city's formative years under French and Spanish control.

St. Louis also experienced an economic boom, which expanded the need for fresh laborers. The United States had extended its reach all the way to the Pacific Ocean by 1848, when the Treaty of Guadalupe Hidalgo that ended the U.S.-Mexican War of 1846–1848 ceded to the United States the region identified today as the American Southwest. The treaty finalized control of the territory visualized under the banner of Manifest Destiny, and the nation extended its reach "from sea to shining sea." St. Louis had already established itself as the major north-south gateway along the Mississippi River. After 1848, it became a major portal of Western expansion as well.

Unlike the Scottish and English immigrants who came to the mill towns of New England, the bulk of German and Irish immigrants to St. Louis preceded the appearance of organized soccer in Great Britain. In fact, by the time soccer reached U.S. shores, most St. Louis immigrants were second-generation Irish and German Americans. Lacking the kind of organic impetus that existed among the Scottish and English immigrants in northeastern mill towns, the Catholic Church's involvement in community affairs propelled an interest in St. Louis soccer. Viewing organized soccer as healthy for the body, mind, and soul both individually and collectively, the Catholic Church took the initiative in developing competitive teams and a city league. The church's influence can be seen in the names of early St. Louis soccer teams, among them St. Leo's, St. Theresa's, St. Rose's, and Christian Brothers College.

The first official soccer match in St. Louis pitted the Athletic Club against the Mound City Club in 1881.[14] By 1886, St. Louis operated a city league and crowned a champion each successive year. Because soccer didn't exist in the lower plains, matches were confined to the city. Intense rivalries across St. Louis drew substantial crowds to the games. One match in 1887 reported 6,000 fans in attendance. Due to the league's amateur status, travel expenses remained virtually nonexistent; financial support came easy. For years, until the city improved its means of travel, St. Louis remained an isolated, yet vibrant, soccer center. Because travel to the northeast was expensive and cumbersome, the St. Louis teams didn't participate in the AFA Cup competitions. Although reputable teams existed in Philadelphia, Chicago, Cleveland, New York, and elsewhere in the last two decades of the nineteenth century, none of those organizations matched the extent and enthusiasm of the St. Louis soccer landscape. For decades, St. Louis teams played some of the best amateur soccer in the United States, and many of the most talented players to grace the early twentieth-century soccer pitches in the country came out of that milieu.[15]

Though not as extensive, other soccer venues existed alongside those from large cities. In the early nineteenth century, select universities competed in a number of football contests. As in England, rules varied widely and matches typically resembled a hybrid of soccer and rugby. Teams could score goals by both kicking and running with the ball. In 1862, the Oneida Football Club formed in Boston, drawing players primarily from the area's elite secondary schools. Once a week they would challenge local makeshift teams. Because their challengers were disorganized and poorly trained, Oneida dominated play. Over a three-year period, Oneida's opponents failed to score a single goal.

In 1866, Beadle & Company of New York, adapting guidelines established by the London Football Association three years earlier, published a set of rules for both association football and rugby football. Three years later, in 1869, Rutgers University defeated Princeton 6–4 in what is generally considered the first-ever American football match. In 1969, the National Football League celebrated the sport's centennial. The match from 1869 still resembled a hybrid, however, containing elements of both the handling game and the kicking game. Teams consisted of 25 players. They advanced the ball only by kicking or heading it. If a player caught the ball in mid-air or after the first bounce, that player was entitled to a free kick; if he missed the ball, a free-for-all exploded. Players scored points by kicking the ball through their opponents' goal, which consisted of two posts 25 feet apart. The match ended when one team reached six points. In reality, this early form of American football was closely attuned to what eventually evolved into soccer.[16]

Other universities such as Yale, Columbia, and Pennsylvania State also established football clubs. Like their Ivy League counterparts, these universities rarely followed a consistent set of rules. In the 1870s the football played at universities in the northeast favored the handling game. On November 13, 1875, Harvard met Yale in New Haven in a game that more closely resembled modern American football. Playing with teams of 15 players and a mutually drafted set of rules that allowed the ball to be both carried and kicked, Harvard trounced Yale "four goals and four tries to zero." In these kinds of matches a team scored a goal when a player propelled the ball with his feet or head through the opponent's two goal posts; a team scored a "try" when they carried the ball across the opponent's goal line, giving the carrying team a free kick. The try resembled the modern extra point in American football, granted when the ball is kicked through the goal posts. In 1876, Columbia, Harvard, Princeton, and Yale formed the first Intercollegiate Football Association, agreeing on rules that closely resembled rugby football. Over the next several decades, rule changes, as well as alterations in the shape of the ball, moved the sport further from the kicking game, which we've come to know as soccer. Ultimately soccer, or any other sport vaguely resembling it, essentially disappeared from the college sports landscape. Not until 1902, when an English exchange student named Richard Gummere initiated a Haverford College team in a local Philadelphia amateur league, did the sport reappear in a university setting.[17]

In the final decade of the nineteenth century, U.S. soccer remained primarily in the northeastern towns of English and Scottish immigrants, in Irish and German St. Louis, and in other expanding urban areas across the country that attracted Great Britain's immigrants. Soccer had arrived on the shores of the United States through these immigration channels earlier than in any other soccer nation outside of Great Britain. Early soccer in England, Scotland, and the United States remained amateur, with costs absorbed primarily by company sponsors. Talented players on company teams often received perks in terms of hiring preferences, workloads, and work hours, but they still maintained their nonprofessional status. As the popularity of the sport spread in England and Scotland, sponsors felt increasing pressure to pay players in order to help them develop individual and team skills. Simultaneously, the owners of teams saw possible financial opportunities due to the sport's expanding popularity. By 1888, the English had formed their first professional league; the Scots followed with their own league in 1890.

Ironically, the National League of Professional Baseball initiated the first drive to professionalize soccer in the United States. Professional baseball clubs and players had existed since the 1860s, but prior to 1891 professional teams and players had come and gone due to wavering public support and poor management. In 1894, owners of six baseball teams representing the 12-team National League organized the first professional U.S. soccer league. They called it the American League of Professional Football Clubs, and announced that play would begin in October 1894, after the conclusion of the baseball season. The baseball owners showed little interest in supporting soccer, but they saw such a league as a potentially profitable way to utilize professional baseball stadiums that would otherwise lay dormant during the offseason. Although American football had grown increasingly popular in universities, no movement emerged to professionalize that sport; college teams were firmly established in their own campus stadiums. Baseball owners had little choice but to turn to the only other sport hinting at signs of popular appeal.[18]

The six baseball teams that first professionalized soccer operated in the northeast, in the vicinity where the small mill towns had popularized the sport. The actual stadiums in which the soccer teams were scheduled to play, however, were located in New York, Boston, Philadelphia, and other urban areas. Relocating to these larger arenas threatened small-town rivalries and identification with already established neighborhood clubs. While amateur teams from Kearney, Pawtucket, Fall River, and Bedford had attracted crowds in the thousands, this support failed to matriculate into the larger cities. Poor attendance, bad planning, inadequate financing, and misguided scheduling doomed the effort to professionalize almost from the start. Within one short and unenthusiastic season, the league folded.

Despite this dismal failure, the idea of professionalizing soccer still held widespread appeal. Within months enthusiasts initiated a second attempt, but on a much smaller scale. This new attempt looked more promising because it included an already established player and fan base. The National Association Foot Ball League began play in March 1895, with five teams: Brooklyn Wanderers, New Rochelle FC, Kearney Scots, Centerville FC (Bayonne, New Jersey), and Americus AA (West Hoboken, New Jersey). Primarily a New York City metropolitan league, the newly formed NAFBL misrepresented a more inclusive "national" league.[19] By the same token, it took its cue from "National" and "American" baseball leagues, whose teams represented regions east of St. Louis and no farther south than Washington, D.C. Of course, terms like "National" also reflected a coded attempt to manufacture a collective soccer identity. Despite its misrepresentation, the NAFBL stands as one of the earliest professional soccer leagues in the world. It survived both the shifting sands of the U.S. economy and the country's professional sports landscape until the beginning of World War I.

Unfortunately, this second attempt at professionalism coincided with the Panic of 1893, a severe economic downturn in the country that hampered high-level sports. Such bad timing represented a missed opportunity to place professional soccer securely alongside professional baseball and university football. For more than three years, the United States suffered the collapse of 15,000 companies, 500 banks, and a significant percentage of railways, the primary overland transportation system.[20] Unemployment escalated and labor unrest caused many solvent industries to spin out of control. Strikes inundated steel mills, railway car plants, and textile industries in places like Fall River and New Bedford, where amateur soccer had flourished. The economic downturn meant less financial support from businesses and smaller audiences for sports, soccer included.

By the mid–1890s soccer remained on the fringes of sports-conscious

Americans, and few thought the decade a propitious time to launch a new professional enterprise. Also, print media had long promoted baseball as the "true American" sport. Similarly, football played in universities had evolved beyond its rugby origins to attain a distinctly American footprint. Unfortunately, soccer had not escaped the lingering perception of being a foreign sport at worst, and a sport played by recent immigrants at best. Had some brilliant entrepreneur steeped in marketing found a way to tap into the base that had been secured in New England, St. Louis, and other regions of the country, the history of soccer in the United States might have been very different.

The primary soccer venue for most teams formed in the 1880s remained the AFA Cup. Due to the economic turmoil of the 1890s, this American "championship" struggled and finally disappeared in 1899. Although teams from Kearny, Fall River, and other towns continued to play, the period between 1899 and 1905 saw diminished competition. Elsewhere in the world, soccer planted its roots.

The British carried the game to other corners of the globe, including Continental Europe and South America. By 1900, national football associations had emerged in more than a dozen countries, mostly in Europe but also on distant shores in New Zealand, Argentina, Chile, and Uruguay. On May 21, 1904, representatives from six national football associations and an unaffiliated representative from Spain met in Paris and formed the Fédération Internationale de Football Association, more commonly known by its acronym FIFA. Over 100 years later, this organization still controls international soccer competition. Like Spain, Germany did not have an official representative at the meeting. But that same day the Germans cabled Paris indicating that they, too, would join the federation. Curiously, British FAs from England, Ireland, Scotland, and Wales remained aloof, perhaps sensitive to upstart European nations taking the lead in organizing a worldwide governing body of a sport they felt they had invented.

This international effort seemed to revive interest in the United States, although the tour of an amateur English team called Pilgrims Football Club through Canada and the United States in 1905 generated more enthusiasm. After several matches in Canada, the team arrived in Detroit with much fanfare. It trounced the local team 10–2. This score was a harbinger of things to come. While scheduled matches in St. Louis expected better competition, the Pilgrims relentlessly attacked their Midwestern opponents. Newspapers reported that the St. Louis goalie feared for his life after his team lost their first match 10–0. Exposed to the British style of play heading into their second meeting, St. Louis still lost 6–0. In just three matches in the United States,

PFC had outscored their U.S. opponents 26–2. The lopsided stats effectively exposed the true state of U.S. soccer.[21]

The tour continued to Chicago, where an amateur all-star squad lost 6–0. Playing the next day in the stadium of the Chicago White Sox, the same team managed a 2–1 upset. The winning streak proved short-lived. Traveling to Philadelphia, Boston, and New York City, the PFC continued to dominate its opponents in the same unbalanced way.

One of the most interesting legs of the PFC tour included a lone match in Fall River, an early cradle of U.S. soccer. After play in the six largest cities in the United States, the match in the small Massachusetts town corroborated the kind of soccer that had existed there for the last 20 years. An overflow crowd of 7,000 fans, described as the largest audience to attend a match in Fall River, crowded into the local stadium to watch an intensely competitive match that remained undecided until the very end. The English team managed a hard-fought goal in the last five minutes to squeak out a 4–3 win.[22]

Although the amateur Pilgrims FC marched triumphantly through the U.S. soccer landscape, the attendance at the matches told the real story. Precise figures are unavailable, but various accounts report 10,000 fans in attendance in Detroit; 15,000 to 28,000 in St. Louis; 5,000 in Chicago; and 10,000 to 15,000 in Philadelphia. The attendance in Fall River showed that small towns could also attract enthusiastic crowds. While baseball games still averaged a larger attendance in 1905, the figures for the 23-game tour indicated the possibility of a larger soccer fan base than previously imagined.[23]

At the same time as the PFC's tour, U.S. government and sports officials leveled a series of complaints against college football for its overt violence. Around the time the Pilgrims played in St. Louis, President Teddy Roosevelt met in the White House with appropriate representatives to discuss the recent upsurge in football injuries and related complaints.[24] The group included Walter Camp, considered by many the "father" of American football for his significant contributions as an organizer, player, and coach of the game. Roosevelt demanded that Camp and other leaders address the growing violence, cheating, and unsportsman-like behavior associated with collegiate football. Although Roosevelt believed the increasingly popular game served an important function in the development of masculine character, he also feared that the growing discourse around violence in the sport could lead to its demise.

In fact, as the PFC prepared for its matches in New York City, the *Harvard Bulletin* published an article critical of the current state of football. Claiming that the game required "the constant attention of skilled surgeons" and identifying the playing field as a "hospital clinic," the article concluded,

"When, however, a game becomes so dangerous that several players are sure to be hurt in every contest ... it is time to admit that something is wrong." But violence was not the only problem. The article also suggested that football distracted students who "for weeks ... talk and think about nothing but football."[25]

Harvard president Charles W. Eliot led an unsuccessful attempt to ban football on campus. Such a move smacked of controversy, since Harvard's role in the development of the sport had been so crucial. Eliot said of football, "No sport is wholesome in which ungenerous or mean acts which easily escape detection contribute to victory."[26] To be fair, Eliot's criticism exceeded the morality of this one sport. He also objected to throwing the curveball in baseball because its basic intent was "to deceive."

Nevertheless, in 1905–1906 a number of universities, including Arizona, Baylor, California, Nevada, Northwestern, South Carolina, Stanford, and Temple, eliminated their football programs. Over the next few years they gradually reinstated the sport. Although American collegiate football never faced a real nationwide danger of elimination, the criticism leveled at football could have potentially opened a larger social space for the sport of soccer at this time.

Despite the rumbles over American football, soccer at universities remained almost imperceptible. Haverford College, which had fielded a student team in a local amateur league in 1902, became the first intercollegiate U.S. champion in 1905 when it defeated Harvard 1–0. Some members of the Haverford team had studied at Cambridge, where they had honed their soccer skills. Haverford won the initial intercollegiate championship three straight times. The title "intercollegiate champion" was misleading, however. By 1908 only eight universities fielded competitive soccer teams. No university west or south of Pennsylvania played the sport. By 1918, the number of universities playing soccer had increased by a mere four teams. Such slow growth indicated that the collegiate space for soccer would remain dormant for years.

The excitement created by the relatively large crowds watching the Pilgrims tour did provide some initial optimism for soccer, however. A New York journalist wrote that "the general public paid no heed to the sport until the advent of the Pilgrims team."[27] Fred Milnes, an on-again, off-again English player generally considered the driving force behind the Pilgrims FC matches, claimed there was "little doubt that the outcome of our tour will be the adoption of the British style of play in the States."[28] Various discussions in Chicago, New York, and Philadelphia centered on the development of competitive, inter-city systems as well as the formation of an effective national organization of soccer interests. This renewed interest in soccer, stimulated by the English team's visit, the development of FIFA at the international level, and the ineffective (yet public) criticism of American football, led to a slow but rising development in the soccer landscape.

In 1906, the AFL revived its Cup championship after a seven-year hiatus. The West Hudson AA, a team that came out of the same Scottish immigrant milieu as the earlier Kearney teams, won the first Cup. West Hudson went on to win two additional American Cup championships over the next four years. The final in 1908 between the West Hudson AA and the True Blues of Paterson drew a more-than-respectable crowd of 10,000 people. In 1912, West Hudson managed the first "double-double" in U.S. soccer history, winning both the AFL Cup and the NAFBL championship.[29] The professional league, which had started play during the precarious U.S. economy of 1895, had limped along since then and still represented only the second professional U.S. sport, after baseball, to survive into the twentieth century.

Through the first decade of the 1900s, soccer still resembled a jumbled landscape. Most large cities hosted a variety of ad hoc adult amateur teams. The professional league still functioned, although most salaries were insufficient to support individuals, much less families, for the entire year. The American Football Association still proclaimed itself the organizational head of U.S. soccer, even though it lacked true authority and was often embroiled in internal politics. The American Amateur Football Association was established in 1911 and held its own "American" Cup competition in 1912 and 1913, even though 23 of the 27 teams that entered were from New York. The competition rarely drew more than a few hundred fans and never really challenged the AFA, which supported more than 80 amateur and professional teams. The infant AAFA, however, argued that the AFA had ignored amateur football and challenged the AFA's assumed right as the governing body of U.S. soccer.

At FIFA's annual meeting in the summer of 1912 in Stockholm, both the AAFA and the AFA requested membership in FIFA, which would provide one of them with the internationally recognized right to control the U.S. soccer landscape. Thomas Cahill, the organization's secretary, represented AAFA. The AFA sent Frederick Wall, secretary of the English Football Association, with which the AFA had maintained loose ties since its founding over two decades earlier. FIFA representatives were reluctant to become embroiled in the conflict between the two organizations, and ultimately postponed full membership in hopes that both sides could present a unified application.[30]

Over the next several months, negotiations between the two sides faltered. In December 1912 the AFA decided against further talks about a merger. Unfortunately, because the bulk of organized soccer in the United States was still amateur, the AFA's draw-a-line-in-the-sand approach backfired. As more city soccer associations jumped ship and threw their support behind the AAFA, the new association organized a "national soccer congress" in New York City on April 5, 1913. With other soccer organizations the AFA reluctantly tagged along, although its president, Andrew Brown, admitted that he held antagonistic feelings toward the entire affair. It was too late to grumble, however. The congress overwhelmingly supported the creation of a new national governing body, eventually called the United States Football Association (USFA), and agreed to forward minutes of the meeting to FIFA with a fresh membership application.[31]

The infighting continued, with the AFA refusing to join hands, or feet, with the majority. All the same, FIFA granted the new organization provisional acceptance in Norway the following summer. Knowing that the AFA National Cup had been the most successful soccer venue up to this point, the newly formed USFA wasted no time creating its own competition, calling it the National Challenge Cup. Although the AFA continued its own Cup competition, the USFA Challenge Cup now gained the prestige and power of its association with FIFA. The AFA was now permanently "offside" and its demise just a matter of time.

The USFA invited 247 amateur and professional soccer teams to participate in the first Challenge Cup. Forty teams from seven states accepted the invitation, making it more "national" than any previous AFA Cup. Eleven of the 12 professional teams in the NAFBL declined to participate, likely due to their historical allegiance to the AFA. Only the Brooklyn FC, the top team in the professional league, bucked the tide and accepted the invitation. Competition began in the fall of 1913, and by spring the field had been reduced to eight quarter-finalists. Two Brooklyn-based teams—Brooklyn FC and Brooklyn Celtics—and the New Bedford FC (Massachusetts) and Niagara Falls Rangers pushed through to the semi-finals. Both Brooklyn teams were undefeated that year. The professional team, Brooklyn FC, had marched through the 1913–1914 season of the NAFBL with an unblemished record of 12–0–2. The Brooklyn Celtics, the top team in the New York Amateur Football Association League, had a record of 15–0–1 for that year. Both Brooklyn teams won and advanced to the finals. On May 16, 1914, 10,000 fans jammed into the small stadium in Pawtucket, Rhode Island, and watched an exciting match won by the professional Brooklyn FC 2–1.[32]

The first USFA Cup competition was a financial and morale-building success. The AFA Cup continued that same year; Bethlehem Steel FC, a team that would dominate U.S. soccer over the next 15 years, won the event.

Although the company had started a team in 1909, it came into full prominence during the 1913–1914 season, winning both Philadelphia's Allied American Football Association league championship with a perfect 13–0–0 record and the AFA Cup, defeating a team from Tacony, Pennsylvania. The *South Bethlehem Globe* headline read, "Bethlehem's Soccer Team Wins Championship of America." An estimated 15,000 fans watched the match.[33] Obviously, the two Cups still competed with each other over which event defined the true "national" championship.

Both competitions continued until 1929, when AFA's Cup phased out of existence. Teams could enter both competitions, and many did. Bethlehem Steel FC won AFA's newly named American Cup six times—in 1914, 1916, 1917, 1918, 1919, and 1924. They also won the USFA-sponsored National Challenge Cup in 1915, 1916, 1918, 1919, and 1926 before dissolving their team four years later. Winning one or the other Cup competition six straight years and both Cup competitions in 1916, 1918, and 1919, Bethlehem Steel could legitimately claim to be the true American champion. Other, older teams like Kearney Scots, Fall River Rovers, Brooklyn Celtics, and West Hudson FC continued to win and challenge Bethlehem FC's preeminence, but in those years no other soccer team in the United States achieved comparable success.

The Bethlehem Steel FC had started out with much more modest goals, designed mainly to promote company virtues of exercise, teamwork, and loyalty. A South Wales immigrant named Horace Edgar Lewis came to work at Bethlehem Steel in 1906 and picked up the game from other immigrant workers. Together they initiated an informal company team. The team eventually joined the Allied American Football Association League of Philadelphia, and by 1912 it finished runner-up in the league's championship competition. With the American Cup championship in 1914, the team achieved soccer prominence; the owner of Bethlehem Steel, Charles Schwab, donated $25,000—an enormous sum at that time—to be used to promote sports among the workforce. Schwab, who had a reputation for ruthless union busting and questionable business practices, realized that the publicity that came from sports translated into good business. Given the success of the soccer team and the considerable number of British immigrants who worked at the company, soccer received a significant portion of the generous donation. The money added considerably to building the team's subsequent success.[34]

The U.S. entry into World War I in 1917 impacted many soccer teams and leagues. The Southern New England League suspended play altogether for two years, taking the powerful Fall River Rovers with it. Many teams that had competed for years never returned after the war ended. Bethlehem Steel, as might be expected of a steel company during war, continued its soccer team as if nothing had changed. The team won both Cup competitions in 1918 and 1919 against a diminished field of 40 entries. As one of the few nationally recognized teams, BS continued to draw large crowds wherever it played. In the 1919 final for the Challenge Cup held in Fall River, an overflow crowd exceeding 9,000 saw Bethlehem FC defeat Paterson FC by a score of 2–0.[35] Although the team would go on to win two more Cup championships in the 1920s, the victory in 1919 marked the zenith of its career.

As the reigning U.S. champions, Bethlehem Steel FC team members added yet another feather to their collective soccer cap when they accepted an invitation to tour Scandinavian countries that summer. For the tour, they added several professional players from other teams, including Archie Stark, a talented 21-year-old player who would go down in history as one of the country's greatest players. BS also recruited Harry Ratican, owner and player for Ben Millers, a top St. Louis team. Ratican was probably the best American-born forward of the day. In a month-and-a-half tour, Bethlehem marched triumphantly through Denmark and Sweden, losing only two of 14 matches and demonstrating that U.S. teams could compete with some of the best teams that mainland Europe had to offer.[36] On the strength of that performance, Bethlehem was invited to tour in South America the following year, but South American sponsors canceled at the last minute. One can only speculate on the kind of upswing that could have resulted had the United States successfully toured South America on the heels of its Scandinavian rout.

By this time the Challenge Cup had surpassed the older American Cup in both prestige and financial success. The 1920 competition was particularly significant because it saw the first entries from the St. Louis league. Although recognized as one of the power centers of U.S. soccer, St. Louis—partly because of its location and partly because of city pride—had remained largely insulated from soccer played in the rest of the country. But improvements in transportation technology and infrastructure, coupled with the growing prestige of the Challenge Cup, enticed St. Louis to join the fray. Although soccer leagues had started to appear in western cities like Los Angeles, San Francisco, and Denver, distance prevented those teams from integrating into national competition. Professional baseball faced the same problems, and its leagues focused attention on the nation east of the Mississippi.

Ben Millers, the best team in St. Louis, won the western draw and was poised to play Fore River, eastern champions from the greater Boston area. Usually finalists played the championship match in a neutral location, but the USFA welcomed the participation of St. Louis teams by holding the last match in their city. The decision proved a financial success when more than 12,000 fans watched Ben Millers slip past their East Coast rivals 2–1.

Not only was the match seen as a competition between two rival soccer centers, but it also symbolized two styles of play linked to national identity. All of Ben Millers' players were native-born, with nine from the squad described by the *New York Times* as "Irish-Americans." The entire Fore River team consisted of Scottish and English immigrants. As the *New York Times* reported on May 10, the day after the match, "It was a triumph not only of the Middle West over the East, but of the American style of the association kicking game over the so-called 'old-country' style." The article described the "old-country" style as a "close combination, short passing game," whereas the American style was a "more aggressive, dash and shoot, long driving game." The article also asserted that the Ben Millers players exhibited more speed and stamina against the greater technical ability of the Fore River players. Accurate or not, the piece suggested an obvious hint of pride in an "American" victory over the "old country." Irish American Jimmy Dunn appropriately scored the winning goal with what was described as a "vigorous toe."[37]

* * * *

At the end of "the war to end all wars" and the beginning of the "Roaring Twenties," soccer in the United States appeared poised to seize the imagination of America along with short skirts, ragtime music, the Charleston, talking movies, and optimistic times. The United States had been the first country outside of Great Britain to form a national soccer association, albeit one in name only. After Great Britain, it also fielded a professional soccer league, although the league went through various phases and struggled mightily. Likewise, the United States had been one of the first 20 countries to be accepted into FIFA, even before the great soccer country of Brazil. In many cases crowds drawn to major soccer competitions compared favorably with the crowds attending professional baseball games (although, spread out over a 152-game schedule compared to most soccer leagues' 13- to 18-match schedule, baseball still ranked first in popularity). The formation of the U.S. Soccer Association in 1913 had ameliorated the previous anarchy of leagues and teams, and soccer in the United States soon demonstrated to the larger world that it might very well be able to compete on other pitches around the globe.

Most modern Americans know very little about these positive steps forward and still consider soccer a recent sport in the United States, gaining prominence only after it hosted the 1994 World Cup. Even individuals familiar with contemporary U.S. soccer often suffer from a loss of long-term memory.

Yet, with all of these advances leading up to 1920, enthusiasts anticipated the next decade with even more relish as U.S. soccer experienced a desire to seize the moment and make the soccer pitch an integral part of the nation's growing sports landscape.

Today, if one visits Fall River, its vibrant soccer history is nowhere to be seen. The 100-plus mills that once dominated the cityscape are either torn down or sit like ghost-town shells. The city's website, which boasts videos on local recreation, visitor attractions, and economic development, mentions neither the textile industry nor soccer. The Fall River Rovers, the Fall River Olympics, and the Fall River East Ends have literally been wiped from the city's past and present identity. The Fall River stadium that saw so many classic early battles and AFA and Challenge Cup finals is long gone. There are no remaining echoes of the screaming (and often rowdy) fans that packed the stadium.

Similarly, what's left of the 13-acre site of the Clark Thread Company is now a hodgepodge of industrial companies. In 1978 the few remaining buildings became part of the U.S. Register of Historic Places, ensuring preservation of the architecture that supported American soccer's birthplace. But a concrete parking lot covers the Clark Field that once witnessed the subsequent growth of U.S. soccer. People who use the lot know next to nothing about the area's soccer tradition that started some 120 years ago. The fragile, historical threads that connect the Napoleonic Wars to the Clark Thread Company in Scotland, and ultimately to the introduction of the association kicking game in the United States, have been cut by the so-called scissors of progress.

Even in St. Louis, the country's first "soccer city," the past presence of soccer is nearly invisible. The only sports mentioned on the city's website are professional baseball, football, and hockey, as well as the higher-revenue sports fielded by area universities. The "Explore St. Louis" website is more of the same. On similar digital sites the public face of St. Louis is a city with an incomplete history, a fact consistent with the cultural ethos of a country that typically values the future more than the past.

4

History of U.S. Soccer: The Golden Years

Many contemporary soccer fans in the United States fantasize about a future in which soccer occupies a prominent space in the country's sports landscape. They imagine a time when a financially viable soccer league finally exists, drawing large crowds of loyal, rabid fans chanting team anthems and waving banners and flags as vigorously as enthusiasts do in other parts of the world. They foresee a time when over-the-hill players from abroad—the Beckhams, the Péles, the Chinaglias, the Beckenbauers—no longer claim an essential space in U.S. soccer, but are replaced by younger, top-level athletes from around the world who are drawn to the United States because of its quality of play. They look forward to when U.S. professional teams compete on a level pitch with established European and South American superpowers; when the U.S. Men's National Team, like its female counterpart, advances at least to the semi-finals of the prestigious World Cup.

Soccer skeptics, however, deride such fantasies as delusions of deranged maniacs. They claim that soccer always has been, and always will be, a marginal sport tainted by an alien cultural heritage and un–American values. As Tom Weir wrote in *USA Today* in December 1993, before the United States hosted its first World Cup, "hating soccer is more American than apple pie, driving a pickup, or spending Saturday afternoons channel surfing with the remote control."[1] In other words, soccer is for alienated misfits, not real men and women.

One thing is absolutely clear about these polarizing viewpoints: soccer fans and skeptics alike are misguided prisoners of an ahistorical perspective. A brief skim through the annals of history indicates that the 1920s were one of the most exciting times in American soccer, and that a culminating third-place finish in the 1930 World Cup proved that the U.S. Men's National Team could compete against the world's greatest soccer players. While soccer was still fraught with difficulties as the country emerged from World War I, the sport flaunted an unparalleled success that not only pleased enthusiastic fans but also silenced the most ardent doomsday critics.

A sense of change, economic prosperity, and postwar optimism characterized the 1920s. More and more Americans sought lifestyles centered around electricity, telephones, and automobiles. The motion picture industry flourished, and celebrities like Clara Bow, Mae West, Mary Pickford, Rudolph Valentino, John Barrymore, and Charlie Chaplin became household names. The radio transformed mass communication, making information, entertainment, and advertising more accessible and instantaneous. Fashion for both men and women redefined the "proper" male and female looks, and Art Deco, exemplified by the Chrysler Building in New York City, redefined architecture. The first great sports icons—Babe Ruth, Jack Johnson, Jack Dempsey, Joe Louis, Red Grange, and Knute Rockne—carved out their legendary and often mythological space in popular American culture.

High-level soccer joined the parade. Although first- and second-generation immigrants still fielded most professional and amateur teams, soccer had not yet capitulated to the degrading status of "foreign sport." Since it first appeared in the 1880s, soccer had carved out an imperfect but positive space in the growing, lucrative business of organized sports. By 1919, professional soccer players were drawing salaries as high as $6,000 a year, comparable to the average pay for professional baseball players. The U.S. Challenge Cup competition attracted crowds as big as those watching other high-level competitive sports. Both corporate and individual team ownership confirmed that soccer was a sound investment.

Thomas Cahill, secretary of the United States Football Association (USFA) for a number of years, was the prime mover and shaker who propelled U.S. soccer to the next level. Cahill and his associates at the USFA felt they had laid the successful groundwork for something more polished and profitable, and they were determined to make professional soccer the winter-time choice of sports-hungry Americans. Born in Yonkers, New York, to Irish immigrants and raised in St. Louis, Cahill was immune to media attacks labeling soccer a sport promoted by "foreigners." He grew up in an American city where most soccer players shared his sentiment. He was an ideal candidate for leading the charge.

In 1920, Cahill told the *St. Louis Dispatch*, "My idea is to put the game on a paying basis, while I also have in mind a plan to form a national soccer league."[2] Although the professional NAFBL had competed vigorously since 1895, Cahill imagined a larger, more *truly* national and financially viable league that would build on the foundation already in place. A well-rounded athlete noted for his distance running, Cahill first played soccer as a young man in St. Louis. He also loved baseball, and later owned and managed several semi-professional teams in his Midwestern hometown. Taking his cue from the successful model of professional baseball, which was already called "the national pastime," Cahill realized that in order to put soccer on sound footing, the sport needed first-class stadiums and an expanded season. Arguing for a kind of "trickle-down" effect, he noted that "the professional game [of baseball] has developed the amateur interest to such an extent that every American boy plays baseball from the time he is able to toddle."[3] He dreamed of the same for soccer.

In the spring of 1921 Cahill's dream came true when he helped form the American Soccer League (ASL). The initial organizers of the league chose the word "soccer"—a British slang reference to the game—"because it would discriminate between the American game of football and soccer, the rugby game being considered football in the American sense."[4] Although attempts to organize the first professional American football league were just getting started, university football was already a wildly popular sport, routinely drawing 20,000 fans and more at major universities. The Yale-Princeton battle in 1920, for example, attracted an overflow crowd of 78,000; the Harvard-Yale game that same year drew 75,000. The initial game in Stanford's new stadium in 1921 against the University of California filled the stands with 62,000 fans, immediately prompting plans to expand the facility's capacity. In selecting the word "soccer" over football, the organizing officials of the ASL recognized the public relations need to distinguish their sport from the rising tide of "the other football."

The national governing body of the sport recognized by FIFA, however, stuck with the title "United States Football Association." In retrospect, this divergence in name by the professional league from that of the FIFA-recognized governing body of U.S. soccer may have been a harbinger of the conflict between the two entities that emerged in the late 1920s. The USFA was destined to change its name to the U.S. Soccer Football Association in 1945 and to the U.S. Soccer Federation in 1974, but in 1921 it refused to budge from the original name.

Starting modestly in a concentrated area of the northeast, the eight-team ASL drew from regions with established soccer traditions. From New England came Fall River United and J & P Coats of Pawtucket; from New Jersey, Harrison

FC and Jersey City Celtic. Todd's Shipyards of Brooklyn and NYFC in the Bronx represented New York, while Philadelphia FC and Bethlehem Steel rounded out the league. Only J & P Coats and Bethlehem Steel had advanced to the round of sixteen in the previous year's AFA Cup, and the winner and runner-up of the USFA 1920 Challenge Cup—St. Louis's Ben Millers and Fore River—failed to enlist teams. Other successful teams in the nation's recent premier tournaments were also absent from the initial roster of ASL teams. There were no Fall River Rovers, no Kearney Scots, no West Hudson AA of past glory.

Bethlehem Steel, the most successful team in recent years, had anticipated a big draw in the league. Surprisingly, it withdrew from competition before play even started. Bethlehem had always attracted large crowds from out-of-town matches, and the team wanted the new league to develop a policy allowing visiting teams to share revenue portions from home gate receipts. The majority of teams, especially the Fall River and Pawtucket teams that had developed loyal fans over several decades, advocated home teams keeping all gate receipts. The policy favored by the majority won out, and Bethlehem Steel withdrew in protest.[5] The Holyoke Falcos took the open spot, and the league soon announced a 28-match schedule, with each team playing seven other teams in four different matches.

More than a handful of Bethlehem Steel's top players disapproved of their team's withdrawal from the league and subsequently joined the Philadelphia FC, which went on to defeat the New York FC in the league's first championship match. Bethlehem Steel eventually succeeded in getting the league to change its revenue policies and re-entered the league the following season. The soccer powerhouse finished second over the next three seasons.

As with many new enterprises, the league got off to a shaky start. Attendance fluctuated, and several teams either withdrew from the league or folded altogether. Even though they won the first championship, Philadelphia FC reported a $10,000 loss. Cahill fought hard to promote patience and optimism. "One need not be possessed of the gift of prophecy to look into the future and see ... a steady and rapid growth of the American Soccer League," he wrote.[6]

Despite this confidence, Cahill and his colleagues had to contend with the ongoing USFA. The older Challenge Cup continued its success, claiming a $100,000 profit from gate receipts in 1922–1923. A record 132 teams entered that year's competition. Over 100,000 fans attended Challenge Cup matches, and more than 10,000 paid to watch the final in Harrison, New Jersey, between Paterson FC and Scullin Steel. Scullin Steel had sponsored a team in the St.

Louis Soccer League in 1918, and they became one of the city's most successful clubs. They won the city title in 1919, 1921 and 1922 in a four-team league and advanced to the 1921 Challenge Cup, losing in the final. Winning the Cup the following year, they were poised to defend their title in 1922–1923.[7]

Unfortunately, the match ended in a draw and the USFA demanded a rematch in Harrison. Several Scullin Steel players also played baseball and faced an approaching season. Soccer authorities in St. Louis requested that the Cup match be played in St. Louis, but the USFA insisted the final remain in the East. As a result, Paterson FC claimed the national championship by forfeit and the wedge between soccer in the East and the Midwest sunk even deeper. This disarray in what the USFA promoted as the most important venue in soccer competition also gave more ammunition to the more vocal critics of soccer, who viewed the disappointing decision of crowning a national champion by forfeit as one more indication of soccer's inherent weaknesses.

The real fallout centered on the USFA, the ASL, and the strong personalities that ran each organization. At the annual meeting of the USFA, a month after the Challenge Cup debacle, the St. Louis delegation, still angry over the impasse that had led to their city's team forfeit, pushed for a change in USFA leadership. Peter Peel of Chicago was ultimately elected president. Cahill, who advocated fiercely for the professional league as a means of expanding greater national interest in the sport, was a long-time adversary of Peel and others associated with him. Peel's election marked the beginning of a power struggle that would ultimately have devastating effects on the future of American soccer.

As the association's secretary, Cahill maintained his cadre of supporters in the USFA. But his fate was sealed. He wrote in his annual report the following year that "a campaign of hate ... by a little clique [seemingly] actuated ... the idea that if they cannot rule, it is their special province to ruin." At the next annual meeting, Cahill lost his position as secretary for "insubordination and incompetence." His removal divided the delegates to the USFA and established a deep bitterness between the country's official governing body and the professional league that had looked so promising.[8]

Although Cahill still had his supporters within the USFA, he turned his attention even more fervently toward the infant ASL. Enhancing the financial viability of the league became a top priority. Whether intended or not, this financial emphasis led the ASL clubs in 1924 to withdraw from the brightest star of the USFA—the annual Challenge Cup competition. In public the clubs argued that the financial incentives to continue participating were insufficient, but the rift between Cahill, his supporters, and Peel's organization lurked in the shadows. The ASL decided to hold its own knockout competition, a move it believed would draw larger crowds and greater shares of gate receipts. When the professional teams from St. Louis joined the Challenge Cup exodus, the USFA was left high and dry, depending on a mix of amateur and semi-pro teams to compete in its "American Soccer Championship." The relatively unknown Shawsheen Indians of Massachusetts won the 1924–1925 Challenge Cup by defeating the Chicago Canadian Club 3–0. A sparse 2,500 fans watched the match—a considerable dip in numbers and gate receipts from the 14,000 who had attended the previous year's final.[9]

Although ASL teams reentered the Challenge Cup competition the following year, the resentment between the two main soccer organizations in the United States festered. Soccer fans, either oblivious to the raging battle between the USFA and ASL or simply uninterested in internal politics, turned out in pre-squabble numbers. Bethlehem Steel, in its last substantive national hurrah, dominated Ben Millers of St. Louis with a lopsided 7–2 trouncing. An enthusiastic crowd of 18,000 witnessed the slaughter.[10]

Meanwhile, the "other" football struggled to professionalize. In 1919 the National Football League formed with 14 teams, but league organizers couldn't agree on set schedules or a minimum number of games. With some teams playing only one legitimately recognized game and others claiming matches against non-league teams, chaos reigned during the first few NFL seasons. In the first season of the NFL, for example, several clubs claimed they had finished first, and the league didn't crown a champion until five months after the season ended. By the mid–1920s, the NFL improved its organization, although most teams struggled financially and attendance rarely reached 10,000. In contrast, a crowd of 10,000 had become routine for many professional soccer teams. Comparing the NFL with the ASL in the 1920s, a prognosticator would most likely have predicted a brighter future for professional soccer.

For its first three years of existence, the ASL remained an eight-team league. Only three original teams survived into the third season. One of the teams that folded after the first year included Fall River United, which had finished one notch from the bottom, winning only five out of 24 matches, including one by forfeit.[11]

Unlike other teams that came and went with the wind, however, Fall River boasted a winning soccer tradition and large fan base. They were never destined to disappear from the soccer radar. Within a year the team rose from the dead and formed a new identity: the Fall River Marksmen. The new name conjured up images of goal scorers hitting their target time and again. It also recognized the team's new owner, Sam Mark.

Often called Fall River's "leading athletic promoter," Mark was the driving force behind the new Fall River team.[12] He also promoted himself unabashedly. Claiming the remnants of Fall River United, as well as fresh players, the Marksmen moved into a newly constructed stadium named after its owner. A grand 15,000-seat facility, it was located across the river in Tiverton, Rhode Island. A law in Massachusetts still prohibited "frivolities" like soccer and other sports from being played on Sundays, which confirmed turn-of-the century journalist H.L. Mencken's definition of Puritanism as the haunting fear that someone, somewhere, was having a good time. This law in Massachusetts and other states deterred the development of professional sports because it removed from game calendars the one day a week that workers were free of labor. Mark managed to avoid the law and still draw on Fall River's fan support by locating the new stadium across state lines, where no such law existed.[13]

The future didn't look bright for the newly constituted Fall River team, however. Not only had the first-year team compiled a miserable record, but the town of Fall River had also fallen on hard economic times. The economic boom sweeping the country had bypassed the old mill center, shifting its fabric industry south, where construction and labor costs were much cheaper. Such economic uncertainty didn't bode well for sustaining an ongoing fan base, even if the team could reverse its dismal record from the preceding year. The four-decade soccer legacy of the town appeared threatened, nearing its demise.

One of the new players Mark recruited was Harold Brittan, who led the ASL champion Philadelphia FC during the first season with 27 goals. Brittan, who hailed from Derby, England, had played a number of unremarkable seasons for Chelsea in the English first division before coming to the United States and signing with Bethlehem Steel. He was expected to play for Bethlehem when they reentered the league, but Mark lured him to Fall River after buying out his contract. The Marksmen were not disappointed. In Brittan's seven-year career in the ASL, the center-forward scored 135 goals in 168 matches.[14] He ranked as one of the top five professional U.S. goal scorers in a match-to-goal ratio—more than .80 goals per match. As a point of comparison, Lionel Messi, one of the most prolific goal scorers in contemporary soccer, has recorded 160 goals in 210 matches with Barcelona, or a match-to-goal ratio of .76.

The Fall River Marksmen quickly supplanted Bethlehem Steel as the premier soccer team in the league. Their first year they finished third behind J & P Coats and Bethlehem Steel, with 15 wins and 5 draws in 28 matches. With Brittan and a staunch defense leading the way, they won the league championship in 1923–1924, winning 19 and losing only two matches in 27 games.

Brittan finished the season as the third leading goal scorer, but the Marksmen's fierce defense led the charge, as they allowed only 19 goals in 27 matches. The team's success ensured near-capacity attendance at home matches, despite the economic slump facing the town.[15] The Marksmen also drew substantial away crowds. While Fall River continued its path down unemployment, local soccer managed to thrive. Perhaps soccer provided the right diversion, and maybe even a sense of hope and meaning to carry a once-thriving town through economic and social hard times.

On a grander scheme, the league continued its roll. The following year (1924–1925), the ASL expanded to 12 teams and a 44-match schedule. Fall River repeated as league champion and also won the Challenge Cup title to become the undisputed king of U.S. soccer.[16] Tom Mark's investment in the team and a new stadium had paid off. Decades after Fall River's central role in establishing U.S. soccer, the town had regained its prominent space in competitive sports.

The Fall River Marksmen witnessed a "three-peat" as they literally devastated the opposition with an impressive 30–2–12 record the following season. An intimidating wall of forwards led the charge. At that time most teams in the United States played five forwards, three mid-fields (or half-backs) and two defenders (or full-backs). The forwards held down the outside-left, inside-left, center, inside-right, and outside-right positions. Four of the five Fall River forwards scored 92 of the team's 142 goals that year. James "Tec" White initiated the assault, scoring 33 goals. Brittan followed with 21, and Dugald "Dougie" Campbell and Tommy "Tucker" Croft had 19 apiece. The team dominated play and boasted the strongest collective play on a U.S. pitch until that time.[17]

The Marksmen stars typified standout players from other major teams. Although many ASL players were second- or even third-generation immigrants born in the United States, others were imported from the British Isles. Tec White had played several years with the Albion Rovers of the Scottish League and even participated in the finals of the Scottish Cup in 1920. He also played for Maidstone United in the English southern league before coming to the United States to play for the Marksmen. Born in Paisley, Scotland, Dougie Campbell had moved to the United States with his parents as a youth. Tommy Croft played professional soccer in Ireland before immigrating to the United States, best known in that country for scoring the winning goal in the Irish team's only victory against the English national team. Brittan, too, had played professional soccer in England.[18]

In fact, more than a few players from the British Isles found American soccer attractive. Reports filtered across the Atlantic about the quality of play in the United States, and the pay was often better than that in the British and Scottish leagues. The lure of the ASL was so pervasive in Scotland that the Scottish Football Association denounced the "American Menace" of U.S. soccer.[19] Scotland argued that the ASL was stealing top-level players from the homeland, some of whom allegedly broke contracts to accept more lucrative offers in the United States. Hearing such complaints, FIFA even considered a rule requiring immigrating professionals to live abroad for one year before playing in another country.

Scottish player Johnny Ballantyne was a case in point. In 1924, the millionaire president of the Mystic Steamship company, A.G. Wood, bought an expansion team named the Boston Wonder Workers. Signing several prominent players from other ASL teams, Wood also used his money to lure top European players, including Ballantyne, who was under contract with the Scottish club, Partick Thistle. Ballantyne broke his contract and boarded the next steamer. He starred for Boston the next three seasons before finishing his career with Scottish and English teams. As Ballantyne explained years later, "The contract came ... and I had to make my mind up suddenly. I [hoped] to make about 12 pounds a week in America. What chance [had] I of doing that here?"[20]

Economic incentives often dictated play during this early period in "world" soccer. Charlie Shaw, a Scottish-born goalie who had played professionally in both England and Scotland, moved to the United States in 1925 to play with the ASL New Bedford Whalers. He spoke for others when he commented, "Of course I'm sorry in a way to leave the Old Country ... the minimum I should earn [in the United States] is double what I had last season from Celtic and the maximum is double the highest salary I have ever earned in one year ... I'll be in clover in a year or two."[21]

As word spread beyond Great Britain about ASL opportunities, players from other countries seized the soccer day and pay. From Egypt came Tewfik Abdullah, who played with several Scottish and English teams before seeking greener pastures in the United States. Herbert Carlson, who played 20 times for the Swedish national team and was the top goal scorer in the 1920 Olympics, played 268 games with several ASL teams from 1924 to 1931. Norwegian-born Werner Nilson shared the top goal scorer award in 1928 and enjoyed a 10-year career in the ASL. János Nehadoma, born in Budapest, Hungary, played professionally in Italy before coming to the United States. In three years he scored 80 goals in 105 matches before returning to Italy to play for Livorno and Florentina; he finished his career as coach of Atalanta.[22] These professionals characterized the caliber of player attracted to the United States in the 1920s. It is also important to point out that most of these players immigrated to the United States during the best days of their careers, not in their twilight. In other words, unlike the Beckhams of the last 20 years, they played their most impressive soccer in the United States *before* returning to Europe to finish their careers.

While it is difficult to objectively assess the quality of play in the ASL by today's standards, it's clear that professional soccer in the United States didn't lag far behind its counterparts in other parts of the world. During the first half of the decade the ASL had clearly come into its own. The historical connections of U.S. soccer to Scotland and England meant that most professionals from abroad who were drawn to the ASL came from those countries. Names like McAuley, McGhee, McGregor, McLeavy, McNab, and McPherson punctuated the rosters of ASL teams. Despite this influx of quality professionals from abroad, making an ASL team never carried a guarantee. In January 1924, the *New York Times* reported that there were occasions "when a player from the other side of the Atlantic Ocean has come to this country to find that the competition was stronger than he expected and has returned again without having gained a position as a player."[23]

With the ascendency of the Fall River Marksmen and a host of other players, the player of the ASL decade, Archie Stark, learned his soccer skills in the United States. Born in Glasgow, he immigrated to the United States in 1912 with his parents. He began playing soccer at an early age with Kearney Scots, a traditional powerhouse of the NAFBL. He was one of the youngest members of the 1915 Kearney Scots team to win the Challenge Cup competition. His ASL career began in 1921–1922 with the New York FC, leading them to a second-place finish as the team's top goal scorer. In his third season, he led the league in goals, with 21 in New York FC's 27 matches.[24]

These first few years were a mere prelude of what was to come. With the expansion of the league to 12 teams and a schedule of 44 games in 1924–1925, Stark signed with Bethlehem Steel after his former New York club reformed under new ownership. Although Bethlehem finished second to the powerful Fall River Marksmen, Stark set a single-season ASL record by scoring 67 goals in 44 games, an amazing average of 1.52 goals per game. The second-place scorer, Andy Stevens, who played for the Boston Wonder Workers and New Bedford Whalers, lagged far behind with 33 goals. Stark's performance is even more impressive when considering that it took the third-place finisher Brooklyn Wanderers' entire team to match Stark's 67 goals.[25] New York sportswriter Ed Sullivan recognized Stark's dominant play by calling him "the Babe

Ruth of soccer." Stark finished his career in the ASL in 1931 with 253 goals in 293 matches, records for both games played and total goals scored in the ASL.[26] By comparison, the great Italian striker Giorgio Chanaglia, who played eight seasons for the New York Cosmos in the late 1970s and early 1980s, scored a career 243 goals. His most prolific year was 1980, when he scored 50 goals in 39 matches.[27] When looking back over the century, it's impossible to determine the better scorer of the two. The level of competition, style of team play, rule changes, and even weather all factor in to the way one ultimately performs. Yet Archie Stark clearly stands as one of the top players, especially among American citizens, to ever play professional soccer in the United States.

* * * *

Another measure of U.S. soccer's success included the international matches played during this era. Between 1926 and 1931, a number of teams from Europe and South America toured the United States, primarily playing ASL teams and professional organizations in other leagues, but also going up against top amateur teams and squads comprising different ASL teams. While these visiting teams often returned home with more wins than losses, the fact that they came at all indicated their recognition of the sport's growing popularity. For most visitors, this popularity translated into financially viable tours. Although many of the touring teams didn't play the best U.S. teams, the level of competition they did encounter demonstrated the overall strength of American soccer at that time.

In 1926 Hakoah Vienna, former champions of the Austrian league, played eleven matches in New York, Philadelphia, Providence, Newark, St. Louis, and Chicago. Six of the matches were against ASL teams whose win-loss records ranked at the bottom of the league. Only the Providence Clamdiggers, who tied Vienna 2–2, had a winning record, finishing fifth in the league during the 1925–1926 season. Three of the matches were against teams that had a combined ASL record of 26–78–15 the previous year. One can only imagine what might have happened if Vienna Hakoah had played a team like the Fall River Marksmen, who had lost only two matches the previous year. A telltale sign is Vienna's 3–3 draw with the ASL Newark Skeeters, a team that Fall River beat four consecutive times in 1925–1926 by a combined goal score of 20–2.[28]

Vienna's second match on May 1, 1926, at the Polo Grounds in New York was particularly notable, for two reasons. First, a U.S. team called the New York Stars, comprising players from two ASL teams, handed Vienna a resounding 3–0 defeat. Second, and more important, a crowd of 46,000 fans jammed into the home stadium of baseball's New York Giants (one of the New York soccer teams was also called the Giants) to witness the shutout. That record attendance stood some 50 years until the Péle era of the New York Cosmos in the 1970s. Two other matches drew crowds of over 30,000; another attracted 25,000. Soccer had never seen such a sight, and it would be more than four decades before the sport saw such attendance again.[29]

Although it might be convenient to attribute these crowds to the growing popularity of soccer, this representation is somewhat misleading. Vienna Hakoah had toured the country in the past and attracted fans everywhere. Comprised entirely of Jewish players, they always drew large crowds in New York and Philadelphia, home to significant Jewish populations who were not ordinarily soccer fans. Attendance at other matches in St. Louis and Providence attracted respectable but less spectacular crowds. Nevertheless, wherever Vienna played they managed to receive media publicity, which provided the ASL another opportunity to assimilate into the larger sports landscape.

In 1927, the Uruguayan national team toured the United States, playing nine matches against ASL teams. Uruguay had already evolved into one of the best national teams in the world. They won both the 1924 and 1928 Olympics. Capitalizing on those victories, the Uruguayan national team would go on to win the first FIFA World Cup in 1930.

Similar to Vienna Hakoah, Uruguay played the majority of matches against middle- or low-ranking ASL teams. Two matches pitted the South Americans against stronger ASL opponents. The Fall River Marksmen, who finished in third place during the 1926–1927 season, managed a 1–1 draw against the Uruguayans at Marks Stadium in Tiverton. The Boston Wonder Workers, who had finished second to Bethlehem Steel, beat Uruguay 3–2. Although the national Uruguayan team finished the tour with 5–2–2 record, almost every match proved competitive.[30]

In 1928 a team of Brescia, Bologna, Milan, and other Italian professionals toured the United States. The Italians escaped with three wins and two losses. Two of their victories came against the New York Nationals, last-place finishers in the ASL. The Italians lost to the two strongest ASL teams they faced—3–2 to the Brooklyn Wanderers, and 4–2 to the Fall River Marksmen.[31]

Finally, in 1931 Vélez Sársfield of Buenos Aires, one of the founding members of the Argentine Primera Division, undertook a 25-match pan-American tour of Chile, Cuba, Mexico, Peru, and the United States. The Argentinians lost only one game in the entire excursion, to the Fall River Marksmen on February 22.[32] Only six days earlier Sam Mark had agreed to move his team from Fall River to New York, renaming them the New York

Yankees. The declining economy of Fall River had finally taken its toll. The victory against the top-level Argentinian squad marked a last hurrah for the mighty Marksmen, descendants of a long soccer tradition that had witnessed the birth and growth of U.S. soccer.

Adelino "Billy" Gonsalves and Bert Patenaude, two of the finest American players to ever grace a soccer pitch, scored five Marksmen goals that day against the powerful Argentinian team. Unlike the Scottish and English immigrants who populated most ASL teams, Gonsalves and Patenaude were raised in the United States. Gonsalves was born in Portsmouth, Rhode Island, in 1908, two years after his parents immigrated from the Portuguese island of Madeira. His family later moved 12 miles north to Fall River, the heart of U.S. soccer country. Growing rapidly into an intimidating physical specimen at 6'2" and 200 pounds, Gonsalves played for the Fall River Pioneers, a local amateur team, at the age of 14. Working his way up through semi-pro leagues, the 19-year-old Gonsalves signed with the ASL Boston Wonder Workers in 1927. In his initial appearance with Boston, he scored his first professional goal two minutes into the match. Overnight he gained a reputation as someone who could score, pass, dribble, and control the ball. After two years with the Boston club, he played for his "home" team, the Fall River Marksmen. He starred on the 1930 national squad, considered by many soccer historians the best professional soccer team in U.S. history. Like Archie Stark, he courted the nickname "Babe Ruth of soccer." His shots on goal intimidated his opponents, as Walter Dick, who played with Gonsalves on the U.S. national squad, attests: "Gonsalves was the greatest shooter I ever saw, and with either leg.... His power was murderous on goalies and whoever got in the way."[33]

Patenaude was born in Fall River in 1909. His parents were French Canadian and immigrated to Massachusetts in search of economic opportunities. For a soccer player, Patenaude grew up in the right place at the right time. Fall River provided the proper soccer training, and by 1928 he was playing professionally for the Philadelphia FC. Patenaude came into his prime during the two seasons he teamed with Gonsalves on the powerful Marksmen team. From 1928 to 1930, he scored 57 goals in 62 ASL matches with the Marksmen. His numerous achievements included scoring five goals in each of four different matches, a feat never again matched by any other U.S. player.[34]

* * * *

Gonsalves and Patenaude's most notable achievement, however, came during the 1930 World Cup, held in Uruguay. Since its formation in 1904, FIFA had anticipated hosting some form of world championship. For almost three decades logistical problems of transportation, financial issues, and internal political intrigue delayed such a plan. By 1930, against significant odds, FIFA finally garnered the support it needed. Italy, the Netherlands, Spain, and Sweden offered to host the world tournament, but FIFA selected Uruguay, nestled near the southern tip of South America. Unlike Europe, Uruguay had avoided the brunt of Depression woes and not only committed to underwriting travel and hotel expenses for international teams but also agreed to construct a new stadium in Montevideo to host the tournament. More a symbolic center than a financially sound governing body at the time, FIFA found the Uruguayan offer irresistible. The soccer organization also recognized the caliber of Uruguayan soccer, evidenced in its winning two Olympic gold medals in the 1920s.

Strapped by the Depression, much of the world found it difficult to embrace such a long trip to South America for an untested "World Championship." Seven national teams from South America—Argentina, Bolivia, Brazil, Chile, Paraguay, Peru, and Uruguay—as well as Mexico and the United States, eventually committed national teams to Montevideo. European teams were less enthusiastic. Two months before the July tournament, not a single European country had entered the event. These countries also recognized that their European leagues started in August a few weeks after the Cup, which made entering the tournament even more problematic. In addition, England, which had periodically pulled out of its FIFA affiliation, rarely embraced the organization's claim to "govern" international soccer. As the founder of modern soccer, Britain influenced several of its neighbors to abstain. In the end, Belgium, France, Romania, and Yugoslavia agreed to participate. The final tally included 13 entries out of 41 active FIFA affiliates.

The teams from Belgium, France, and Romania departed together on the SS *Conte Verde* from Barcelona. FIFA president Jules Rimet sailed with them, as did Belgian referee John Langenus. Soccer officials also carried along the first FIFA World Cup trophy, the *Goddess of Victory*, designed by French artist Abel Lafleur. The steamship stopped at Rio de Janeiro to pick up the Brazilian team, finally arriving in Montevideo on July 4. Almost 15,000 Uruguayans turned out to greet the arriving teams.

It came as no surprise that Gonsalves and Patenaude made the U.S. team. However, Archie Stark, the career goal leader in the ASL, rattled fans when he declined the invitation to participate. Stark had played for the national team in 1925 against Canada, scoring five goals in a 6–1 victory. Ten years older than Gonsalves and Patenaude, Stark's goal scoring had declined over the previous five years. Thinking about his future, he had opened a garage in

Massachusetts and worried that leaving the country might jeopardize his life after soccer. One can only speculate what Stark's presence might have added to the U.S. attack.

With such a small competitive field, FIFA placed the teams in four groups—three groups of three teams each and one of four teams. The United States was coupled with Belgium and Paraguay in group four, avoiding the Argentinian and Uruguayan powerhouses in the earliest stage.

On July 13, 1930, the U.S. team played its first World Cup match against Belgium. The crowd of 18,500 endured a brief snow shower before the match, which made the U.S. players feel right at home, since most of them had played in the northeastern United States during cold winter months. Both teams appeared nervous and cautious. As halftime approached, Gonsalves unleashed a ferocious shot that careened off the post. Positioned in the right place, Bart McGhee, an ASL New York Nationals standout, netted the rebound. Moments later, Tommy Florie of the New Bedford Whalers scored, putting the United States in front 2–0 at halftime. In the second half Patenaude scored another goal on a header. The U.S. defense held firm and the team won easily 3–0.[35]

The first three goal scorers for the U.S. national team in a World Cup match exemplified the mix of players on the squad. Some historical revisionists suggest that the 1930 U.S. national team was really a team of "foreigners" and cannot rightly claim the title of a true national team. The truth is that, of the 16-member squad, only six were born in England and Scotland, and those had immigrated to the United States to play soccer or to follow families. All of them had played in the ASL for a number of years. Bartholomew McGhee typified this group. Born in Edinburgh, he grew up in a soccer family. His father had captained an early Scottish team that played in the 1887 Scottish Cup final. The older McGhee eventually immigrated to the United States; young Bart followed a few years later. By age 19, Bart McGhee was playing professionally in the ASL. Ten of his fellow players on the U.S. squad, including Florie and Patenaude, were native-born. Florie, who served as captain of the team, was born in New Jersey to Italian immigrant parents and had spent his entire professional career in the ASL.[36]

On July 17, the United States met Paraguay, a much stronger team than Belgium. The previous year, the Paraguayans had placed second to Argentina in the South American championship and were considered one of the top teams in the tournament. The Gonsalves-Patenaude combination proved devastating. With the Paraguayan defense trying to prevent Gonsalves from unleashing his powerful strikes, Patenaude received two perfectly placed crosses from left halfback (midfielder) Andy Auld of the Providence Gold

Bugs, which resulted in two goals during the first 16 minutes of the match. In the second half, Patenaude scored again, performing the first World Cup hat trick. The final score was a convincing 3–0 shutout. Considered underdogs, the U.S. squad could now boast that their brand of soccer could take on that of the very best soccer nations.

The United States advanced to the semi-finals with Argentina, Uruguay, and Yugoslavia. Although Yugoslavia, which had surprised everyone by defeating Brazil 2–1 in the group stage, would have been the more ideal opponent, the United States was pitted against Argentina, the South American champion. Argentina had scored 10 goals in three group stage matches and, with Uruguay, was clearly a Cup favorite. But it also had shown moments of defensive weakness in a 6–3 win against Mexico, whose team had lost all three of its group stage matches. Whatever optimism the U.S. team had gained from its two impressive victories quickly evaporated on July 26. Over 70,000 fans crammed into the new Montevideo stadium to watch the events unfold.[37]

With only 10 minutes elapsed, goalie Jimmy Douglas, who had helped shut out the previous two opponents, severely strained a knee. Born in Kearny, New Jersey, Douglas played for the New York Nationals in the States and was the grandson of a player from the original ONT 1880s team. Playing "one leg" for the rest of the 80-minute match, Douglas's mobility was severely limited. To make matters worse, within minutes center halfback (midfielder) Raphael Tracey sustained a broken leg and was removed from the game. Rules at this time did not allow substitutes for any reason, even serious injury, so the United States had to finish the first half with ten players, a badly hobbled goalie among them. With such misfortunes, the United States was down 1–0 at halftime.[38]

Early in the second half, left halfback Auld, who had delivered two beautiful assists to Patenaude against Paraguay, received a severe kick to the face; he played the remainder of the match with a towel stuffed in his mouth to control the bleeding. With only ten players, including an injured midfielder and a crippled goalie, the United States folded against the more powerful Argentinians, who scored five second-half goals to take a 6–0 lead. Forward Guillermo Stabile, known by his nickname *El Filtador* (the Filter) because of his slick moves, scored two of those goals on his way to winning the tournament's top scorer award. In the eighty-ninth minute, the United States prevented a shutout when 21-year-old James Brown, the youngest player on the team, scored from his outside right forward position. Brown had moved to the United States three years earlier from Scotland and began playing professionally with ASL's Newark Skeeters and the New York Giants. He later moved to England and finished his professional career with Manchester United, Tottenham Hotspur, and Brentford.[39]

In the other semi-final, Uruguay beat Yugoslavia by an identical score of 6–1, setting up a final between the tournament's pre-favorites. As in most sports, superstition factored in to the skill and preparation of both squads. Argentina and Uruguay agreed to play the final with an Argentinian ball during the first half and a Uruguayan ball for the second half. Switching balls would eliminate any suspicion of chicanery. Playing with its own ball, Argentina led at halftime 2–1. Uruguay, however, dominated the second half with its own ball. They scored three unanswered goals and were crowned *Goddess of Victory,* the first FIFA World Cup Champions. The United States finished third over Yugoslavia due to an advantage in goals scored vs. goals given.[40]

Despite the disappointing semi-final loss, the U.S. team members could hold their heads high. Even though only 13 teams had entered the tournament, the United States managed its highest finish ever in World Cup competition. On its way home, the team stopped in Brazil for a number of exhibition matches. They lost 4–3 to the Brazilian national team that had been such a disappointment in the World Cup, with Patenaude scoring two goals and Gonsalves one. Over the next several weeks they played six matches against a variety of Brazilian professional teams. The United States felt the officiating was unbalanced, with no less than 12 goals called back. In one match against Santos, the U.S. team actually ended the game ahead 4–3, but during a postgame briefing the referee announced that he was disallowing the final goal and declared the match a draw.[41]

Nonetheless, players, coaches, and league officials felt a shot of adrenaline from the third-place World Cup experience. While significant problems still plagued soccer in the United States, there was little doubt that soccer had finally staked a claim in the U.S. sports landscape. It wouldn't take long, however, for the optimistic rush of the World Cup experience to disappear.

* * * *

The ASL continued its success in the latter half of the 1920s. Each year teams folded, moved, and were renamed, but a growing stability in team rosters continued to emerge. By the 1927–1928 season, 10 of 12 teams from the original 1924 expansion remained in the league, showcasing the same names. A new owner purchased Indiana Flooring of New York and renamed it the New York Nationals.

In 1927–1928 the ASL adopted an expanded two-season schedule. Originally 30 matches composed each half, but after two teams folded the remaining teams played over 50 matches that year. With the new two-season format, the league staged its first championship playoff, which included the first- and second-place finishers in each half. The Boston Wonder Workers defeated the New Bedford Whalers in the final by a score of 4–2.[42]

The season ended on a note of optimism. An expanded schedule that began in September and ran into May established soccer as a professional winter sport that only marginally interfered with professional baseball. Although not at full capacity, attendance had stabilized enough to produce a degree of security. U.S.-born players continued to emerge in greater numbers. The future looked bright.

As for Mother Nature, weather continued to be a problem. For most teams, the first half of the season carried over into the first week of January, and while most teams didn't start the second half until mid–February, the unpredictability of the winter months continued to create problems with scheduling and attendance. Rarely did all teams play the same number of games, since weather conditions caused cancellations that were rarely rescheduled. Even when matches were played during winter months, severe cold kept large crowds from attending. Nevertheless, the financial picture for most teams remained adequate, and the level of soccer flourished both at home and internationally. It's little wonder that no one predicted what came next.

A lingering antagonism between the ASL and the USFA resurfaced with unexpected fury in the fall of 1928. The reasons were varied and complex: conflicts over scheduling Cup competition during the ASL season; incompetent management within the USFA; competition over the control of organized soccer in the United States; and ASL feistiness resulting from its growing success. In October of that year, the ASL once again instructed its clubs to forego the Challenge Cup. Three ASL teams—Bethlehem Steel, Newark Skeeters, and the New York Giants—defied the edict and entered the competition. The ASL fined each club $1,000 and suspended them from the league. The suspended clubs appealed to the USFA to intervene on their behalf, but the ASL ignored a demand for reinstatement. This rejection led to the ultimate reprisal: the ASL was booted out of the USFA, leaving it to operate as a rogue league, unaffiliated with both the U.S. national soccer association and FIFA.[43]

The USFA also went a step further. Grabbing the three renegade teams and several semi-pro teams from the Southern New York Soccer Association, the USFA helped to form the Eastern Soccer League, whose season ran parallel to that of the well-established ASL. With an "I'll show you" attitude, the ASL applied for membership in FIFA, but the request was predictably rejected. Like two feuding, out-of-control toddlers trying to decide on the next toy to throw at one another, the two central soccer organizations in the United States continued their battle throughout the 1928–1929 season. That battle is known in the annals of soccer history as "the Soccer War."

Once again the ASL dwindled to eight teams, but they managed to compile a 53-game schedule. The Fall River Marksmen, led by Tec White and Bert Patenaude, reasserted themselves as champions. Ex-ASL power Bethlehem Steel, led by Archie Stark, won the championship of the Eastern Soccer League that was recognized by the USFA.

By the summer of 1929, officials of both leagues and the USFA began to sense the futility of the conflict. Both leagues suffered financially, as did the quality of play. The reputation of the USFA also declined as it clumsily tried to deal with an administrative and financial disaster. As in all wars, everyone loses and the damage can't be immediately repaired, nor can memories be easily erased. Many fans grew tired of the internal politics of the sport, and those members of the media still hostile to soccer fanned the flames of discontent.

With momentum for a truce building, the ASL and the ESL began their fall schedules in August under the shadow of the previous year. Both leagues hoped to regain the momentum that professional soccer once had. The ASL signed an agreement on October 9 and came back into the national soccer fold licking its wounds with its tail between its legs. The agreement called for play in both leagues to end while a new organization, the Atlantic Coast League, was formed, with play beginning immediately. With the Soccer War nearly over, few could have known what was coming.

The Fall River Marksmen played their final match in the ASL fall season at home against the Brooklyn Wanderers on Sunday, October 20, winning 6–2 on the strength of Bert Patenaude's four goals. In the midst of the turmoil and confusion surrounding the league, the Marksmen were on their way to winning their third straight ASL championship.[44] The next Thursday, signs of gloom hit the horizon, wreaking financial havoc on the New York Stock Exchange. Fear gripped the nation. The following week, on October 28 and 29, the stock market fell over 23 percent, and the Great Depression started its roll. Professional soccer, wallowing in its divisive pettiness, took a deep plunge.

No one knows how much money the owners of ASL and ESL teams actually lost during the Depression, but the cost was significant. The new Atlantic Coast League began play with 11 teams on November 9, completing a schedule that ran through spring season. The Marksmen easily won the season championship, but the weight of the Depression greatly affected the financial support and gate receipts necessary to sustain the league. By the fall of 1930, after the national team's success in Uruguay, the league reclaimed its original American

Soccer League title. However, the name change never recaptured the league's previous glory.

Over the next several years the ASL limped along. By 1931, the league supported a mere seven teams, and attendance at matches dropped precipitously. The powerhouse teams of the 1920s were a relic of the past. Bethlehem Steel had folded and the Fall River Marksmen became the New York Yankees, deserting one of the cradles of U.S. soccer in the same way the mills had deserted the town a decade earlier. On January 4, 1932, only 3,000 fans attended the last championship match played in New York City. The New York Giants, having lost the first match 8–3 to the New Bedford Whalers, won by a score of 6–0 to claim the championship on a 9–8 aggregate advantage.[45]

Baseball, "America's sport," also struggled to survive. The summer before the Wall Street crash, five teams had averaged over 10,000 fans per game, the Chicago Cubs leading the way with an average of 19,041. By 1932, only two teams averaged over 10,000, and the Cubs' average had plummeted to 12,658, a decline of one-third. By 1933, the New York Yankees led the league in attendance with an average 9,707 fans, a decline of almost 50 percent from the league-leading Chicago Cubs four years earlier.[46] The firmer ground that baseball occupied allowed it to survive, but only just. Professional soccer wasn't so fortunate.

Although the ASL continued to exist in name until 1983, it never renewed the grandeur of the 1920s. Semi-professional teams like the Kearney Scots in the 1930s, the Philadelphia Americans in the 1940s, the New York Hakoah in the 1950s, and the Ukrainian Nationals in the 1960s dominated play and won league championships. These teams and a handful of others kept U.S. soccer alive, but, like a sleeping bear in winter, the sport went into hibernation, losing its visibility in the national sports consciousness outside the cave in which it continued to exist. Soccer would slowly emerge from that cave after World War II, gradually gaining strength from the 1960s onward. But the promise of the 1920s was broken, and soccer in the last half of the twentieth century would have a very different look and feel.

* * * *

The history of the American Soccer League and the 1930 U.S. national team is part of this country's sports amnesia. When one of the foremost historians of U.S. soccer, Colin Jose, was conducting research on the ASL in 1969, he received a list from the league at that time detailing the winners of the ASL championship. The list started in 1933. Imagine his surprise many years later when he came across articles in the *New York Times* chronicling the ASL of the 1920s. How could this be, he asked, when according to the ASL's own records the league began in 1933? Intentionally or not, the ASL had erased its official memory of the best years of its existence.[47]

Whether cause or effect, this institutional amnesia is linked to the space occupied by soccer in the popular consciousness of U.S. sports fans. In the minds of most Americans, soccer is a recent foreign import into a sports landscape long occupied by baseball, basketball, and American football. Both contemporary advocates and critics of soccer argue that the sport's marginal space results from its "recent" appearance in the United States, since there is little room for a "new" sport given that the Big Three have always dominated that landscape. The history of U.S. soccer through the 1920s paints a very different picture, however.

Because the past is always reconstructed through the lens of the present, this amnesia—or, to some, dementia—may be related to the current cultural space occupied by U.S. soccer. Filling a primarily white, middle- to upper-middle-class niche, contemporary soccer may want to forget its rich past. The successful years of early U.S. soccer were anchored in a fundamentally different cultural space—a working-class space, healthily sprinkled with immigrants and sons and grandsons of immigrants. The criticism identifying U.S. soccer in these early years as a foreign sport peopled with foreign players is patently false. By the close of the 1920s, there were as many, if not more, native-born players in the ASL and on the U.S. national team than players born abroad. Recognizing the success of this era might require rethinking the class-based formula for success that typically dominates the soccer landscape today, which is reason enough for those who have an investment in the contemporary structure of U.S. soccer to conveniently forget the past.

5

History of U.S. Soccer: Lost Years, Renewed Hopes

Thomas Cahill, whose dreams of establishing a competitive U.S. soccer program briefly materialized in the 1920s, died in a nursing home on September 29, 1951. He was 86 years old. With the exception of family and close friends, his death went largely unnoticed. Today his passing is listed on the website HistoryOrb as one of the "famous deaths for year 1951," along with such notables as writer Sinclair Lewis, German auto innovator Ferdinand Porsche, philosopher Ludwig Wittengenstein, Indian writer Abanindranath Tagore, and star baseball player "Shoeless" Joe Jackson.[1] Although the United States Football Association sent a floral arrangement to his family and a representative to the funeral, few Americans appreciated Cahill's "fame" at the time of his death. For reasons known only to the organization, the USFA had erased the history of U.S. soccer before 1933, along with Cahill's legacy. Even in St. Louis, where he'd first learned the game, his passing slipped by largely unnoticed.

In the early 1920s, when he had dreamed about a successful American soccer tradition, Cahill audaciously claimed that he could assemble a team of U.S.-born soccer players who could equally compete with any team from Great Britain. "In goal shooting, speed, aggressiveness, and other factors America is equal to or better than the old country today," he proclaimed.[2] Despite the various successes of American soccer in the 1920s, Cahill never validated his remarks. Nor did he get an opportunity to test his assertion. The Glasgow Rangers were the only team from the British Isles to tour the United States in that decade, and they played most of their matches against mediocre ASL teams.

Years passed, and amid the twin disasters of the Depression and World

War II soccer faded from the U.S. sports landscape. Cahill's vision of establishing an internationally competitive national team faded with it. Exactly 15 months before his death, however, the unheralded visionary must have experienced a renewal of the old soccer glory, if only for a few days. On June 29, 1950, U.S. soccer briefly emerged from its obscurity of the previous 17 years to catch the fleeting attention of the sports world. In the first FIFA World Cup since the end of World War II, held in Brazil, a rag-tag U.S. national team made up of semi-professional journeymen beat a heavily favored English team by the score of 1–0. It was the first time England had faced a United States national team.

At mid-century England was on top of the soccer world. They were a clear 3–1 favorite to win the 1950 World Cup. Their national team had compiled a 23–4–3 record in post–World War II competition, including a 4–0 victory over a strong Italian team and a 10–0 drubbing of Portugal in an international friendly. English papers called them "The Kings of Football," and the rest of the soccer world agreed. The English national team was especially hungry for a championship because the Brazilian tournament represented their first World Cup competition, having bypassed the three 1930s Cups due to irreconcilable differences between the English FA and FIFA. The "inventors of modern football" still felt their own national cup competition was much more important than the neophyte World Cup, but by 1950 they were ready to showcase what they considered their soccer superiority to the rest of the world.

The United States formed its squad almost overnight. Because there was no true professional league at that time, players represented a variety of semi-professional and amateur teams. The ASL still existed, but players were paid on a per-match basis—usually $25 per appearance—and had to maintain second jobs to support themselves. The initial hurdle the team faced included convincing employers to hold their jobs for the three months they had to commit to the national squad. Walter Bahr, a Philadelphia schoolteacher and semi-pro player who later coached soccer at Penn State, recalled years later that the USFA paid him $100 a week, more than double what he earned as a teacher. However, the school system was reluctant to release him from his contract before the end of the school term. It finally relented when a qualified substitute was found.[3] Several other players turned down offers to join the team because they couldn't afford to forfeit permanent employment. Obviously the honor of being selected to the U.S. national team held little merit for employers.

In order to qualify for the World Cup, the United States had to play a three-team round-robin tournament against Mexico and Cuba. The event required each team to play two matches each against the other two teams. Two of the three would qualify for the Cup. Because Mexico was considered the superior of the three teams, the real contest revolved around the United States and Cuba. Like the United States, Cuba promoted baseball as a national sport, and its soccer program had garnered little attention outside the Caribbean. Cuba did receive minimal recognition when it entered the 1938 World Cup, although only 16 teams competed in that event. Most Latin American countries boycotted that Cup, citing European favoritism when FIFA selected France to host the international tournament. Cuba beat Romania to advance to the round of eight before Sweden convincingly eliminated them with an 8–0 trouncing.[4]

Mexico hosted the three teams in its mile-high national capital. A second-place finish for the United States seemed reasonable, but assembling a national team at the last moment was not a promising way to begin. The United States lost its initial match to a stronger Mexican team 6–0. Facing off against Cuba, they could only manage a 1–1 draw, barely escaping elimination. In the second match against Mexico, the United States showed modest improvement, but still lost 6–2. In the rubber match with Cuba, the U.S. offense scored four first-half goals. They went on to win 5–2, advancing to the June 24 start of the tournament in Brazil.[5]

The United States' qualification boosted the players' confidence only slightly. FIFA seeded the U.S. team at the bottom, alongside Mexico, Turkey, and India, the latter two countries withdrawing before the start of the tournament due to travel costs and related issues. Before departing for Brazil, U.S. coach Bill Jeffrey allegedly described his players as "sheep ready to be slaughtered." Looking ahead to the inevitable match against England, U.S. baseball player–turned–goalie Frank Borghi later noted, "I was hoping I could hold them to four or five goals."[6] The *Belfast Telegraph* called the U.S. national team "a band of no-hopers," while the English *Daily Express* wrote that it "would be fair to give [the United States] three goals of a start."[7] Even with such foreboding, the team anticipated its appearance with dignity.

When the United States met England in Belo Horizonte, Brazil, both teams had already competed in their first matches. England had defeated Chile 2–0; the United States had lost a heartbreaker to Spain 3–1. The U.S. squad actually led Spain 1–0 in 80 minutes of play, but with just 10 minutes left in the match, Spain scored three goals in a span of eight minutes. Despite the two-goal loss, the U.S. performance against a more experienced Spain gave the American team a spark of confidence. At the same time, the squad also knew that Mexico, whose team had outscored them 12–2 in two qualifying matches, had lost both its matches—4–0 to Brazil and 4–1 to Yugoslavia.[8] Such news inspired little optimism.

At the start of the match the 30,000-seat stadium in Belo Horizonte reported a meager 10,000 in attendance. The mainly Brazilian crowd rooted for the United States because they knew that a showdown with England would promise a more competitive match for their own team.

England began the match with such confidence that they held out one of their superstars, Stanley Matthews, for an anticipated meeting against Spain. Walter Bahr, an American midfielder and inside forward, later recalled that "for the first 20 minutes, England was all over us.... We were fighting for our life."[9] In the first 12 minutes England attempted five shots on goal. Two shots hit the post, one sailed over the net, and two others went wide.[10] U.S. goalie Frank Borghi, who drove a hearse for his uncle's funeral parlor in St. Louis when he wasn't playing soccer, saved another shot. The United States managed only one shot on goal while England continued its relentless first-half attack.

In the thirty-eighth minute of play the United States struck. Receiving a throw-in, Bahr took an ambitious shot from 25 yards out, angling it toward the post. The English goalie leaped to the right to block the ball, but U.S. forward Joe Gaetjens, a Haitian immigrant who studied accounting at Columbia University and worked as a dishwasher on the side, dove headlong for the shot. It grazed his head enough to deflect the ball to the left of the goalie, who was unable to change direction. The ball found the net, and the United States led 1–0 as the first half ended.[11] The Brazilians went wild.

Despite the lead, the United States still lacked confidence. Bahr remembers that the team thought "the floodgates would open" in the second half.[12] Harry Keough, a defender and U.S. postal worker from St. Louis, recalled, "For us to be ahead at the half was one thing; for us to hold it was another."[13] The underdog U.S. team entered the second half with obvious trepidation.

As news of the U.S. lead spread in Belo Horizonte, the stadium attracted more fans. A few minutes into the second half, local Brazilians who had anticipated an English slaughter arrived to cheer on the American underdogs. Although Bahr's setup and Gaetjen's header had scored the goal, the hearse-driving Borghi turned out to be the real hero of the match. The man who had hoped to hold "The Kings" to four or five goals had shut them out for 45 minutes. That stellar performance continued in the second half. In the fifty-ninth minute, England received a direct free kick. Stanley Mortensen, a top scorer for the Blackpool professional team, fired a fierce strike toward the American goal. Borghi miraculously saved it. The English grew desperate and imagined the worst. Their final chance came in the eighty-second minute, when U.S.

defender Charlie Colombo brought down Mortensen with a rugby-style tackle outside of the penalty area. Colombo, perhaps in homage to his Italian surname, wore lightweight boxer gloves on the pitch and was known for his tough, physical play. He later joked that the Italian referee had congratulated him on his rough tackle, saying "Buono, buono" for taking down the Englishman.[14] The English side screamed for a direct penalty kick, but the referee held firm. An English player lofted the free kick toward the U.S. goal, where a teammate headed the ball toward the corner of the net. Again Borghi deflected it away with another remarkable save. The English players claimed the ball had crossed the line before it was deflected, but the referee ruled no goal.

The lead held, and when the final whistle blew the United States celebrated an unprecedented victory against the world's best team. Delirious Brazilian fans hoisted Gaetjens on their shoulders and carried him off the field. The U.S. team followed, stunned by their achievement.

One would think that such a startling win would have been major news in the United States. It wasn't. The only U.S. reporter attending the match was Dent McSkimming of the *St. Louis Dispatch,* who had to pay his own way to Brazil. The *New York Times* published a two-paragraph story about the victory, and other American newspapers attributed the lone U.S. goal to the wrong player.[15]

The U.S. team played Chile three days later. In the forty-eighth minute the Americans tied the score 2–2 on a penalty kick by Joe Maca, who had honed his soccer skills in Belgium before moving to the United States. A win would have sent the United States to the knockout round. Unfortunately, six minutes later Chile scored a goal, and then managed another two before the final whistle blew. The 5–2 whipping sent the U.S. team home.[16]

Surprisingly, England met the same fate. A shocked crowd of 74,000 in Rio de Janeiro watched as Spain defeated the "Kings of Football" 1–0. The defeat marked the beginning of a number of disappointments for the English national team, who had to wait until 1966 to win their one (and only) World Cup title.

The U.S. team returned home to the obscurity surrounding U.S. soccer at this time. Walter Bahr noted that the only person to greet him at the airport upon his return was his wife.[17] There were no reporters waiting to interview members of the team; there was no band or parade; there was no invitation to the White House. The improbable victory was forgotten almost as soon as it happened, except by those who had fought so hard to win. "One thing that bothers me is people in our own federation have referred to our victory as a fluke," Bahr noted. "It was no fluke. Things happen in sports. The ball can bounce any way."[18] Reporter McSkimming would later say that the U.S. victory was so unbelievable that it was "as if Oxford University sent a baseball team over here and it beat the Yankees."[19]

If the national team was invisible in 1950, despite its surprising victory over England, it disappeared completely over the next four decades, failing to even qualify for the World Cup until 1990. During the time of the U.S. disappearing act, England exacted considerable revenge, beating the United States in four international friendlies by a combined score of 29–4, including a 10–0 drubbing in 1964. From 1994 to 2008, the United States fared a little better, losing all three of their international friendlies with England, but only by a 6–1 combined margin. The United States and England did not meet in tournament competition again until the 2010 World Cup. By this time the U.S. national team had picked up steam while the English were floundering in Cup competition. The 2010 match ended in a lackluster 1–1 draw.

The few remaining players of the 1950 team finally got their interviews in 2005 after the release of *The Game of Their Lives*, a film based on the book of the same name that Geoffrey Douglas had published nine years earlier. The book and film briefly immortalized the famous U.S.-England match and brought fleeting attention to the players. Walter Bahr, at age 82, noted ironically in one interview that "the older I get, the more famous I become."[20]

* * * *

While semi-professional soccer and the U.S. national team were closeted away in relative obscurity, the landscape of soccer was expanding in one unforeseen and significant direction that would transform the social landscape of the sport. Through the mid-point of the twentieth century, soccer had never gained a significant foothold in universities and colleges. After disappearing entirely in the latter part of the nineteenth century in favor of rugby and American football, university soccer reappeared briefly in the early twentieth century, beginning at Haverford College in Pennsylvania. By 1920 there were over 20 university teams, mostly in small private colleges like Haverford and Christian Brothers College in St. Louis, as well as a few elite, more prominent universities, including Columbia, Harvard, Pennsylvania State, Princeton, Stanford, and Yale. With so few university and college programs, scheduling competition proved difficult, resulting in a majority of matches being played against local amateur teams. Few teams played more than eight to ten matches a year.

In 1926, the Intercollegiate Soccer Football Association was formed, with membership extending to a dozen universities in the northeast, but there was virtually no oversight of schedules, coaches, rules, and referees. Players and coaches usually had little experience with soccer prior to their university experience, and many soccer programs were an extension of general physical education. Soccer played in most universities was largely recreational.

The World War II years reduced the minimal growth of university soccer during the late 1930s and 1940s. Walter Bahr, a Philadelphian and one of the heroes of the 1950 World Cup U.S. National Team, remembered his days playing at Temple University during the war: "We ... never fielded eleven experienced players.... Our goalie was a big guy from the basketball team; we had a guy from the gym team and another guy from the track team—fast but with no soccer skills. All were good athletes, but not soccer players. At this time, many of the soccer-playing kids from our ethnic neighborhoods didn't finish high school, let alone think about college."[21]

This system began to change in the early post–World War II years. At the end of the war in 1945, only 42 universities and colleges fielded soccer teams. By 1954 that number had tripled to 125, and by 1958 it almost doubled to 235. At a time when soccer seemed to be retreating from the landscape it had occupied earlier in the century, it was expanding on university and college campuses, a space that had remained quietly dormant for so long.[22]

Several changes affected this renewed development in university soccer. First, the Servicemen's Readjustment Act, better known as the GI Bill, opened the door to university and college enrollment. Prior to World War II, only 4.6 percent of the U.S. population over the age of 25 held university degrees. Attending a university was not only relatively expensive but also not seen as a necessary advantage for entering the workforce. Following the war, however, the expanding U.S. economy in manufacturing and service sectors made a university degree much more attractive.

Over seven million veterans took advantage of the educational benefits given to them through the GI Bill, changing the social and economic mix of students on university campuses. Students no longer came solely from elite and middle-class backgrounds. An increasing number of these new students had lived in urban ethnic enclaves where soccer had thrived for generations, albeit informally. In addition, many GIs had been exposed to soccer when stationed overseas in countries where soccer truly was *the* national pastime. GIs abroad could play soccer because it was cheap—all that was needed was a ball and an open field.

The university student population also changed with the arrival of additional international students. Decolonization and globalization, spurred by dramatic advances in transportation and communication technologies, were transforming the social and economic world landscape. With a robust U.S. economy propelling the country to the forefront of global politics and economics, students from Europe, South America, Asia, and Africa sought greater opportunities in the U.S. educational system. Many of these students brought their passion for soccer to university campuses.

By 1957, the percentage of adults in the United States with a university degree had grown to 7.6 percent. The influx of students from different socioeconomic classes, veterans, and international students helped propel university soccer to a new level. By 1970, the number of university and college soccer teams had swelled to 473.[23] University soccer was now firmly entrenched as a non-revenue college sport.

This growth period was also a time of radical experimentation with the long-accepted rules of international soccer. While U.S. universities had modified some regulations in the 1920s, the tremendous postwar growth encouraged even greater tampering with accepted practices. Universities continued to operate with 22-minute quarters, a practice that some schools had adopted in the 1920s. Other modifications included a two-referee system, a liberal system of multiple substitutions, one-handed throw-ins, kick-ins rather than throw-ins, and even the abolition of the off-side rule that some coaches had curiously identified as "a drawback in the promotion of soccer."[24] Some of these changes were confined to specific collegiate divisions and rarely codified, but they were also symptomatic of the autonomy of university soccer and its lack of integration within the national structure of the U.S. Soccer Football Association (the new title for the preexisting USFA).

This tampering with the rules created confusion. First-generation students who had come up through home-grown urban soccer communities, as well as soccer-novice veterans and international students privy to their own brand of soccer, found it difficult to adjust to these changes. They were used to playing soccer as it was played in the rest of the world, as prescribed by FIFA. But because university soccer had developed separate from the USSFA, and because universities boasted no long-standing soccer tradition, such experimentation continued. The USSFA worried that the lack of FIFA-sanctioned rules would hamper otherwise talented university players when they transitioned to the U.S. national and Olympic teams, which played by international rules.

By the mid–1950s, an increasing number of players who had come up through the university ranks made it to the national team and Olympic tryouts. This represented a dramatic change from previous years, when players came up primarily through the urban semi-pro and amateur leagues. At this time, the Olympics still had strict rules prohibiting "professionals" from competing, barring some of the best U.S. players, who were playing at the semi-pro level. Three of the seven collegiate players invited to tryout camp advanced to the 1952 Olympics in Helsinki: Billy Sheppel of Seton Hall, Larry Surock of the University of Baltimore, and Jack Dunn of Temple.[25] Unfortunately, the addition of university players didn't help matters. Italy dismantled the United States in its only match by a lopsided score of 8–0. The 1956 Olympic squad also touted three ex-collegians: Dick Packer and Ron Coder of Penn State and Zenon Snylyk from the University of Rochester. The Americans lost their only Olympic match in Melbourne to Yugoslavia 9–1. Despite these embarrassing losses, by 1960 a full quarter of the players brought to Olympic tryouts came from university soccer.

A mix of players populated the growing university soccer landscape. Most quality teams still recruited veterans who had either picked up soccer while abroad or played in urban ethnic leagues prior to military service. In addition, a number of first-generation university students who had grown up in communities with long soccer traditions took their skills to university campuses. Also, successful teams usually enlisted several international players; some schools showcased a preponderance of foreign players. For example, the University of San Francisco, which won 55 straight matches from 1948 to 1953 and another 41 straight contests from 1954 to 1959, relied almost exclusively on foreign-born players. Still other players advanced through the ranks of a growing number of high school teams, particularly in elite prep schools. Tom Fox, who played at Williams College during the late 1950s, recalled that "none of us played soccer until prep school in New England. We never played soccer on Sunday or club soccer."[26]

The effects of this migration of the cultural landscape of soccer from community-based teams with established traditions to university-based settings linked with the growing collegiate sports landscape could not be foreseen. The migration illustrated the beginning of a geometric shift in the soccer pyramid. For decades, soccer in the United States was accessible to almost anyone who wanted to pursue it. Anchored in ethnic, working-class communities of large cities like New York, Philadelphia, Chicago, and St. Louis, and in smaller enclaves like Fall River and Kearney, soccer personified a right-side-up pyramid where anyone who had the inclination and skills as well as the drive and passion to play the sport could participate. Now, the pyramid was shifting toward its current upside-down configuration as it became a sport intrinsically linked to the university landscape. The pipeline of soccer success shifted away from the streets and amateur and semi-pro leagues to the university, laying the groundwork for the development of a youth soccer program that would feed and ultimately reinforce the emerging cultural landscape of the sport.

* * * *

Two dramatic technological changes propelled the expansion of the U.S. sports culture during the 1950s: commercial airline travel and television. Prior to this time, the national sports industry faced financial and geographical limitations. Gate receipts were the only means of profit, traveling was expensive in terms of both money and time, and competition was generally local or regional. Commercial air travel and television changed this arena, propelling the expansion of the sports landscape into cultural corners that had previously been semi-arid wastelands. Air travel opened the door to truly national sports by reducing the vast distances that separated the East Coast from the West Coast and everything in between. Television dramatically expanded the audience base for sports as well. Fans in Tupelo, Butte, El Paso, and countless other American cities could now follow their favorite teams and athletes with a flick of the dial. The massive sports industry that we see today is the result of such innovation.

Although commercial air travel existed prior to World War II, the industry expanded dramatically after 1945. The need for military aircraft during the war years had accelerated both the quality and quantity of production, and that trend continued in the private sector as countries recovered from the devastation of the war. The first jetliner, the de Havilland Comet, was introduced in 1952. It was followed rapidly by other innovations, such as the Russian Tupolev TU-104 and the U.S. Boeing 707, the first two commercially successful jet airplanes. The developing airline industry had the immediate effect of alleviating travel problems for teams, a factor that, in turn, affected scheduling, team and league expansion, and travel expenses.

The evolution of airline travel in the United States affected the development of other professional sports as well. In 1952, the teams of the American and National Baseball Leagues were located in the same major northeastern metropolitan areas where professional baseball teams had been centered since the early twentieth century. Chicago, Detroit, and St. Louis were as far afield as major league baseball had been able to extend itself from its northeastern center. In 1953, thanks to the airline industry, the Boston Braves moved to Milwaukee and the Philadelphia Athletics transferred to Kansas City, inching professional baseball westward.

A West Coast league—the Pacific Coast League, with teams in Los Angeles,

San Francisco, San Diego, Seattle, and other cities—had existed as a "minor" league for almost as long as its professional East Coast rivals. The Pacific Coast League competed with the more financially secure American and National leagues for players and media attention, and there was the lingering threat that the PCL would form a third, independent major league. This competition was quelled in 1958, when the Brooklyn Dodgers moved to Los Angeles and the New York Giants settled into San Francisco. The PCL thus remained a minor league system.

The same trend occurred in the National Football League. The Los Angeles Rams, added to the league in 1946, became the first non-northeastern or Midwestern team to join the ranks of professional football. The San Francisco Giants formed in 1950, and the Dallas Texans in 1952. (The latter team lasted only one season.) The real expansion, however, came in 1960 with the creation of the rival American Football League. In addition to teams in the northeastern hub of New York, Boston, and Buffalo, the new league fielded teams in Houston, Dallas, Los Angeles, Oakland, and Denver.

The National Basketball Association evolved through a merger of several smaller leagues in 1949. The expansion westward occurred later than those in baseball and football, with the early 1960s seeing the Minneapolis Lakers moving to Los Angeles and the Philadelphia Warriors arriving in San Francisco. Later, that decade also witnessed the addition of teams in Phoenix, San Diego, and Seattle.

Such expansions were unthinkable prior to the development of the airline industry. For the first time, professional sports were truly national in scope. This expansion of established professional sports into a national geographic and cultural landscape did not go unnoticed by the few sports entrepreneurs who were thinking of resurrecting professional soccer.

The acceleration of the television industry coincided with the growth in air travel. In 1950 there were only 6 million TV sets in 9 percent of U.S. households. One year later 23.5 percent of U.S. households owned at least one TV set, and by 1955 that number had increased to almost 65 percent. By 1960 almost 90 percent of American households owned a total of 53 million televisions, or one TV for every 3.4 persons in the country.[27]

The first sports events to be televised occurred in the neo-natal year of 1939, when TV was still experimental. On May 17 of that year, NBC broadcasted a collegiate baseball game between Columbia and Princeton in New York City. The summer of 1939 saw several more sports broadcasts: the Max Baer–Lou Nova heavyweight fight in Yankee Stadium; the finals of the Eastern Grass Courts Tennis Championship from Rye, New York; and the first professional baseball telecast matching the Cincinnati Reds and Brooklyn Dodgers. The Gillette Cavalcade of Sports, the first scheduled program that showed a variety of sporting events, first aired in 1944. However, these broadcasts were limited to the few households that owned television sets in and around New York City and the northeastern United States.[28]

The real explosion began in the late 1940s and early 1950s, as TV ownership rapidly became a symbol of postwar prosperity. While television can be viewed as an engine that propelled the expansion of the sports landscape, the reverse might be true as well. As pioneering NBC television sports director Harry Coyle once observed, "Today, maybe sports need television to survive, but it was just the opposite when it first started. When we put on the World Series in 1947, heavyweight fights, the Army-Navy football game, the sales of television sets just spurted."[29] Regardless of the prospective cause and effect, the result remained the same. For better or worse, television and sports were married forever. By 1962, the three major networks invested over $80 million in the mutually beneficial arrangement. This investment provided professional and collegiate sports with much-needed revenue, placing them on a more secure footing than could be realized from gate receipts alone.

By 1969 the gross revenues of network sports approached $180 million for the three major networks. Writing in *Variety*, Murray Horowitz noted that "TV has made 14 carat gold out of posts, putts, pucks, bats, and balls.... Now there is not a major sports event in the United States that does not have some tie with TV. The reason is simple: money."[30] The Age of Big Business had arrived securely in the U.S. sports landscape.

Moreover, the advent of the space age in the 1960s led to the launching of communication satellites that enabled American TV to broadcast international sporting events. The opening ceremony of the 1964 Summer Olympics in Tokyo was broadcast live via Syncom III satellite at 1:00 a.m. EST, although the remainder of the Olympics appeared on NBC via videotape flown to Seattle. By 1965 the Early Bird satellite made transcontinental sports broadcasting commonplace. In 1966 ABC aired a number of sporting events from abroad, including Le Mans Grand Prix from France, the British Open from Scotland, the Irish Derby from Dublin, a boxing match from Frankfurt, and a U.S.-U.S.S.R. track meet from Kiev. Not even the Cold War could dampen the televised sports fever that was infecting the United States.

NBC broadcasted one additional transcontinental sporting event that same year: the first soccer match televised in the United States. Although the 1954 World Cup in Switzerland was the first televised soccer broadcast, that showing was limited. The 1966 World Cup in England has been called the first globally televised soccer competition, with an audience of over 400 million viewers in 75 countries worldwide. While much of the world enjoyed watching multiple matches, American viewers were limited to the final game played on July 30 between England and West Germany. Broadcast at noon on Sunday with a two-hour tape delay, NBC intentionally scheduled the event immediately preceding its baseball game of the day in hopes of increasing the number of viewers. Because the actual match went into overtime, NBC edited the televised version to fit into its time frame. An estimated nine million viewers, however, watched England's exciting (and controversial) 4–2 overtime victory.

Although nine million viewers in the United States might seem comparatively small, it was enough to interest potential financial backers of the sport, especially those who had maintained soccer aspirations. Actually, that number of viewers constituted over 4.6 percent of the total population, a percentage that translates into over 15 million viewers given the total population of the country today. At the time, it was certainly sufficient to feed financial appetites.

This expanding sports landscape, fueled by television, air travel, and the postwar economic boom, along with the relative success of the 1966 World Cup television experiment, reignited professional soccer in the United States. It didn't happen overnight, nor did it happen easily, but it did happen. Now that sports had joined the ranks of Big Business, the new initiative required not only a love of soccer but also entrepreneurs who believed in potential profit.

* * * *

One such entrepreneur included New York–born Bill Cox, who had made his fortune as a lumber company executive and art dealer. Cox loved sports and had dabbled financially in the sports industry for some time. In the 1940s he purchased the Philadelphia Phillies, but he was forced to sell only eight months later when National League authorities discovered that he was betting on his own team. He tried investing in professional football, but in the 1950s he discovered soccer. Catching games as he traveled to Brazil, England, and Spain, Cox was willing to use his penchant for betting to kick-start professional soccer in the United States one more time. He was impressed by the passion of fans and the capacity crowds at matches in Rio de Janeiro, London, and Madrid, and convinced that both could be replicated in the United States given the right business strategies.[31]

Unaware of the history of soccer in his own country, Cox viewed soccer as a "new product" that required a proper introduction into the sports marketplace. With the advances in commercial aviation, a number of top international teams found it financially profitable to tour the United States in the 1950s, including Manchester United, Tottenham Hotspur, Celtic, Napoli, Munich 1860, and others. The financial success of these tours didn't go unnoticed by Cox and his affiliates. Cox prepared his strategy, creating a professional league of international teams so that Americans could witness first-hand how the sport should be played.

Cox called the mechanism for delivering this new product the International Soccer League, which operated from 1960 to 1965. Teams like the English West Ham United, the Brazilian Bangu Atlético Clube, the Polish Polonia Bytom, the Czech Dukla Prague, the Austrian Rapid Vienna, and others rotated in and out of the league. Initially, the teams played in New York City, but eventually their schedules expanded to Chicago, Philadelphia, and even Los Angeles. In addition, Cox usually included one American all-star team in the competition, although that team always featured a significant contingent of international players. Cox even managed to secure regional television contracts.[32]

While the venture occasionally drew crowds of 25,000, the ISL was not a booming financial success. However, it was not a financial disaster, either. In the end Cox lost money, but he viewed the loss as an investment in something much bigger: building the infrastructure for a bona fide U.S. professional soccer league. The ISL would serve as a catalyst for developing soccer fever in the United States, but the goal always included a professional American league. After five bumpy seasons, Cox felt the time was ripe.[33]

As Clive Toye, a soccer writer for the *Daily Express,* the largest circulation newspaper in the English-speaking world, recalls, "In the spring of 1966 [Cox] arrived with a whole new bunch of Americans in tow, with the story he had told me five years earlier now coming to life."[34] The men accompanying Cox included investors and soccer supporters from St. Louis, Atlanta, Texas, California, and other states. They were there to announce the formation of a professional American soccer league, to begin play in 1967.

As Toye began running stories about the plan in the *Daily Express*, he and Cox received phone calls from players and coaches from around the world looking for new career opportunities. Toye remembers an initial call he received from Phil Woosnam, a Welsh player for West Ham United, who would become the first player-coach for the Atlanta Chiefs in the new league and later coach the USMNT in 1968. At the time, neither Toye nor Woosnam had any idea what might develop over the next years.[35]

Cox was such an enthusiast (with dollar signs embedded in his eyes) that he announced the league while forgetting essential details, such as securing the blessing of the USSFA, the governing body of U.S. soccer. Since its inception, the ISL had had an uneasy relationship with the official American soccer bureaucracy, which frowned upon a soccer league in the United States comprised almost entirely of foreign teams. Another problem was that none of the potential investors had assembled a team. They had announced the new league with considerable fanfare, but there were as yet no coaches or players.

At this time the USSFA sought proposals from potential investors who could guarantee not only the formation of a coast-to-coast professional league but also television contracts and an enthusiastic fan base. Three different groups submitted proposals, including the one headed by Cox. Big sports money led the competing groups, which included owners of baseball's Atlanta Braves, Baltimore Orioles, and Houston Astros and NFL franchises the Washington Redskins, the Los Angeles Rams, and the Pittsburgh Steelers. Seeing the potential from big investors and feeling its oats, the USSFA demands escalated. In order to be sanctioned as *the* American professional league, the USSFA demanded a $25,000 franchise fee from each team, plus 4 percent gate receipts and 10 percent of television contracts.[36]

The Cox investment group withdrew and plowed ahead with its own plan to form an independent professional league, the North American Professional Soccer League (NAPSL). The USSFA selected a group headed by Jack Kent Cooke, who already had considerable financial investments in the Washington Redskins, the Los Angeles Lakers, and an expansion NHL franchise. Cooke's was the only group willing to meet the USSFA financial demands. By August, Cox had united with other investors who'd rejected the USSFA "offer" and renamed their league the National Professional Soccer League (NPSL). They would begin play in April 1967. Thumbing their noses at the national governing organization, they also announced a $1,000,000 annual television contract with CBS. Despite its renegade status, the NPSL had outmaneuvered the opposition. The TV contract might as well have been a knife in the back of the USSFA.[37]

By this time, Clive Toye had joined forces with Bill Cox. He recalls negotiating with Bill McPhail, head of CBS Sports: "All was going well until Bill McPhail ... asked, OK, how do we stop the game for commercials?"[38] Eventually they reached a compromise, which involved fitting referees with electronic devices hooked up to broadcast directors who could signal referees when to pause for commercial breaks. This compromise led to some curious soccer moments, when referees actually encouraged injured players to remain on the ground long enough to air a commercial.

Both sides drew a line in the sand. The USSFA-sanctioned league conveniently adopted the name the United Soccer Association (USA). Once again professional soccer was embroiled in the politics of power and money. With the USA already running behind the Cox group, they announced a schedule that would begin in the spring of 1967. Instead of building entirely new teams, however, the league borrowed the old ISL model of importing international teams, providing new "American" identities superficially consistent with the acronym USA. Ireland's Shamrock Rovers became the Boston Rovers, while England's Wolverhampton Wanderers transformed into the Los Angeles Wolves. Stoke City adopted a new name—the Cleveland Stokers; Brazil's Bangu ended up as the Houston Stars. And so on. No one could predict which league would triumph over the other.

The fateful day arrived on Sunday, April 16, 1967, when all 10 teams of the renegade NPSL took to their respective fields. The Philadelphia Spartans, playing in Temple University's 20,000-seat football stadium against the Toronto Falcons, led attendance that day with a respectable 14,200 fans. Other stadiums appeared almost empty. The 4,700 fans at the 100,000 Soldier Field, home of the Chicago Bears, were almost invisible to the hometown Chicago Spurs. The New York Generals, playing in the rented Yankee Stadium, fared only slightly better with a small crowd of 7,800 in a stadium that held 67,000 people.[39] The nationally televised game on CBS saw the Baltimore Bays defeat the Atlanta Chiefs 1–0 before a crowd of only 8,434. Northern Ireland international Danny Blanchflower, who did the play-by-play with CBS sports announcer Jack Whitaker, vocally criticized the level of play demonstrated to a nationally televised audience. The *New York Times* echoed Blanchflower's lack of enthusiasm for the televised match: "Everyone was an unknown and the action had no compelling interest. A flick of the wrist and Richie Allen was hitting a home run for the Phils ... and Wilt Chamberlain was wolfing in rebounds."[40] With a long-term contract with the NPSL, CBS did the only thing it could: it fired Blanchflower.

Two weeks later, the 10 teams of the USA took the field. Initial attendance figures provided more optimism to team owners. Brazil's Houston Stars drew almost 35,000 to the Astrodome, but just as many fans came to see the stadium that Roy Hofheintz, the team owner, had advertised as "the eighth wonder of the world." In retrospect, the event is remembered more as the first soccer match ever played on artificial turf. The initial appearance of the USA's New York Skyliners drew 21,000 to Yankee Stadium. The novelty soon disappeared, however. Houston's attendance leveled off to a respectable 12,000, but the Skyliners eventually played before fewer than 5,000 fans per game.

By mid-season, teams in Detroit and Boston drew gates of less than 1,000 fans.[41]

The response to declining attendance in both leagues typified American gimmickry. Halftime fan contests, "ethnic" nights, roving jazz bands, free babysitting services, dancing girls in sexy costumes, prizes of all sorts, and even rumors that 7'1" Wilt Chamberlain was about to be signed to play goalie didn't change the downward trajectory of attendance figures. The public face of owners and league administrators remained optimistic, claiming that most first-year "products" struggled to find a niche in a competitive market, but many owners worried privately. More importantly, egotistical sports entrepreneurs were quickly realizing that two competitive leagues in an untested market meant inevitable suicide. Market saturation reflected a grim reality. Ultimately such cut-throat competition indicated that neither side had won. NPSL teams had lost $5 million, and the USA slightly less.[42]

With threats of lawsuits hovering in the air, cooler heads prevailed. The two sides eventually reached a compromise and merged to form the North American Soccer League. No one could predict it at the time, but the NASL was destined to ride a roller coaster for another 16 years, resurrecting similar hopes that had died 35 years earlier. Seventeen surviving teams from the 1967 disaster banded together into four divisions, with plans for a 32-matches-per-team schedule to begin the following spring. Although many of the NPSL's international players remained in the new teams' shuffled lineups, the new league abandoned importation of wholesale squads from abroad.

The problem of market saturation still remained, however. The NASL would play a total of 272 regular season matches, with predictable results. Attendance figures remained skeletal. The finals between the Atlanta Chiefs and the San Diego Toros averaged only 12,177 fans for two matches. Atlanta eventually won by an aggregate score of 3–0.

Only five of the 17 teams survived into the 1969 season, and some of those were living on borrowed time. Because of the reduced number of teams, the league tried to stir interest by staging a competitive round-robin "International Cup" between British imported teams, each team identified with one of the five remaining American teams. Atlanta represented Aston Villa; Baltimore, West Ham United; Dallas, Dundee United; Kansas City, Wolverhampton Wanderers; and St. Louis, the Kilmarnock FC. With moderate attendance, the hoped-for spark never developed. Attendance for the regular season remained marginal. Kansas City barely edged out Atlanta for the league championship in a shortened, 16-match schedule. Dallas held down the middle and St. Louis and Baltimore fought for last place, losing a total of 24 of 32 matches. By the end of the season, what little hope had survived the three seasons of professional U.S. soccer had turned to despair.[43]

The following three years saw teams coming and going, with schedules vacillating between 14 and 24 matches per team. The six championship matches, played from 1970 to 1972, drew a meager average of 5,888 fans. Regular season attendance fared even worse. The highest-paid player during the 1970 season was Victorio Casa, a one-armed Argentinian striker who played for the Washington Darts. He barely made $15,000.[44] Most players held second jobs either in the United States or in their home countries. Others were on loan from international clubs whose seasons had finished by the time the NASL season started. The earlier belief that soccer could thrive in the United States had changed to the desperate hope to survive.

For obscure reasons, the 1973 season showed signs that the tide was turning slightly. The eight teams that survived the 1971 and 1972 seasons continued, joined by Philadelphia, an original 1967 NPSL entrant. Attendance edged up. The single championship match played in Dallas between the Dallas Tornadoes and the Philadelphia Atoms drew 18,824 fans, still low for the championship of a national sport but an improvement over past years. The upstart Philadelphia team defeated Dallas by a score of 2–0, earning that year's championship crown.[45]

Because hope springs eternal, the slight improvement in attendance led to a sudden expansion in the league. While teams from Atlanta and Montreal folded, the league added teams from Baltimore, Boston, Denver, Los Angeles, San Jose, Seattle, Vancouver, and Washington to form a 15-team league that once again spanned the country. The 1975 season witnessed yet another explosion as the league added teams from Chicago, Hartford, Portland, San Antonio, and Tampa Bay, although the schedule remained modest, with each team playing 22 matches.[46] The expansion strategy added substantial amounts of money to NASL coffers, as franchise fees had grown from $10,000 to $250,000 in a relatively few years. In hindsight, one wonders whether the growth was too much too fast.

In 1975, an international star player joined the still struggling NASL. For the moment this event was more important than expansion and gave rise to even greater hopes for professional soccer in the United States. His name was Edson Arantes do Nascimento, and his *nom de guerre*—Péle—was already synonymous with soccer. Péle joined the New York Cosmos, a legendary team that would dominate NASL competition for years. With Péle and other international imports, the Cosmos generated unprecedented enthusiasm as well as plans and profits for professional soccer in the United States. At last, it appeared that professional soccer had finally arrived in the U.S. sports landscape.

6

History of U.S. Soccer: The Cosmos Years

At age 34, Pelé was obviously beyond his prime, but his name was legendary even in the soccer-poor United States. Starting his professional career at the unprecedented age of 16 with Santos, a team that dominated Brazilian soccer in the late 1950s and 1960s, Pelé quickly established himself as a once-in-a-century player. Santos competed in the highly competitive top-flight league in the state of São Paulo and Pelé led the league in scoring each year between 1957 and 1965, beginning in his first professional season. In 1958, at age 17, Pelé led Santos to victory in the Campeonato Paulista, the league championship, by scoring 58 goals in 30 matches. The record stands to this day. That same year he became the youngest player ever to play in a World Cup match, the youngest player ever to score a World Cup goal, the youngest player in World Cup history to score a hat trick, and the youngest player ever named "Young Player of the Tournament." At age 17 he also led Brazil with six World Cup goals in four matches, cementing the title of teenage star of Brazil's first World Cup championship team. Although Brazil repeated the same feat in 1962, Pelé suffered an injury in the second match of the tournament and had to watch from the bench. Another injury sidelined him in the 1966 World Cup, and Brazil exited early. Brazil's 1970 World Cup team, often referred to as the greatest soccer team ever assembled, won the country's third World Cup over the previous four tournaments, and Pelé was named outstanding player. Tarcisio Burgnich, the ace Italian defender who was given the task of marking Pelé in the final, said after Italy lost 4–1, "I told myself before the game, 'He's made of skin and bones just like everyone else'—but I was wrong."[1]

His legacy and fame soundly established, Pelé retired from Santos in 1971. Brazil had ensured that Pelé would remain in the country for his entire professional career by declaring him a *Tesouro Nacional*—a national treasure that could not be legally exported to another country. What was unknown to Brazilian officials and most of the world was that an NASL team calling itself the New York Cosmos had been courting Pelé since his retirement. New York had fielded a team called the Generals during the first two years of the league, but that team had folded for the 1969 and 1970 seasons. Resurrected as the Cosmos in 1971 with an audacious eye on Pelé, team officials selected Brazil's colors as their own. That same year, Clive Toye, who had left the Baltimore club to help form the Cosmos, met Pelé before an exhibition match between Santos and Deportivo Cali of Colombia at Yankee Stadium. He informed the soon-to-be-retired star that the Cosmos were "retiring" his number 10 jersey in his honor.[2] What Pelé thought of his jersey being retired by a team he had never played for, or ever heard of, is not known. What *is* known is that four years later Pelé and his number 10 jersey emerged from retirement to join the NASL Cosmos.

Signing the richest contract ever in U.S. sports at the time—somewhere between $4.5 and $7 million, depending on how it was computed—Pelé announced, "My contract is not just to play for the Cosmos; it is to promote soccer in America."[3] Pelé joined the team for the final nine games of its 22-game season and scored five goals with four assists—hardly the spectacular showing that had been expected. He played his initial match in the dilapidated, Depression-era Downing Stadium on Randall's Island before a crowd of 21,000, more than four times what the Cosmos had drawn in their previous outing. Toye recalls, "Watching Pelé play at Randall's Island is like seeing Baryshnikov dance in a Times Square honky tonk joint."[4] CBS paid $50,000 for television rights and relayed the telecast nationally (and in 11 other countries). An estimated five million viewers tuned in. Because the TV networks had not figured out how to telecast soccer matches without commercial breaks, television audiences were deprived of Pelé's first Cosmos goal: the network unceremoniously broke for a commercial break.[5]

With a record of 10 wins and 12 losses, New York finished the 1975 season with a twelfth-place finish in the 20-team league, an improvement over the previous season's dismal 4–14–2 record but hardly something to justify Pelé's financial package. The record didn't matter, however. Though they remained a mediocre team, Pelé had turned the Cosmos into the darlings of a suddenly interested media. If his first year with the Cosmos hadn't transformed their on-the-field play, Pelé's mere presence fulfilled the more important part of his contract: the promotion of soccer. *Sports Illustrated* featured Pelé and the Cosmos in one of its issues, and the newly invigorated team made newspaper headlines wherever it played. Attendance improved significantly for home games, and crowds turned out to see the Cosmos and Pelé when they traveled: 22,000 in Toronto, which had drawn only 5,000 previously; 35,320 in Washington, up to that point the largest crowd in NASL history; and 20,000 in Boston, playing in a stadium with an official capacity of 12,500.[6] Because the Cosmos basically fielded the same team as the year before, it was obvious what important factor produced an increase in ticket sales. The other Cosmos players stood in awe of his presence and often stopped on the field to watch Pelé maneuver the ball.

Pelé worked the same magic off the field. At the White House he shook hands with President Gerald Ford. He cavorted with Hollywood celebrities and appeared on late-night and early-morning television shows. For fans, Pelé sightings shared the same status as Elvis sightings.

Pelé and the Cosmos soon toured in Europe and the Caribbean, creating the same frenzy witnessed in the United States. The first stop on the tour was Sweden, the site of the 1958 World Cup, during which the 17-year-old Pelé had burst onto the national stage. Swedish prime minister Olof Palme noted, "When I tell my family I am meeting kings and queens, presidents and prime ministers, they shrug their shoulders. When I told them I was coming here to meet Pelé, they all wanted to come."[7] Everywhere the Cosmos went, Pelé attracted the same attention.

The buoyant soccer hopes of the late 1960s had met the experience of disappointing gate receipts, off-and-on TV contracts, folding teams, inadequate stadiums, and a lukewarm media, resulting in futile pessimism. Now Pelé was starting to turn things around, or so the optimists thought. More fans than ever showed up to buy tickets, and wealthy investors started calculating how to share the action. The NASL top brass assumed that Pelé would draw fans to the stadiums and the excitement of the games would take care of the rest. The tide had turned, and once again the future of American soccer looked bright.

Bloated with confidence and drunk with publicity, the Cosmos decided they had outgrown Downing Stadium, which seemed a ghastly insult to the greatest player in the world. They eventually signed a deal to play in Yankee Stadium. The per-game cost for the fabled stadium came close to the season-long cost of Downing Stadium, but nothing seemed too good or too expensive for the reenergized team. They also went on a player-signing binge. A major catch included midfielder Ramón Mifflin, former captain of the Peruvian national squad. Several other prominent South American players signed, no doubt attracted by the rapidly expanding NASL salaries as well as the chance to play with Pelé.

The real find was a disgruntled Italian star named Giorgio Chinaglia, who led Lazio to its first Italian Serie A championship in 1974. Despite being at the zenith of his career, Chinaglia was unhappy in Italy. His volatile, competitive personality had created a hostile relationship with Lazio's cross-town rival Roma and its fans. After scoring a goal against Roma in a Copa Italia match early in his career, he ran directly in front of the section of the Stadio Olimpico reserved for Roma fans, yelling, "Look at me. I am Giorgio Chinaglia. I beat you."[8] Whether or not the rumors of physical threats to him were real, the media reported that Chinaglia had started carrying a pistol in his car. What Roma hated, Lazio loved, but in soccer-divided Rome his unabashed bravado created equally unabashed hatred in much of the media and citizenry. Moreover, in the 1974 World Cup, Italy removed him in favor of a substitute in a match against Haiti, and his violent outburst in the dressing room effectively banned him from future caps (that is, appearances) on the national team. By 1975, married to an American wife and fluent in English from his early years in Wales as a kid, Chinaglia prepared for a move to what he hoped would be less hostile terrain. Likewise, the Cosmos were anxious to add a "second Pelé" to their roster.

The top brass of the Cosmos got a taste of Chinaglia's personality when he arranged, at his own expense, to be flown to the United States in a private jet, leaking his time of departure to the Italian media so that he would be conveniently photographed for his Columbus-like journey to "The New World." He also took out a full-page ad in Rome's *Corriere dello Sport* listing the reasons for his departure. The Cosmos spent a precious $750,000 on a transfer fee to Lazio, but they bargained an $80,000 yearly salary with Chinaglia, a fraction of what they were paying Pelé. Immediately, the Italian became an inside favorite with Steve Ross, CEO of Warner Communications and owner of the Cosmos. This relationship continues to mystify those who knew both men, and it stands as a contributing factor to the demise of the Cosmos (as well as the NASL).

The Cosmos' investment and risk-taking paid immediate dividends. In 1976 the team finished the season with the second best record in the NASL, slightly trailing the previous season's champs, the Tampa Bay Rowdies. The Cosmos led the league in goals scored (65 goals in 24 matches), with Pelé scoring 13 goals and dishing out 18 assists in 22 matches. Chinaglia led the league with 19 goals in 19 matches, complemented with an impressive 11 assists of his own. Pelé earned the honor of being named the league's outstanding player.[9]

The ripple effect of signing these superstars and others a few notches down in the hierarchy of world soccer also continued to be felt. The all-time NASL single-match attendance record, set the previous year in a match between New York and Washington, was shattered in half a dozen or more matches. The Seattle Sounders led the way with 58,128 in their new Superdome home for a pre-season friendly against the Cosmos. The first-year Minnesota Kicks, playing in a region best known for its relative absence of soccer, drew 46,000 to see the Cosmos and 49,572 in a playoff match with San Jose.[10] The Cosmos/NASL strategy seemed to be kicking in. The trick was balancing increasing profits from gate receipts with escalating salaries and transfer fees. This balancing act kept the league precariously skating on thin ice.

Surprisingly, Tampa Bay eliminated the Cosmos in the championship playoff round. The departure of the league's primary public relations face disappointed fans and owners alike. Even more disappointing was that the league's least favorite team, the Toronto Metros-Croatia, won the championship by beating an upstart Minnesota team 3–0 before a measly 25,765 fans in the Superdome and a small CBS television audience. League officials could only dream about what might have transpired had the Cosmos reached the finals.

The next year the Cosmos added a "third Pelé," German superstar Franz Beckenbauer, to the team. At age 31, Beckenbauer had not quite exhausted his playing with Bayern Munich, but he definitely had reached the downside of his career. His credentials were every bit as extraordinary as his personality was reserved (at least compared to those of Pelé and Chinaglia). A three-time World Cup All-Star team member with over 100 caps for the German national team, Beckenbauer was twice named European Player of the Year. With Pelé and Chinaglia up front and Beckenbauer directing the action from the middle, the Cosmos appeared to have the "Holy Trinity" of NASL soccer.

Other NASL teams tried to follow the Cosmos' example. The Los Angeles Aztecs signed Irish superstar George Best (known for his off-repeated statement "Maradona good, Pelé better, George Best") in 1976, and they added Johan Cruyff, the Dutch magician of total football, the following year. Other teams with shallower pockets managed as best they could through loans or transfer fees.

Sports fans-in-the-know widely predicted that the 1977 season, the last of Pelé's three-year contract, would be the Year of the Cosmos. While Beckenbauer was not due to join the team until after the season started, the Pelé-Chinaglia combination was projected to peak. In building their team around aging superstars, however, the Cosmos had failed to measure the impact of competing personalities, nationalities, and styles of play. Although they worked well together the first year, neither Pelé nor Chinaglia enjoyed sharing the limelight. Pelé skipped the entire pre-season and showed up right before the start of the regular season, slowed by both his age and lack of conditioning. Chinaglia flaunted his close relationship with Steve Ross, strutting around the locker room in a silk dressing gown, with a bottle of Chivas Regal—Ross's favorite brand—conspicuously displayed in his locker. Rumors abounded that Chinaglia had become the *de facto* manager of the team with Ross's secret blessing.

Their antagonism often erupted on the field, spreading to other players. The other South Americans on the team started passing more frequently to Pelé, either in deference to his soccer stature or in preference for a regional identity. The three Americans who played regularly and a contingent of Englishmen rarely seemed in sync. When he joined the team, Beckenbauer reportedly expressed shock at the disarray.

The feud finally erupted in the locker room after a match. Chinaglia berated Pelé for not sharing the ball more, and Pelé replied that it was because the Italian gambled by taking shots from impossible angles. Chinaglia, a tall, imposing figure who towered over the well-built but shorter Pelé, went nose-to-nose with Pelé and shouted, "I am Chinaglia. If I shoot from a place, it's because Chinaglia can score from there!" Shaking his head, tears welling in his eyes, the Brazilian icon quietly left the locker room.[11]

Despite the turmoil, the Cosmos continued to draw huge crowds to their matches. Over 45,000 attended Beckenbauer's league debut in Tampa, a 4–2 loss for the Cosmos. A month later a crowd of 62,394 in New York witnessed a hat trick by Pelé as the Cosmos trounced Tampa Bay.[12] Their season home average inched toward a record 40,000.

Nearing the end of the season, the dissension had produced a mediocre 12–10 record and the Cosmos were in danger of not making the playoffs. In July the team acquired the brilliant Brazilian sweeper Carlos Alberto, and the coaching staff moved Beckenbauer to center midfield. Beckenbauer's precise passing and play-making abilities seemed to ignite both Pelé and Chinaglia and the team finished strong, winning three of their last four matches to make the championship playoffs.

Finally playing like the team that everyone had anticipated, the Cosmos dispensed of Tampa Bay 3–0. They smashed Fort Lauderdale, champions of the Eastern Division, 8–3 and 3–2, and later rolled over Rochester 2–1 and 4–1 to set up a meeting with the Seattle Sounders for the NASL Championship, now called the Soccer Bowl in imitation of the NFL's popular Super Bowl. The fans came in even greater numbers. A record 77,691 supporters in New York witnessed the butchering of Fort Lauderdale; 74,000 attended the

Cosmos' home victory against Rochester. These incredible numbers—over 150,000 in two matches—remain a high-water mark for U.S. soccer.[13]

Unfortunately, the NASL, in all its infinite wisdom, pre-selected Portland's rickety Civic Stadium, originally built in the 1920s for greyhound racing, as the site of the Soccer Bowl finals. The stadium held only 27,000, although 8,500 temporary seats were added. In hindsight, the Seattle Superdome would have been a grander and more profitable venue, pitting the home team against the legendary but underperforming Cosmos. Still, the match received all the hype it deserved. The Pelé-era Cosmos had finally made it to the finals and Seattle, a solid team with an excellent attendance record since it joined the league in 1974, participated for the first time.

Promoters billed the match as the "underdog vs. the superdog." The superdog, of course, indicated the star-studded Cosmos. Underdog Seattle players were not even well known in the countries from which they came. The Sounders starters were mostly second- and third-tier British players whose lack of fame and common backgrounds were probably their strongest assets. Most of the fans in attendance supported Seattle, but they also wanted to see Pelé go out in style. Sounders coach Jimmy Gabriel, an Englishman, scoffed at the latter sentiment, stating, "Pelé won enough medals."[14]

The Cosmos prevailed by a score of 2–1, with Chinaglia scoring the winning goal on a header from a cross by Steve Hunt, who had scored the initial Cosmos goal on a still-legendary mistake by Sounders goalie Tony Chursky. In a scoreless first half, the Sounders outplayed the Cosmos. In the second half Chinaglia sent a long looping pass down the left side, hoping that the English forward Hunt could outrun the defender. Chursky wasn't taking any chances and raced to the edge of the box, spearing the ball safely in his arms before Hunt could reach it. At full speed, Hunt raced past the goalie to the end line and started walking back on the field. Chursky casually carried the ball a few steps, and then rolled it to the edge of the penalty area, looking downfield for an open teammate. Suddenly, Hunt appeared from behind Chursky, tapping the ball away from the startled goalie and netting it for the Cosmos' first goal. That goal is now immortalized as one of the costliest mistakes a professional goalie has ever made.

With the star-studded Cosmos crowned champions, the media went overboard. In its September 5 recap of the championship match, *Sports Illustrated* referred to the ramshackle Civic Stadium as "the place where soccer in North America had its coming out party." According to *SI*, the match signaled "the culmination of a season that has changed the face of the sport in the U.S."[15] Actually, this event marked the tenth year of the NASL, during which time teams had come and gone. And while most teams were still losing money, the Cosmos represented only one of several solvent league teams. Yet the hyperbole struck a chord. With players like Pelé, Chinaglia, Beckenbauer, Cruyff, Best, and Alberto joining a number of top-level players from around the world, as well as a handful of Americans who could compete at the same level, the quality of play in the NASL captivated fans. Record crowds at matches confirmed that Pelé and others could sustain interest over time. The flurry of positive publicity provided sudden credence to NASL Commissioner Phil Woosnam's bold but misguided claim two years earlier that "I am totally confident that soccer will be the biggest sport in this country, and that the United States will be the world center of soccer."[16]

The problem with such optimism centered on isolating the Cosmos' success rather than looking at the reality of the entire league. Warner Communications had deep pockets that enabled them to attract high-quality players with name recognition. Few teams could match that economic clout. With the help of media publicity, money, a bit of bravado, and the Pelé brand, the Cosmos built a highly successful fan base in New York and around the country. Before the 1977 season, the Cosmos' single-game home attendance record was 28,436 in their 1976 home opener with Pelé aboard. Attendance in 1977 exceeded that figure in 11 of their 17 home matches, culminating in the August 14 crowd of 77,691. While other teams occasionally experienced crowds of over 30,000, the league as a whole still averaged only 14,000 per match. The Cosmos' average attendance had experienced a dramatic increase from 3,500 in the pre–Pelé year of 1974 to over 10,000 in 1975, 18,500 in 1976, and 40,000 in 1977. The upward slant of the Cosmos' attendance graph certainly signaled a reason for optimism, but the trajectory for the league as a whole was less impressive—from 7,500 in 1975 to 8,000 in 1976 to 14,500 in the banner year of 1977.[17]

Pelé's career in the United States wasn't quite finished. Two months after their victory in the NASL championship, the Cosmos hosted a match with Pelé's former Brazilian team, Santos. It was a touching and deserving farewell to a player who had accomplished what the Cosmos and American soccer had asked of him. At the Meadowlands in New York, 75,000 fans bid Pelé a warm *boa viagem.* In a constant downpour that failed to dampen the spirits of anyone on the field or in the stands, Pelé played the first half with his Cosmos teammates and the second half with Santos. He scored for the Cosmos, who completed the match with a 2–1 win. ABC outbid the other networks for television rights, broadcasting its first live soccer match and adding enough ritual fluff to please even the most lethargic viewer. Celebrities like Danny Kaye, Barbra

Streisand, Robert Redford, and Muhammad Ali paraded before the camera as recently converted soccer enthusiasts. Still, the night belonged to Pelé. The more sentimental types in the crowd even said that the raindrops were "God's tears" shed over the departure of Pelé from the United States.[18]

The following season, there was trepidation over an NASL without Pelé. Would it continue its upward momentum? Could it stand on its own feet? After the 1977 season, Clive Toye proudly declared, "The crowds went out to see Pelé in 1975 and 1976, but in 1977 they went out to see soccer."[19] Beneath the surface of these bold public relations statements, insiders expressed grave concerns. The league formed a long-range strategic planning group, which concluded that of the 18 active clubs, "six are doing well. Six are okay and can be improved. Six either have to be moved to better markets or taken over by new owners or dumped."[20] According to Toye, who served on the planning committee, two key recommendations emerged: (1) the league should not expand, and (2) the focus should shift from the national TV market to local and regional markets.[21] After all, what is the national interest in seeing Tulsa play Fort Lauderdale? Both recommendations, however, were ignored. The lure of bringing in millions of dollars through expansion fees tempted too many backers. Besides the money, the image of an expanding league would communicate to the nation that all was well.

With an entry fee now in the millions per team, the NASL still managed to expand to 24 teams and a 30-match schedule. There seemed to be no shortage of deep pockets. With unabashed optimism, the expansion Detroit Express leased the 80,500-seat Pontiac Silverdome. The expansion Colorado Caribous jumped into Denver's 75,000-seat Mile High Stadium. The veteran Los Angeles Aztecs moved confidently into the 104,696-seat Rose Bowl. Everyone involved seemed to predict an epidemic of soccer fever.

The Cosmos stood as the team to beat. Their 1977 performance had finally caught up with their reputation, and anticipation was high despite Pelé's absence. The team invested heavily in signing Manchester City's Dennis Tueart and Red Star Belgrade's Vladislav Bogićević, excellent players but hardly likely to become household names in the United States. It was indeed time for the league to stand on its own merits. The Cosmos lived up to expectations, sweeping past Fort Lauderdale in their opener 7–0 and attracting 71,000 to an early home match against Seattle, whom they manhandled 5–1. By the end of the regular season, they had achieved a 24–6 record, scoring 88 goals to their opponents' 39. The next leading goal-scoring teams, Vancouver and Detroit, lagged far behind, with 68 goals in 30 matches.[22]

Freed from his brash competition with Pelé, Chinaglia continued his barrage, managing 34 goals and 11 assists in 30 matches. Hunt, who'd played a tertiary role behind both Pelé and Chinaglia the preceding year, added 12 goals and 12 assists to become a legitimate scoring threat. Adding Tueart's 12 goals meant that the trio scored almost two-thirds of the Cosmos' total goals.[23]

Although collectively the NASL drew 5.3 million spectators to its games, many teams continued to struggle. Average attendance at the league's 360 regular season matches still attracted only 14,000, down slightly from the preceding year. Expansion teams like the Caribous, San Diego Sockers, Houston Hurricanes and Memphis Rogues regularly lured no more than 5,000 fans to their matches. The bottom also fell out of some veteran teams. The Chicago Sting at times played before a paltry 1,500 fans. The Los Angeles Aztecs, playing in the cavernous Rose Bowl, often played before 100,000 empty seats. The Cosmos, however, still reigned supreme. Their 1978 home attendance increased to an average of over 50,000, a 25 percent increase over 1977.[24]

The Cosmos marched to their second championship in post-season play, beating their archrival Tampa Bay Rowdies in the final, 3–1, before 74,901 wild New York fans. Both Chinaglia and Tueart had scored four goals apiece in the first five playoff matches, but this time the Italian's one goal took a back seat to Tueart's two goals and one assist. Once more the Cosmos were atop the American soccer world, and soccer seemed to be fulfilling predictions made by Commissioner Woosnam and *Sports Illustrated* as it climbed up another rung on the sports ladder.

In October 1978, Commissioner Woosnam announced the acquisition of a prize that would be the league's crowning glory: a television contract. ABC signed an agreement to televise nine NASL matches per season, including the Soccer Bowl, over the next three years. The financial benefits to the league were modest, with each team receiving only approximately $30,000 per year from the league's coffers. By comparison, NFL teams received about $6,000,000 apiece per year from their television contract. Nevertheless, the contract was perceived as an essential step forward in the league's progress and a major publicity coup.

The 1979 season began with the momentum of the previous season and the new television contract still going strong, but unforeseen circumstances soon intervened. Players in the NASL had watched from the sidelines as player associations in other American sports gained power during the 1970s, resulting in a doubling of professional baseball salaries from 1967 to 1975 and a five-fold increase in professional basketball salaries during the same period. The average NASL salary hovered around $20,000 (and that figure was inflated due to high-end salaries of the relatively few big foreign stars), while average salaries in the big three U.S. sports had moved into the \$75,000–\$100,000 range.[25] With salaries for most professional soccer players hovering far below those of their colleagues in other sports, the NASL players voted overwhelmingly to strike for higher wages. The owners balked, and when push came to shove, on opening day players crossed the few picket lines in droves.

Actually, 85 percent of the league's players were foreign citizens, many of whom supplemented their salaries from professional leagues in their home countries with summer salaries in the United States. The 15 percent who claimed U.S. citizenship didn't have deals quite so sweet. The international players, who on average drew higher salaries than their American counterparts, had little stake in a long, drawn-out battle with owners. So the threat of a strike fizzled almost before it began.

In previous years tension had grown between the majority of foreign players and the minority of U.S. players. Bobby Smith, from Trenton, New Jersey, and a defender for the Cosmos from 1976 to 1979 complained about the league being run by British coaches and a British commissioner. "The British coaches," he said, "don't feel any obligation to develop American players. They expect an American player to walk straight into the first team after he's drafted. If he doesn't do that, they don't want him ... a majority of the foreigners don't care about the league or protection of the players."[26] This sort of bitterness overlooked the obvious fact that the NASL was a business and that the coaches couldn't be faulted for wanting winning teams. The NASL had increased the minimum number of Americans on the field at any one time from two to three, but many teams got around that requirement by using naturalized citizens. At the time, the obvious way to have winning teams that exhibited reasonably high-quality soccer was to import players from abroad. The best professional teams in Europe had developed this model years earlier.

* * * *

The only real pipeline for American players was the rapidly expanding university system. Although the U.S. Youth Soccer Association formed in the early 1970s and had expanded the youth development system considerably by the end of the decade, the potential impact of that system had not yet been felt. University players, many of whom had minimal prior experience with competitive soccer on a higher level, emerged from that soccer pipeline ill prepared to compete professionally. The soccer experience of university players at most schools hovered between 12 and 20 matches per year, often against mediocre teams led by inadequately prepared coaches. Coming out of the university pipeline at 22 years old, an age at which international players already had played at a highly competitive level, university-trained soccer players tended to be inferior. The NASL wasn't secure enough to have its own player development system, and teams could ill afford to spend precious time and resources developing American players.

On the whole, the Cosmos international players were the highest-paid players in the league and thus had the most to lose with a strike. When they drew 72,000 fans to their first match, any lingering thoughts of a strike in New York or elsewhere evaporated quickly.

Once again the high-flying Cosmos dominated league play. At 24–6 they finished at the top of the league and led other teams with 84 goals in 30 contests. Chinaglia topped the league in scoring, with 26 goals in 27 regular season matches. In just four seasons with the Cosmos, he had already scored 108 goals in 114 regular season and playoff matches.[27]

In the semi-finals, Vancouver surprisingly derailed the Cosmos' march to a third straight championship. Team officials considered filing suit against the NASL, claiming that the officiating in Vancouver reflected bias by Canadian referees.[28] Júlio Mazzei, who had worked his way up from Pelé's interpreter to the newly created position of technical director, sulked, "I don't think they [the league] wanted the Cosmos in the final."[29] The response of the Cosmos' top brass to the loss indicated quite vividly that the Cosmos had grown too big for their soccer britches.

Actually, the league had scheduled the Soccer Bowl for New York again, partly in anticipation that the Cosmos would make it to the finals. Although 66,000 tickets were purchased for the final, only some 50,000 actually showed up, undoubtedly because of the Cosmos' failure. Vancouver beat Tampa Bay 2–1, but when the trophy was presented to the Soccer Bowl 1979 champions, chants of "Cosmos, Cosmos" spread through the stands, followed by a chorus of boos. Vancouver coach Tony Walters said, "It was like, 'forget the rest of the NASL; it's only the Cosmos.'"[30]

Discontent with the Cosmos spread throughout the league, exposing an obvious love-hate relationship with the reigning champions. Most enthusiasts recognized that the publicity stirred up by the New York team over the past several years had been important to the league in both the short term and the long term. Yet there was a growing sense that this route to success had its liabilities. One New York newspaper even asked, "Is it time to break up the Cosmos?" Many claimed that the Cosmos threatened the overall viability of the league by luring international players to America with outrageous salaries. This system wasn't a bad thing in and of itself, but the reality was that it put the rest of the league at an extreme disadvantage. The same New York newspaper wrote, "The creation of a team like the Cosmos violates a basic American axiom—fairness."[31]

Commissioner Woosnam predictably defended the Cosmos, noting that they had helped build the league and that dominating teams in sports come and go. "I think the rate of success always varies within the league," he said.[32] It was true that in the 12 years of the NASL, the Cosmos had won only three championships (1972, 1977, 1978), but no other team had won more than a single Soccer Bowl, and no team could match the Cosmos' 48–12 regular season record and 172 goals over the past two seasons.

There may have been a bit of envy in the growing conflict, but the issue of income disparity was undeniable. Other major sports handled the corrosive impact of financial inequities by creating salary caps for teams, resulting in a relative spreading of the wealth. Despite the general American view that individuals and businesses should be praised for their accumulation of wealth, sports that are as American as apple pie have, for a long time, recognized that extreme inequities can be damaging.

As the NASL prepared for the 1980 season, the soccer establishment saw reason for hope despite the friction. Although several teams acquired new owners and others shared financial instability, the lineup for the league matched that of the previous year. This consistency produced at least an image of stability. Yet the spending spree continued. Teams like Dallas and Chicago tried to keep pace with the Cosmos by enticing top players from West Germany with large salary offers.

To prepare for the 1980 season, the Cosmos played a demanding schedule of international friendlies. Although they had been competing in friendlies for several years, the long 1980 schedule was the most grueling yet. In preceding years they had traveled to Asia to play relatively easy teams like Singapore, Hong Kong, and South Korea. Beginning in February 1980, they stepped up the competition. Significant away matches included a 2–1 victory over Brazil's Santos and a 1–1 draw with Cipoletti of Argentina. At home, the Cosmos fared even better. They beat Germany's FC Cologne 3–1. Less than a month later they organized "The Transatlantic Cup," a competition between the Cosmos, the previous year's NASL champ Vancouver, Manchester United, and Chinaglia's old nemesis, Roma. The Cosmos striker scored two goals as the Cosmos defeated Manchester City 3–2 and then extracted revenge from Roma with a hat trick in a wild 5–3 victory.

Once more the Cosmos swept through the league. Chinaglia still excelled at age 33, and this season proved to be his best ever. In 32 regular season matches he scored 32 goals and dished out 11 assists, participating directly in half of the Cosmos' league-leading 87 goals.[33] Again, New York's 24–8 record topped the league. They swept through the first six post-season playoff matches, led by Chingalia's unbelievable 16 goals, including seven goals in one match against Tulsa. Their opponents in the final, the Fort Lauderdale Strikers, had struggled through a regular season record of 18–14, but they also had scratched and clawed their way to the final. *Sports Illustrated* noted, "The Strikers had made their way to the final with all the precision, style, and speed of the town boozer footing it home through a snowstorm."[34]

On a steamy day at RFK Stadium in Washington, D.C., a raucous crowd of 50,768 fans defied the mid-day 99-degree, 75 percent humidity weather with enthusiasm. *Sports Illustrated* titled its recap of the match "The Joint Was Jumping." The Strikers targeted Chinaglia. Their two best defenders—Ken Fogarty, an Englishman, and Arsène Auguste, a Haitian—savored the prospect of controlling the Cosmos star. Auguste boasted, "I would love to mark him. If I am there he gets maybe 10 percent of the ball he wants." More cautiously, Fogarty noted, "He's 60 percent of their offense, but when I heard of those seven goals in one game, I thought 'he'd never do that against me.' How would I go home and sleep? How would I pick up my paycheck?"[35]

With Chinaglia on their minds, the Strikers excelled in bottling up the powerful Cosmos offense. They also succeeded in other playoff matches by defending in depth from midfield and using lightning-fast counterattacks on offense. With Fogarty marking Chinaglia and Auguste picking up the Cosmos' most prolific assist players, the first half unfolded "grindingly slow, with long periods of near-walking pace, South American style."[36] Chinaglia managed only two shots in the first half, one of them on a free kick. The first half ended in a scoreless tie. Fogarty appeared on his way to sleeping comfortably that night and picking up his paycheck proudly, but he still had the second half to contend with.

During the final 15 minutes of the first half, the Cosmos found the cracks in the Strikers' defense and their offense became more daring. To fans, coaches, and players, it became more evident that the team that scored the first goal would control the tempo of the match. They didn't have to wait long. In the third minute of the second half, Chinaglia dribbled around a surprised Fogarty and headed toward the goal. Auguste did the only thing he could do—tackle the Cosmos star, just outside the box. While the maneuver saved a certain goal, the resulting free kick provided the opening the Cosmos needed. Chinaglia sent a rocket into the Striker wall and the rebound went directly to the 21-year-old Uruguayan, Julio "Little Cesar" Romero, who left-footed the ball into the net. Romero had joined the Cosmos that year and led the team in assists, with 26 in the team's 38 previous games; yet he scored what even the irrepressible Chinaglia would call "the goal ... that mattered."[37]

With the Strikers forced to desert their defensive strategy, Chinaglia scored in the seventy-first minute with a bullet just inside the box to give the Cosmos an insurmountable 2–0 lead. Just three minutes before the final whistle, Chinaglia scored again and the Cosmos completed their most powerful season with a 3–0 victory in Soccer Bowl 80. Although Chinaglia played in subsequent seasons, he would never match the incredible year he'd just completed: 50 goals in 39 matches. He'd scored 164 goals in 159 matches with the Cosmos, and he was well on his way to being named the most outstanding player in NASL history.[38] The 1980 season represented a high point for both Chinaglia and the Cosmos. Unbeknownst at the time, it also marked the high point of the NASL, poised on the precipice of a rapid demise.

Despite the many markers of a successful year for the NASL, the picture was much gloomier under the surface. Attendance figures remained about the same as the year before, but escalating salaries and expenses led to a $30 million loss for the 24 teams. TV ratings fell dramatically and ABC announced that it would televise only the Soccer Bowl the following season. The league considered axing the most financially weak teams. Some owners even recommended cutting the league from 24 to the strongest 12 teams. Others argued for a mandatory increase in the number of American-born players, who they claimed would better "Americanize" the sport. Unable to reach a consensus, some teams folded and others were sold. After the dust settled, the league was reduced from 24 to 21 franchises, and the number of Canadian-based teams increased from three to five.

The Cosmos continued their winning ways, going 23–9 during the regular season. Chinaglia repeated his onslaught with 29 goals and 16 assists in the 32-match regular season. New York met the Chicago Sting in Soccer Bowl 81—played in Toronto before a crowd of 36,971. Chicago had matched New York's 23–9 record, and this squad was considered the Sting's strongest team since entering the league in 1975. As before, opponents targeted Chinaglia. Shutting him down meant shutting down the Cosmos. Chinaglia had scored six goals in the first five playoff matches, and at age 34 he still proved to be a dangerous threat. The Sting, which had been an offensive-minded team during the regular season, refocused its efforts on defense, and the strategy worked. The match ended in a 0–0 draw, and for the first time a penalty kick determined the NASL championship. Lady Luck prevailed for Chicago and the Sting stung the reigning NASL champs in the shootout. In retrospect, the dethroning of the Cosmos symbolized the decline of the NASL. The Cosmos had dominated the NASL in both image and substance. Their defeat in 1981 served as a harbinger of things to come.

Both the Cosmos and the NASL struggled the following year. Seven teams folded before the start of the 1982 season. Particularly distressing was the loss of teams that had long been part of the league's backbone. Dallas had fielded a team continuously from 1969 to 1981 but folded in 1982. Washington and Los Angeles, both of which had fielded teams for eight seasons beginning in 1974, also faded away. Atlanta, one of the original NASL teams, which had competed from 1967 to 1973 and resurfaced in 1979 for three more seasons, disappeared. The remaining 14 teams managed to maintain a 32-game schedule, and the Cosmos posted their second consecutive 23–9 season. The New York team regained the championship, beating the Seattle Sounders 1–0 in Soccer Bowl 82 on a goal made by none other than Giorgio Chinaglia. By his previous standard, his 1982 performance was a disappointment, with "only" 24 goals in 36 matches. By most ordinary standards, Chinaglia still reigned as king. The glamour and glitz of the NASL seemed to be dimming, however, as only 22,634 fans witnessed the match in San Diego. Even worse, not a single station televised the match.[39]

The writing was on the wall. In 1982 every franchise except Toronto experienced significant drops in attendance. Many league games were played before crowds of less than 1,000. The Cosmos, once proud standard-bearers of high attendance, dropped to an average of 18,000 fans.

With a brave public face, the league stumbled into the 1983 season. Unfortunately, four teams—Edmonton, Jacksonville, Portland and San Jose—folded before the start of the season. Two new franchises were added for a final roster of 12 teams. In addition to a reconstituted California team now called Golden State, an experimental squad known as Team America (based in the nation's capital) entered the league. This team was the brainchild of Howard Samuels, hired to fill the newly created position of league president. Although he remained commissioner, Woosnam was effectively removed from power. As president, Samuels believed the league's problem centered on its inability to sufficiently "nationalize." His outlook reflected the times. The election of Ronald Reagan in 1980 signaled a political and cultural shift to the right. Overt patriotism and flag waving replaced the volatility of the previous decade, and Samuels sensed that a league with more American-born players could piggyback off the new mood of the country.[40] With characteristic bravado, he announced, "It's absolutely true that soccer hasn't made it commercially here, but I'm sure it will make it—and I say to the NFL, watch out because ten years from now we'll be the leaders, on the field and on television."[41]

Samuels proposed to the USSF that the U.S. national team, which had consistently failed to qualify for World Cup competition, be admitted into the NASL. As bizarre as it was—imagine the Spanish national team being admitted to La Liga or the German national team lining up in the Bundesliga—the USSF agreed to the idea. They had nothing to lose, given that the national team continued to perform poorly against weak soccer teams like Bermuda and Canada. If nothing else, it might give them practice against some reasonable foes, although the USMNT losing to Tulsa might not look so good.

If the proposal seemed far-fetched, assembling a team appeared even crazier. Many USMNT members were already contracted to the NASL, and their professional teams were unwilling to release them. Others, like Rick Davis of the Cosmos, felt it was more beneficial to play alongside better foreign players.[42] The fact that the NASL had never paid much attention to the national team didn't make things any easier.

In the end, an all–American team was finally assembled, but it looked nothing like the national squad. Team America ended up with a 10–20 record, scoring an anemic 33 goals and doing little to boost league attendance.[43] One home crowd of 50,000 did witness a 2–1 victory over Fort Lauderdale, but attendance piggybacked off a scheduled concert by the Beach Boys in the same arena. Other Team America matches drew barely 10,000 people.

Once again the Cosmos led league standings with a 22–8 record. They failed to make it past the first round of the playoffs, however, after losing two games to Montreal. They played in front of 20,000 people, considerably less than the 50,000 they had routinely drawn a few years earlier. This marked the last year of King Chinaglia's reign as well. He appeared in only 17 of the Cosmos' regular season matches, racking up 18 goals. He finished his career in the NASL with 193 goals in 213 appearances over eight seasons.[44] Both loved and hated, no one denied his skills or the volatile persona that had ignited the league and inspired thousands of fans across the country.

On October 1, 1983, Tulsa beat Toronto in Soccer Bowl 83. The two teams posted lukewarm seasons, combining for records of 33–27. Surprisingly, 60,041 fans turned out to see Tulsa win the championship in Vancouver.[45] While the number harkened back to the league's glory days, such enthusiasm couldn't remedy the loss of hope and millions of dollars.

With the failure of the experiment in Americanization and the continuing decline in attendance, owners worked on keeping a half-submerged ship afloat in deep waters. Most teams had lost money even during the boom years of 1978–1981, and now a gloomy forecast reached all of them. Regional television contracts dried up. Samuels tried to put an optimistic face on the season, but his voice lacked conviction: "We haven't had a good year. We haven't had a really bad year either, but since it wasn't better than last year I consider it a bad year."[46]

After more than a dozen years of record profits, Warner Communications, the deep pocket of the Cosmos, reported close to a $500 million loss for the first three-quarters of 1983. The $5 million the Cosmos lost in 1983 represented a small fraction of the financial crisis, but under the circumstances CEO Ross's flirtation with his favorite hobby was in jeopardy.[47] With a company in such a financial nosedive, keeping any soccer investment seemed frivolous and irresponsible. Warner thus divested itself of a majority interest in the Cosmos. It eventually handed most of the ownership over to an aging Chinaglia, who had little interest, experience, financial clout, or inclination to salvage the team.

Even with the ship sinking and the upper decks barely above water, the NASL bravely took on another season. Reduced to nine teams, its lowest number since 1973, participants found themselves playing in mostly deserted stadiums. The Cosmos were listless and played as if plagued by a terminal disease. They managed an unimpressive 13–11 record. The rest of the league was just as anemic, with only three teams averaging more than two goals a match. In the final Soccer Bowl, the Chicago Sting beat the Toronto Blizzard at home 2–1 and away 3–2 to claim the title. Only 8,352 fans showed up in Chicago, with 16,821 in Toronto.[48] The Chicago–Toronto matches signaled the end of the NASL, and few fans turned out for the funeral.

After 18 struggling years, the league finally died. Typically, those close to the deceased put a positive spin on the tragedy. Long-time league administrator Ted Howard recalled years later, "I flew over the stadium in the Warner helicopter the night of the first sell-out, 77,691 if I remember correctly. It was a heart stopping sight."[49] Peppe Pinton, who worked in the front office with the Cosmos, remarked, "The Cosmos are like Marilyn Monroe. Everyone remembers."[50] Nostalgic memories might cover the loss, but only for a while, as both memories and loss eventually fade away. Few but the most ardent students of soccer history now know about the NASL, and most of those with direct memories have passed on.

Everyone found somebody to blame for the failure. Some pointed a finger at Commissioner Woosnam for reckless expansion. Others criticized Woosnam's fascination with national TV, claiming he signed contracts that allowed networks to televise matches at odd times. Some former team owners predictably blamed the players' union. Still others blamed the wasted money spent on the NASL's suit against the NFL, which occurred when the football league created an unofficial policy banning NFL team owners from owning any other professional sports teams. The NASL claimed that the restrictions on cross-ownership deprived it of a fair share of the market for "professional sports capital and entrepreneurial skill," and as such violated fair trade practice. After losing in district court, the NASL won on appeal, but the case fizzled as the league spun into precipitous decline. Regarding the demise of the league, some have also pointed to the lack of coordination and even outright hostility between the NASL and the USSF as the primary reason for the league's downfall.

Clive Toye had his own observations: "We've not been able to tell people since 1977–1978 that this is what we stand for.... We lacked consistency, stability and continuity. Every year we had a different crusade that was going to be a panacea for all our ills." He also told a Dallas radio station soon after the collapse of the league, "If one week you're a country and western station, the next week you're a rock 'n' roll station, the next classical and the following an all-news station, you will soon lose all of your listeners. In essence, we've done the same thing with our league."[51]

By March 1985, only Toronto and Minnesota expressed a desire to continue playing. Toye, who had been appointed president of the league after the death of Samuels the preceding fall, read the final obituary. The *New York Times* barely noted that the NASL had disbanded. Vince Casey, a PR man for the league, lamented, "Five, six years after we hit the heights and all we get is a line in the Etcetera column."[52] No one mentioned Pelé. No one shed a tear for the Cosmos. No one cited the crowds of 50, 60, and 70,000 fans. No one applauded the hard work that so many had performed on and off the field. It was simply over, leaving hundreds of players, coaches, and administrators contemplating Toye's bittersweet question: "So what do you do when your entire industry disappears not over time but overnight?"[53]

* * * *

The dream of professional soccer in the United States collapsed at a particularly curious time. By 1980, more Americans were playing organized soccer than ever before. The national youth soccer movement that began in the early 1970s had exploded, and soccer fields were cropping up across the land. The growth in university soccer that began in the post–World War II years had continued year by year. By 1983, universities and colleges supported 523 men's teams and dozens of women's teams. Each year scores of universities added soccer to their sports programs. Yet, in the midst of this phenomenal prosperity, professional soccer withered on the vine.

In examining the NASL decline in the 1980s, soccer historian David Wangerin asks, "Where had all the fans gone? Why was the league losing its appeal when soccer continued to encroach on the conventional pastimes of American youth?" While true, his answer is really no answer at all: "[Pro] soccer seemed to have been a fad.... The awful truth was that most of the 77,691 who had packed Giants Stadium that famous August evening in 1977 were never potential season-ticket holders. Many, in fact, were not likely to pay to watch a soccer match again."[54] But why? Fads do come and go, but some trends move from the margins to the center until they become an indelible part of the landscape they occupy. Why had soccer not become more than a passing fancy when the youth and university soccer world was expanding so dramatically?

The answer to this conundrum lies in the cultural space that soccer was beginning to occupy. The pay-to-play youth club system that was fast becoming *the* route for player development was taking over. Wangerin's observation that "soccer continued to encroach on the conventional pastimes of American youth" is only partially true. The exclusionary nature of the youth development system meant that soccer was becoming more and more defined by its location in a small corner of the American cultural landscape, a corner marked by the material and symbolic dimensions of class. The encroachment of more competitive soccer was not on the "pastimes" of just any American youths, but almost exclusively on those of youths whose parents possessed the class position to make it all possible. Soccer was a "fad" then, as it is now, because most kids (and their parents) who have invested in soccer typically don't do so because of love and passion for the game. They invest because youth soccer is a product to be consumed as a marker of class position.

The intentions behind the club system were sound. In 1969 the USSF and NASL issued a National Development Plan to promote and develop soccer. The first of seven points included establishing "a national youth program ... for boys 7–15."[55] Because no viable infrastructure existed to fund such a program, it was inevitable that bills would be paid primarily by parents. What started as an initiative to promote soccer as an element of mass culture ultimately promoted it as a class-based sport. In essence, the pyramid that had struggled so hard to maintain its upright architecture for almost 100 years was now turning on its head.

Section Three: From the Local to the National

7

Soccer Beginnings: The World of Parks and Recreation

In most countries around the world, the initial foray into children's soccer is simple. The most essential piece of equipment for the sport is a ball. Almost anything that rolls will do—a stuffed sock, a small tin can, a round piece of fruit. Besides players, the only other necessary component is a pitch on which to play. An ideal field includes a space large enough to kick, pass, and dribble the ball. But plenty of substitutes prevail—a vacant lot, an urban side street, even a strip of hard-packed desert sand.

The beginning story for most kids, even those who turn into elite soccer players, is relatively similar. Nwankwo Kanu, a two-time African Player of the Year and a member of Nigeria's national team for 16 years, remembers, "[When] you're so young ... you just play. No referee, no rules. And when I say we played in the street, I mean in the road ... with a rubber ball. If you were lucky, it might be ... something perfectly round. But often the ball wouldn't be like that. You wouldn't know where it was going to bounce."[1]

Italian Fabio Cannavaro, nicknamed Muro di Berlino (The Berlin Wall), and one of only two defenders ever to be named FIFA's Player of the Year, agrees: "I was a *scugnizzo* (a street boy from Naples). We weren't lucky enough to have football pitches.... We played in the street; I mean literally in the street, with the cars going by. We'd use whatever we could find to make goals; normally we'd put down bins or rubbish bags. Or kids would play barefoot and leave their shoes down as goalposts."[2]

Claudio Suarez Sanchez, known as El Emperador (the Emperor), who holds the record for the most caps with the Mexican national team, recalls, "I didn't have shoes.... We played on the street, our little pick-up games: *cascaritas* we call them in Mexico.... You find ... a place to play, and ours was the street ... we'd play, using a few rocks to make goals."[3]

Argentinean superstar Lionel Messi, considered one of the greatest players in soccer today, states that "playing football meant playing in the street, outside my house or anywhere else in the neighborhood where there was a game going on. In those days the road was unpaved, just dried dirt."[4]

In most of the world that's the way it's always been. Soccer is an inexpensive sport, initially learned through informal play. Kids use whatever open space and raw materials happen to be available. An uneven field may not be aesthetically pleasing, the same way a plastic bag stuffed with rags might not serve as the ideal ball. But appearances can be deceiving. Sometimes technical skills involving ball control, dribbling, and accurate passing develop more quickly and just as creatively under less adequate conditions. Moreover, in most parts of the world access to soccer is pervasive, and class barriers rarely get in the way. The sport is facile and spontaneous—nothing fancy, just an unflinching willingness to play.

Learning to play soccer in the United States is rarely the same. Here kids' athletics are increasingly organized, supervised, and systemized. The days of sandlot baseball, schoolyard football, and playground basketball may not be over, but they're rapidly disappearing as sites where children learn to play. Youth sports in the United States are increasingly privatized and commercialized, and with an estimated 60,000,000 American youths playing some form of organized sports, there's lots of money to be made. Behind each of those kids stands a virtual army of parents, coaches, organizations, and corporate sponsors with seemingly disposable income.

While it is impossible to pinpoint exactly when youth sports in the United States transitioned from kid-organized free play to an adult-controlled money-making proposition, the late 1960s and early 1970s mark the most ambitious attempt to organize game play. Of course, it was never a simple either-or situation. The Pop Warner Youth Football League began in 1929, and the first Little League Baseball competition was initiated a decade later. Organized sports in public and private schools at the middle and high school levels date back to the turn of the century. Community establishments such as the YMCA, the YWCA, Boys Club of America, and a host of other organizations have offered systematized sports as well. Yet, despite these formal structures, early exposure to playing sports remained largely conventional until a decade or so after the First World War.

What characterized other youth sports in the United States also defined youth soccer. Players came to know the game pretty much the way kids learned soccer in the rest of the world. In ethnic communities and other soccer-oriented urban neighborhoods, initial excursions onto the pitch were informal and unstructured. Few organized opportunities existed, and most public and private secondary schools rarely fielded organized teams. Since the 1970s, however, American youth soccer has become increasingly entrenched in a sports milieu organized and controlled by adults. While this rigid approach might be well intentioned, it also misses the boat in a number of important ways.

The initial organized experience for most American youths begins between the ages of five and ten years old in a local Parks and Recreation soccer program. No matter who you talk to in this country, a common reply to questions about the first contact with soccer is "I started playing in a Parks and Rec league." Many of these remarks are followed by the words "My dad was the coach." Unlike players in most of the rest of the world, where soccer is first encountered in kid-controlled environments, American kids invariably begin in this more structured arena. These publicly financed programs exist in all 50 states and typically include youth programs in other sports such as baseball, softball, football, and basketball. Because they are publicly financed, participation costs are minimal. Theoretically, the ideology that guides participation emphasizes equal playing time for all kids. It also de-emphasizes competition, keeping score, and winning.

* * * *

Today's Parks and Recreation programs are an outgrowth of three separate, yet intertwined, movements that began in the late nineteenth century. The first was the national park movement. Guided by the dual practical concern for preserving the nation's access to timber and sustaining the environment, the nation's first "forest preserve" was created in 1891 in the Yellowstone Timber Reserve. By the end of President Benjamin Harrison's term, over 13,000,000 acres of wilderness fell under government protection. Future president Theodore Roosevelt published *The Wilderness Hunter* in 1893, which, despite its anti-ecological title, extolled the virtue and necessity of preserving the wilderness for future generations. After camping out in Yellowstone, Roosevelt wrote, "It was like lying in a great solemn cathedral, far vaster [*sic*] and more beautiful than any built by the hand of man."[5] Recognizing the importance of the exploitation of natural resources that built the country, he nevertheless wrote that it "is also vandalism to wantonly to destroy or to permit the destruction of what is beautiful in nature."[6] After assuming the presidency in 1901, Roosevelt established the U.S. Forest Service, 150 National Forests, and five National Parks encompassing some 230,000,000 acres.

An urban park movement, motivated by the creation of green space within America's growing urban areas, accompanied this national park and preservation movement. Although urban parks like the Boston Common, established in 1634, and small city squares existed in most urban areas prior to the 1890s, the urban park movement made significant strides in the late nineteenth century. The acquisition of land to create Central Park in New York City was authorized in 1853. Its designers argued that "the park should not only be an immunity [sic] from urban conditions, but in the laying out of its landscape, features should provide the antithesis of urban conditions."[7] The largest of Washington, D.C., parks, Rock Creek Park, was conceived as early as 1866 and finally approved by Congress in 1890 as "a public park or pleasure ground for the benefit and enjoyment of the people of the United States."[8] During this time many cities initiated plans to set aside green space for the enjoyment and passive recreational activities of urban populations, justified by the virtues of the experience of nature.

The third movement included the urban recreation movement. The development of urban parks and playgrounds, along with growing concern for urban poverty, blight, and crowding, provided the impetus for the organized recreation movement. The initial motivation of this movement was a desire to reduce urban crime and delinquency, while also addressing the needs of economically disadvantaged populations, particularly youth and children. The Playground Association of America was founded in 1906 with the goal of expanding organized recreational activities throughout the country. A primary goal included establishing formal training and education for supervisors of the growing number of organized recreational activities in America's cities. By 1911, training programs for recreation personnel existed at many universities and normal schools. After World War I, the Playground Association of America, now renamed the National Recreation Association, established 26 training schools that offered six-week educational programs for those wanting to gain employment in the expanding world of organized recreation. By 1946, the National Recreation Association reported 78 college and university majors in recreation management, 116 minors, and 33 graduate programs. In that same year, over 700 cities employed more than 5,000 workers in the growing recreation industry. By 1960, over 1,202 city and county recreation programs employed 9,216 personnel.[9]

In 1965, three organizations promoting parks and recreation programs—the American Institute of Park Executives, the National Recreation Association, and the American Recreation Society—joined forces as the National Recreation and Park Association. After more than half a century of expansion,

Parks and Recreation programs had established a firm foothold in the landscape of organized youth recreation programs.

Today, the NRPA claims that four out of five Americans use their local parks and recreation facilities at some point during their lives. The association's goal is the improvement of the overall health and wellness of the nation by combating "some of the most complicated challenges our country faces—poor nutrition, hunger, obesity, and physical inactivity."[10] While county and city Parks and Recreation programs operate a number of related community services, the sponsorship of youth and adult organized sports programs is a primary initiative. Since the 1970s, youth and adult soccer leagues have come to occupy a prominent place in these community-based programs.

Our own local Watauga County Parks and Recreation program serves a county of approximately 45,000 people. With a county-supported budget of $885,532 for fiscal year 2012–2013, the program oversees the operation of a number of county park facilities and operates numerous organized sports activities. From tee-ball to Little League, Parks and Recreation supports baseball teams that include boys from ages 5 to 16. Three softball programs provide opportunities for girls from ages 6 to 16, and adult softball leagues consisting of six divisions of 4–8 teams operate each spring and fall. Two youth football programs—Mite Football and Midget Football—exist for children in grades 3–6. The program supports an adult basketball league and boys' and girls' leagues for youths in grades 5 and 6. Three adult volleyball leagues also operate. Finally, five youth soccer divisions covering ages 5–15 and an adult soccer league include over 70 teams and more than 700 players. Outdoor games, including soccer, are played at five softball/baseball fields, several all-purpose fields owned or leased by the department, and all-purpose fields at the county's seven elementary schools. Indoor games are played at local school gymnasiums through a cooperative agreement with the local county school system. The sports program is operated by three full-time employees and hundreds of volunteer coaches, most of whom have sons or daughters playing on teams.[11]

As is the case in most of the country, local businesses sponsor soccer teams by providing team entry fees and matching T-shirts. In the youth program, individual participants pay a minimal player fee of $33, which, theoretically, makes participation open to youth from any economic background. The soccer program emphasizes recreation over competition. Parks and Recreation employees instruct volunteer coaches not to keep score and that all players, regardless of experience, skills, or athleticism, should play an equal amount of time and in any position that they are willing to play.

* * * *

We began coaching three of our daughters in our Parks and Recreation youth soccer program in August 2005. While neither of us had actually played organized soccer, we'd grown up playing a variety of youth team sports that were more characteristic of our era—baseball, basketball and football. Our interest in soccer was modest, but, having lived and worked in France and Mexico, we were more than casually aware of the global dimensions and passions of the sport. However, a love of soccer was not our primary motivation. Our goal was more modest: provide our nine- and ten-year-old daughters with an opportunity to experience a team sport along with the physical, emotional, and social benefits that we remembered receiving from our participation in athletics when we were young. Our exposure to soccer in Mexico and France, as well as our academic backgrounds in anthropology and ethnic American literature, no doubt influenced the choice of soccer over other available team sports. Of course, we may have also harbored some latent dreams that one or more of our daughters might excel and continue playing soccer at more competitive levels. Our motivations were not unlike those of millions of other parents introducing their children to the world of organized athletics—a mixture of concerns about mental and physical health, belief in the value of team sports, and wandering thoughts of athletic prowess.

The local Parks and Recreation department, like similar programs throughout the country, relies on volunteer coaches. We were accepted as coaches without any questions. We weren't even asked whether we had ever played soccer or knew anything about the sport. Knowledge and experience with soccer were not prerequisites for coaching. Sheer willingness sufficed. Although we had watched soccer on television and seen a few live matches, our basic knowledge of the sport was minimal. We enlisted the aid of a mutual friend and colleague, Andrés Fisher, who'd grown up playing soccer in Chile. He'd also lived for many years in Spain, a country where *fútbol es El Rey.* We hoped that he could teach us, as well as our girls, the basic strategies of team play. We had no idea where this initial, modest interest would lead. Also, although our experience with Parks and Recreation soccer illuminated our own particular circumstances, it was not atypical of the experience of the vast majority of parents-turned-soccer coaches.

One late August Saturday morning we held our first practice. Parks and Recreation assigned our team roster, which included our daughters and seven additional players. Heavy morning dew and a light fog covered the small practice field at Junaluska Park, nestled in a neighborhood a few hundred feet up the mountain from the university where we teach. As we met the nine- and ten-year-old girls who would make up our first team, accompanied by the newly crowned "soccer moms and dads," everyone felt a sense of anticipation and excitement. Throughout the country home-grown players typically get their start in local Parks and Recreation leagues. Ideally, Parks and Rec teams emphasize cooperation, equality, and small skill building. As we looked around and saw the motley crew of shapes, sizes and personalities of our players, the idea of teaching them how to play as a team seemed an immeasurable challenge.

We soon learned what we faced. Only a handful of the girls had ever kicked a soccer ball, and even fewer had actually played on a team. We ran through some basic drills so that the girls could begin to get a feel for the ball and we could evaluate what different players could and could not do. Toward the end of practice, we decided to hold a scrimmage of five against five. Despite their inexperience with the sport, the girls were excited to try something new. We explained various positions and reminded the girls to use the dribbling and passing skills that they'd just practiced. When they actually started playing, however, they forgot everything we had showed them. Like bees after honey, they scurried after the ball. Chaos ruled, but at least they had fun. Every few minutes an on-target pass, a quick dribble around a horde of defenders, or a defensive stop shone through the morning fog, hints of what we hoped would be an enjoyable, successful season.

One nine-year-old player named Audrey, a shy, slightly built, bespectacled girl with thick curly hair, barely moved from her position in the middle of the field. When the opposing team moved the ball in her direction, she would place her hands across her chest and stand motionless, avoiding the action. As we would later learn, Audrey lived with her brother, her mother, and her mom's boyfriend in one of the trailer parks on the outskirts of town. Her mom's boyfriend was a handyman and her mom worked full-time while trying to get her GED at the local branch of a community college. Most of the other kids' parents, like us, worked as doctors, nurses, lawyers, realtors, business managers, and other professionals.

Although we didn't recognize it at the time, what we were beginning to experience even at this local level was the primary dimension of the cultural landscape of youth soccer in the United States. Audrey was not just an anomaly because of her timidity and lack of confidence; she also identified herself through her socioeconomic background. Even at this basic level, soccer in the United States is typically embedded in a class system that's dominated by players (and their parents) from the middle to upper classes. Even though the financial barriers to playing organized soccer didn't exist in the Parks and Recreation program, the cultural landscape occupied by the sport influenced parental and youth choices.

After several practices, we saw considerable progress in fundamental skills and team play. One of the most difficult features of coaching at this level is teaching players about basic positions and the importance of team passing. In their excitement, kids have a tendency to run after the ball, since kicking it appears to be the most active and fun part of the game. Passing and playing defense are basically inconsequential. This is why many Parks and Recreation programs that start kids playing at four or five years old simply call the sport "Kick and Run." We felt one aspect that shouldn't be neglected included learning to play positions as a team, which we emphasized in practice.

With most players, matching specific skills with positions proved a challenge. But there were exceptions. Some of the girls developed a taste for defense. For example, Laura, by far the tallest 10-year-old in the U-10 division, soon realized that her mere presence as a fullback intimidated opponents dribbling the ball in her direction. She also could kick the ball farther than anyone else, so that when she cleared a ball on defense it usually was a long shot downfield, which at this level was sufficiently rewarding in and of itself. Similarly, Alicia, the most purely athletic girl on the team, loved the drama of goalkeeping. She was strong, quick, and aggressive, with natural talent for protecting the goal. Unlike most goalies at this level, she willingly and quite capably dove for balls and used her entire body to block shots.

Although we rotated positions during the course of a game, the success of matching skills to positions soon started to outweigh the Parks and Recreation ethos of rotating players freely between positions. We usually started our three daughters at the front line because they had developed a better sense of the importance of ball control and passing. As both coaches and parents, we often felt self-conscious about this decision, worrying that we were showing favoritism. And as the season went on, some parents even suggested that we were, indeed, doing just that. But as often happens at this level, the line between forwards and mid-fielders usually evaporated quickly, so that multiple players had the opportunity to kick the ball aimlessly in the right direction. With eight players on the field at a time, we typically began with a 3–2–2 formation, with most of the rotation coming between the front line and midfield.

Like many parents whose children play multiple organized sports, our schedules complicated matters. In addition to coaching three of our children on this team, Gregory's oldest daughter played on a U-12 soccer team, while Bruce's son played on a U-8 soccer team. Andrés also faced his commitment to his younger daughter's soccer team. Coordinating the schedules for practices and matches for six kids playing on three different teams proved difficult. The time commitment was huge, as was the struggle to balance our attention to each child's activity.

To our surprise, we marched through the first part of our 12-game schedule with a perfect record. Despite the Parks and Recreation philosophy of not keeping score, everyone did, especially parents and coaches. In the seventh match we faced a team that we'd defeated earlier in the season. As game time approached, however, we were short several players. At the last second, the two cousins whose grandparents owned the local McDonald's franchise that sponsored our team arrived, complaining that their stomachs were bloated because they'd just eaten roast beef sandwiches at a local Arby's. The irony of the moment escaped us as we hurried our team on the field, but the ineffectiveness of two of our players contributed to the first mar on our record—a 2–2 draw. The opposing coach, a woman whose daughter played on her team, and the opposition parents took the draw as a victory, as by this time our team had garnered the reputation of the team to beat.

We recognized that all of us—coaches, parents and kids—had succumbed to the competitive spirit that contrasted with Parks and Recreation ideals. As stated above, although Parks and Recreation officially discouraged keeping score, parents, coaches, and kids did not. Were the kids having fun? Definitely. Did that mean that the score didn't matter? Definitely not. Did it mean that the score was more important for the parents and coaches than for the kids? Probably. The complicated motivations of parents and coaches regarding their kids' participation often got lost in the heat of the competitive moment of winning or losing.

We entered our final game with a 10–0–1 record, with our only blemish blamed mainly on roast beef sandwiches. Our match was against a team whose season record was 10–1–0, their only defeat coming against us earlier in the season by a 2–1 score. The girls on our team referred to our opponents as the "Mean Green Team" because of their green team shirts and rough play. Our previous match had been amazingly physical, especially for 9- and 10-year olds. In this officially "non-competitive" environment where scores and records were not supposed to matter, everyone understood that this was *the* championship match. The culture of competition permeated the playing field.

The match unfolded as expected. The "Mean Green Team" scored first and by halftime we were down 1–2. The third quarter went scoreless as both teams missed opportunities and the goalies made several excellent stops. During the break before the start of the final quarter, we reminded our girls that this was the final 12 minutes of the season and that they should play with the teamwork, energy, skills, and pride that we knew they possessed. Win or lose, we told them, it had been a terrific season and we all had a lot of fun. To our surprise, our team scored three goals by three different players in the final minutes of play. Our defense held the "Mean Green Team" scoreless for the rest of the match. We finished the season with a 4–2 victory and an 11–0–1 record, scoring 49 goals to our opponents' 17 goals. (Yes, we even kept statistics.) We'd captured the imaginary championship that existed only in the hearts and minds of parents, coaches, and players.

Most importantly, we had fun and witnessed the building of modest soccer skills and teamwork. Audrey epitomized that success. Surprisingly, she had emerged from her earlier protective cocoon to score our first goal of the season. Just minutes into the initial game, Audrey fortunately found the ball bouncing off of a player in front of the goal; she easily tapped it into the net. She didn't score again all season, but it didn't matter. That one moment was enough. She had lost the fear and lack of confidence that she'd exhibited on that first day of practice. Later, her mother told us that Audrey slept with her soccer ball and carried it with her wherever she went. She even wore soccer shirts to school. Realistically, Audrey would never develop into a soccer star, or even participate at higher levels of soccer, but that didn't change the fact of that first goal or her comment at the end of the season when we asked her how she felt: "I feel good," she said in her shy but happy voice.

Toward the end of that first season, the idea for a documentary video on youth soccer emerged. As academics, we were inclined to be observers as well as participants. Whether it is a curse or a blessing, the tendency to analyze new circumstances seemed to be in our blood. In that first season, we had caught glimpses of ourselves as soccer dads, critically examining our roles as both parents and coaches participating in a structure of adult-controlled youth sports. We didn't always like what we saw: the competitive emphasis on winning; the criticism of kids who seemed distracted or less capable; the lack of ethnic and economic diversity of players and their parents. Our interest in documenting and analyzing our experience intertwined in complex ways with our interest in continuing what we thought would be another successful soccer season.

Based on the success of that first season, the development of modest soccer skills in our daughters, and our newfound interest in a documentary video, we decided to continue coaching the following year. Our two oldest daughters on the team turned 11, and so we moved up to the U-12 league. This meant that Gregory's youngest daughter, who was still 10, would have to play on a different team. Bruce's son continued to play on another Parks and Recreation team, and Gregory's oldest daughter, age 13, decided to play for the local club team sponsored by the High Country Soccer Association (HCSA). Andrés's daughter also played in a younger league. Our six kids were now playing on five different teams, and the club team's schedule was much more complicated, with twice-a-week, two- to three-hour practices and matches and tournaments each weekend, often demanding out-of-town travel.

At times, it seemed like our lives revolved completely around soccer. The time demands were prohibitive, and we soon became more aware that parents who had multiple kids playing organized sports had to possess both flexibility and energy. Because a lot of our work as university professors revolved around scholarship that required less rigidity and more fluidity, we controlled a great deal of our work time. We couldn't imagine what it must have been like for parents working more physically demanding jobs with little control over an 8–5 work day to manage both the time and energy to support their kids. The cultural capital of time typically possessed by professional, middle-, and upper-middle-class parents and its relationship to organized youth sports grew more readily apparent than ever.

We hoped that our second-year team would maintain the core of 11-year-olds from our first successful team. We weren't that lucky. Our goalie moved and several of our key players were recruited to play for the U-12 HCSA club team. Through a network of peers, parents and coaches, the club system scouted for potential players in the Parks and Recreation leagues, luring young players (and their parents) into the more prestigious arena of club sports where players wore *real* uniforms, were coached by *real* soccer players, and played on *real* soccer fields. This local competition for talented players siphoned off enough kids that the Parks and Recreation program had difficulty fielding team players beyond the age of 12. Our 10- and 11-year-old daughters, as well as Bruce's son, were approached to play on HCSA club teams but chose not to make the leap. Their skills were sufficient to meet that challenge, but they simply weren't interested.

Without our goalie, Gregory's youngest daughter, and the players who left to play for the club system, we were left at the mercy of Parks and Recreation to assemble our team. In our first season, all of our players came from the same elementary school, a factor that had contributed to the team *esprit de corps*. Our new team came from several different schools, and the school cliques were evident from the start. Half of the players had never played soccer before. Moreover, our best and most experienced players were all 11 years of age, and we were now facing teams with talented and experienced 12-year-olds. Still, we made our best effort to, once again, teach and refine basic soccer skills while also teaching team play.

For whatever reasons, the second-year team never really gelled. We lost more games than we won, but that wasn't the heart of the problem. The players and their parents seemed less satisfied with their experience. Parents and players complained more about the player rotations, and some of the players actually started to criticize one another on the field. Some players stopped coming to practices, only to show up at matches expecting to be inserted in the starting lineup. Our frustration with the discord didn't help. We were yelling too much from the sideline and once were called on the carpet by the head of the Parks and Rec soccer program for using profanity. We witnessed a good deal of parental yelling and abuse directed at referees, coaches, and players, and we felt ourselves leaning in that direction far too much. This was supposed to be fun. Compared to the previous year, it clearly wasn't measuring up. We needed to regroup.

Despite the disappointment in our own antics and the lack of team cohesion, the season had its enjoyable moments. Over time, most of the girls improved their skills, and there still was the joy of seeing an occasional brilliant pass, a deceptive dribble, or a decisive defensive stop. We were also busy filming for what was developing into a major project. In fact, in many ways the making of the documentary started to trump our interest in coaching. For better or worse, we drifted deeper into the cultural landscape of soccer than we'd ever imagined.

Gregory's oldest daughter's foray into the world of club soccer also opened our eyes to the nature and power of the club soccer system throughout the country and its contrast with youth development systems in other countries. The direct experience of the financial and time demands of club soccer reinforced our research into the class space occupied by the club system. We began to interview parents and players who had come up through the club system about their experiences. Although the stories were often a complex mix of positive and negative experiences, the information on the considerable amount of money and time invested in these soccer careers were consistently the same.

By the beginning of our third season of coaching, it was difficult to separate our interest in coaching from our interest in our research. In addition to our observations on recreational and club soccer, we latched on to another soccer story in Siler City on the other side of the state, which chronicled the arduous but successful journey of an all–Latino high school male soccer team. The story of these immigrant boys who succeeded outside of the dominant club system resonated with our growing awareness of the cultural landscape of American soccer. The more we pulled on the thread of this local story of soccer, the longer it became. The simple narrative of coaching our daughters in a local Parks and Recreation league had turned into a complex mosaic constructed of layers of social and cultural issues: class, ethnicity, immigration, and much more.

Nevertheless, Parks and Recreation reassembled our third team. Gregory's youngest daughter moved up to our U-12 team, reuniting the successful front line from our first season. As luck would have it, most of the team came from the same elementary school and the individual personalities meshed better than in the previous season. Practices were once again filled with laughter, along with serious drills and exercises—at least as serious as 12-year-olds allowed.

Our attitudes had changed as well. Learning as much from our research as from our critical self-reflections as parents and coaches, we once again started having fun with our daughters and the other girls we were getting to know. We had heard the angry yell of a parent at his own kid: "If you don't play better, there'll be no supper tonight!" We had seen the vicious taunts of parents toward referees, at least once causing one to break down in tears. We had seen ourselves approaching that dangerous edge overlooking the chasm of obnoxious parental behavior, and we were thankful that we had backed away without jumping over the edge.

We never duplicated the successful record of our first season, but it didn't matter. The players never lost their enthusiasm for learning and competing, and their upbeat attitude reinforced our newly rediscovered sense of playfulness and support. Our research had taken us out of the small space of our own immediate lives and opened a panorama of complex, overlapping issues that tied us inextricably to the global arena. We all construct narratives to help explain our lives, and our excursion into the world of parent-coaches led to an unanticipated, serendipitous extension of our personal narratives into a much larger story.

Two of our daughters whom we coached played one more year of organized Parks and Recreation soccer. Because there were not enough boys and girls over 12 years of age continuing in the program, a U-14 mixed league operated with boys and girls allocated more or less equally between teams. Unfortunately, we witnessed some of the same characteristics in their new coach that we, too, had displayed as coaches when we became obsessed with winning. While we never outwardly complained, it was obvious to all of the parents watching from the sideline that the coach not only played his male participants longer than their female counterparts but also positioned his male unit as forwards and strikers in the belief that they were more prone to score than the girls. Our daughters and the other female players were typically relegated to defense. When they entered high school, neither daughter chose to continue playing soccer. After experiencing the sideline hostility of a "seasoned" club coach whose antics we felt were more akin to a wild ape than a concerned mentor working with youth, Bruce's son also left soccer, turning his attention to other physical activities like skate boarding and rock climbing.

Gregory's oldest daughter, who had played one season with the local club team, played two seasons on her high school junior varsity team, where she was named the outstanding offensive player both years. However, she endured considerable pressure from her high school coach to play club soccer, a move expected of high school players who wish to "succeed." While shooting our documentary, we learned that 90–95 percent of local high school players also played club soccer. She stopped playing soccer her junior year because she had no desire to meet the demands of her high school coach to play in the club system. In reflecting upon the different experience of playing for her high school team as opposed to the club team, she noted that on the high school team players felt they were representing a larger community consisting of students and teachers at the school; conversely, players on the club team were representing little beyond themselves and their parents. She felt there was no link between the club system and an identifiable sense of community that she had experienced at the high school.

* * * *

Although our excursion into the world of youth soccer at this level possessed its own unique dimensions, our experience also opened our eyes to the world of organized youth sports. That world seemed to be as much about parents as it was about kids. We even succumbed to certain patterns of that world: the competitive motif, the projection of that internal competitiveness onto our children, the standardization of free play, and the emphasis on winning.

We remembered how we were first introduced to sports: baseball in vacant lots, basketball on the outdoor court at the neighborhood church, football on the elementary school grounds on Saturday afternoons, and volleyball at the local public park. Kids controlled these spaces and learned basic skills on their own, including how to negotiate rules and disputes without adult intervention. We remembered the feelings of freedom and independence that were an integral part of that space. Without creating a romanticized nostalgia for that bygone era or an "essentializing" critique of organized youth sports, we still felt a sense of loss in the transition from free play to organized sports at such an early age. We knew that we could never fully measure what was gained until we also comprehended what was lost. We learned a lot more once we turned our attention to club soccer.

8

Youth Development and Club Soccer

Clint Dempsey—even the most casual U.S. soccer fan knows his name. Born in the small East Texas town of Nacogdoches, Dempsey is the most visible American face in global soccer today. After a three-year collegiate career at Furman University and several seasons in Major League Soccer (MLS) with the New England Revolution, Dempsey hit the big time. In 2007, a struggling, London-based Premier League team named Fulham paid a $4 million transfer fee for Dempsey, the first American to warrant such an investment. It paid off. Dempsey helped Fulham solidify a hold on its precarious position in the English first division. Fulham fans rewarded him by voting Dempsey player of the year in 2011 and 2012—quite an accomplishment for a Yank playing in the country that gave birth to modern soccer. Later, Dempsey signed with Fulham's cross-town rival, Tottenham Hotspur, for an undisclosed amount, undoubtedly the highest salary paid to an American in the history of the game.

In a surprise move in August 2013, Dempsey signed a 3½-year, $24 million contract with the Seattle Sounders of the MLS, making him the highest-paid player in MLS soccer. Dempsey is expected not only to provide a boost to Sounder attendance, already the highest in the MLS, but also to give a shot in the arm to the prestige and overall attendance of the league. Even before setting his boots on an MLS field, he had more than a dozen interviews in major media outlets, including *Sports Illustrated,* National Public Radio, and *Good Morning America.* Despite his successes in England, Dempsey said he wanted to be closer to his family and to return to the United States while he was still in his prime. "I'm not coming here just to chill," he told *Sports Illustrated.*[1]

A member of the U.S. Men's National Team since 2004, Dempsey has served as captain of a squad that many believe has greater potential to succeed on the international stage than any previous team. He has surpassed 100 appearances with the national team, and his 35 goals rank second to Landon Donovan's 56 goals in more than 150 appearances. The 2014 World Cup will be his third trip to the most coveted international tournament.

Few doubt that Dempsey deserves his growing reputation. After Dempsey scored two goals in a recent 4–3 USMNT victory over Germany's national squad, Coach Jürgen Klinsmann commented on his performance:

> Is he highly talented? Does he have all the tools to play at the highest level? Yes. But what is more important, he has the drive. He has the hunger. He's not satisfied. It is just in his inner being, having that inner drive. Having a player like Clint Dempsey is a privilege, and if I look back, I think this is one of the best players in U.S. history.[2]

On a superficial level, the major stops in Dempsey's incredible journey seem to typify American professional soccer players. He first played organized soccer on a local Parks and Recreation team, the Strikers. When he was 10 years old, he began playing in the Dallas club system. His evolving talent earned him a scholarship to Furman University in South Carolina. After three seasons he left the university, for a professional career in the United States. The path from Parks and Recreation to club, university and MLS soccer is the most common pipeline for talented American players. Until recently, this path defined the route of almost every other member of the U.S. national team as well. Because so few American players ever make it to first-level teams in Europe, his past accomplishments in the Premier League testify to Dempsey's superior ability.

Upon closer scrutiny, however, Dempsey's story is an anomaly that illustrates the liability often associated with club development programs in the United States. Because the U.S. system operates like an upside-down pyramid, limiting participation to players with the material means to sustain prolonged involvement, the Clint Dempsey whom the soccer world knows now almost never existed.

The seldom-heard part of his story begins in his family's trailer home behind his grandparents' house in Nacogdoches, a sweltering town of 30,000 people carved out of the tall pine forests that grace East Texas. With 30 percent of the population living below the federal poverty line, Nacogdoches may not be part of Texas's economic boom, but it still has an all–American feel, with an annual hot dog eating contest and a claim as the oldest city and the largest blueberry producer in the state. If outsiders refer to the town as "Nothingdoches," the slow pace of life has advantages that big city folk have trouble understanding.

Clint's father, Aubrey Dempsey, worked in construction and on the railway. His mother, Debbie, worked at a hospital. Although far from poor, family income was limited. With five children, extensive family vacations and luxuries came rarely. Eating out was a rare pleasure, and when the opportunity did arise, the Dempsey kids split meals in order to help pay the bill. To make ends meet, Dempsey's parents worked extra shifts when the opportunity arose.

One thing the Dempsey kids had going for them was athleticism. By the time she was in her early teens, Clint's older sister, Jennifer, had developed into a top-notch tennis player. Clint and his older brother, Ryan, discovered soccer early on. Clint's first soccer memory was seeing barefoot Latino kids playing soccer with a basketball on a nearby vacant lot. Soon he and Ryan were joining them as often as they could. At the time the official Hispanic population of Nacogdoches was only 5 percent. Today, as in so many other small Texas towns, the Hispanic population has ballooned to 17 percent. In Dempsey's youth, it must have been unusual to see two *gringo* kids joining the frequent sandlot *cascaritas.*

An intangible, irresistible force drew Dempsey to soccer. As he later recalled, "I remember everything else as something fun to do. Soccer was something I had to do. It was inside me."[3] That internal affinity for the game soon paid dividends. Dempsey quickly developed the technical skills and bravado that would later characterize his style of play—one that is more akin to the self-taught, intuitive style of soccer in the Spanish-speaking Americas than the more mechanical, conscious style in the United States.

As Dempsey's soccer passion and skills became more evident, his parents realized that his options in Nacogdoches were limited. The small city provided few opportunities to develop as a serious player beyond the informal Parks and Recreation games and sandlot matches. They looked elsewhere for opportunities, including the club system in Dallas, 165 miles northwest of Nacogdoches. Although the distance was daunting, the Dempsey family took the plunge. At the age of 10, Dempsey tried out for a club team called the Longhorns. As his parents recall, the coach gave young Clint a ball, watched him dribble a few moments, and then immediately declared, "I want him." His father responded, "Now wait a second, here. He can have a temper. He's very competitive. You need to look at him some more." The coach replied, "Nope. I know what I see. I want him."[4]

Two to three times a week, Aubrey and Debbie took turns driving the 330-mile round trip to Clint's practices, returning to Nacogdoches late at night. At the same time, Jennifer was moving up in the state rankings of junior tennis players, which meant she needed to travel further to participate in tournaments. Combined with Clint's weekend matches in Dallas and tournaments in other parts of Texas, the logistics and expenses were spinning out of control.

The family sold their boat and Aubrey sold his hunting guns. Family "vacations" consisted of long drives to athletic events, the kids often doing their homework in the car. "I'd look around and see other nurses and what material possessions they had," Debbie recalls, "but I was more concerned that the kids were happy—that they had what they needed."[5]

Despite the sacrifices, their efforts to support both children overwhelmed the Dempseys. Two hard-working parents juggling multiple priorities to make ends meet couldn't be sustained. In the fall of 1995, Debbie and Aubrey pulled Clint from club soccer so that they could support Jennifer's travel, who by age 15 was a state-ranked tennis player. Clint returned to the local game, playing as much as he could in the informal *cascaritas* with Latino kids in the neighborhood.

It was around this time that Clint met the Rivera family. Victor Rivera's two sons, Victor Jr. and Franky, had recently joined their father in Nacogdoches from Chicago, where they had been living with their mother. Their mobile home was located next to the dirt lot that served as the primary battleground for neighborhood *cascaritas.* Victor Jr. and Franky were soon playing side-by-side with Clint and other neighborhood kids.

The Rivera home became a makeshift clubhouse for the young players. Victor Rivera operated a *taquería* in Nacogdoches and he often cooked food for the boys. He affectionately called Clint and a couple of other non–Hispanic players his *bolillos,* after the crusty, white rolls famous in Mexico. Victor, who grew up playing street soccer in Zamora, Mexico, also served as an informal coach for the horde of boys playing daily near his house. Clint watched professional Mexican soccer on television with the Riveras and their friends, listening to countless stories of the exploits of famous Latin American players. He grew especially close to Victor Jr.

While Clint harbored dreams of playing professional soccer, tragedy struck the Dempsey family. Jennifer, who had just turned 16, died suddenly of a massive brain aneurysm. Reeling from Jennifer's inexplicable death, the Dempseys decided to transform tragedy into hope. Once again, they invested in Clint's soccer, and by the next spring he was back with his club team in Dallas. Later, Debbie found a note from Clint in the vase at Jennifer's grave. It said that for the rest of his life, every time he scored a goal he would look to the sky and think of her. Today, playing for the U.S. Men's National Team and for Seattle, Dempsey still keeps that promise.

As Clint progressed through the ranks of club soccer, his parents once again struggled to meet the increasingly steep costs. Besides club fees in the vicinity of $2,000 a season, the Dempseys were investing more than $120 a week in travel. They borrowed money to finance travel expenses and bought a camper to eliminate hotel costs. "My parents were crazy," Clint recently reflected. "With the gas prices now it would be impossible, but back then they did everything they could to make it happen. It was really tough for them because it was 'pay-to-play' in club football and it was expensive."[6]

Despite his return to his club league, Clint continued to play neighborhood soccer. Victor Rivera formed a local team, and Clint and Victor Jr. started to play in the local Latino league against men twice their age. Some of the older players had played in lower-level professional leagues in Mexico, so the competition was intense. Initially, the other teams treated the young players gingerly, but as soon as the Rivera team started winning, they stepped up the play. As a *bolillo*, Clint was a particular target. Alex Romero, an excellent player from El Salvador who played in the league, recalls, "People went out to hurt [Dempsey]." Clint relished the competition. After scoring a goal, he would run around the periphery of the field yelling to families and friends, "Whaaaaat's uuuuuuup?"[7]

When they were 16 years old, Clint and Victor Jr. helped produce a league championship for Rivera's team. Clint's moves and passing and Victor Jr.'s speed provided the one-two punch needed to outwit other teams. To the chagrin of many, the glory was short-lived. Fearful that young Clint would sustain an injury, and because they continued to invest money in the club system, the Dempseys pulled Clint from the local league. He was already receiving letters of interest from major university soccer programs, and his parents couldn't risk that future. Clint remained close to Victor Jr., however, and asked him to try out for the Dallas club team. Victor Jr. had no trouble making the highly competitive squad, even though he'd never played organized soccer outside of the local league. Victor Jr.'s ascension to club soccer undoubtedly surprised more than a handful of coaches and league officials, who were used to cultivating players whose parents had invested tens of thousands of dollars in their kids' careers.

Although Victor Jr. was good enough to make the team and received club financing and logistical support from the Dempseys, the costs proved too burdensome. Victor Jr. left the team after one year of play, prior to the time university coaches might have scouted him. His brother Franky recalled that the decision to drop out "killed [him]."[8] Victor Jr. finished the next year as the leading scorer on the Nacogdoches High School soccer team, but university coaches rarely recruit high school players.

Instead of a soccer future, Victor Jr. settled into work at Nibco, one of the few manufacturing companies in town, and started a family with a wife and young child in Nacogdoches. In many ways, Clint managed to escape an uncertain future in East Texas due to the unfortunate death of his sister. Victor Jr.'s fate was sealed by a different tragedy: the lack of financial resources and an upside-down pyramid.

Years later, Dempsey made his first U.S. World Cup squad. Back in Nacogdoches, Victor Jr. went to a shooting range with friends. According to a police report, Victor's ear plug fell to the ground, and when he reached down to retrieve it his gun accidentally fired, lodging a bullet in his head and killing him instantly. Victor Jr.'s death traumatized Franky and his father, and the twosome gave up on soccer. No more playing, coaching, or watching the sport. The only time pain recedes for the Rivera family is when Clint Dempsey takes the field on the international stage. Those days when Clint and Victor Jr. played together come back again. They don't need to watch Clint play because their memories shape what will happen. "I know where the ball's going to go," Victor Sr. said in a recent article, "where Clint's going to pass it. I just imagine where Victor would have gone and there it goes."[9]

Clint Dempsey's journey can be seen as a success story by those who advocate for the current club system of youth development. After all, he came up through that system, was recruited for a university career through club soccer, and eventually reached the prominence he now possesses. Yet, because of his family's limited financial resources, his talent may never have surfaced had it not been for his sister's death. While the club system enabled him to develop as a player, years of playing *cascaritas* and in the Nacogdoches league provided him with subtleties that are often missing in the game of more traditional U.S. players.

Sports Illustrated calls Dempsey "the U.S.'s most inventive and unpredictable soccer player." Dempsey's style is "self-taught, intuitive, like a jazzman's." Bruce Arena, former coach of the USMNT, puts it more bluntly: "He tries shit." Another former coach of the USMNT, Bob Bradley, says, "Clint's capable of making an attacking play that's a little different, that can create an advantage that can lead to a goal. To have a player who can come up with something different at the right time, that's still such a special part of soccer."[10]

In Dempsey's case, it's an instinct born of tragedy, sacrifice, hard work, and countless hours spent dribbling and controlling the ball across rough fields with inventive opponents. It's an instinct absorbed as much from a relationship with the Riveras, the hours of *cascaritas,* and the dynamics of the Latino league as from what he was able to learn within the club system. "You have to take risks," Dempsey says simply.[11] It's a style that echoes Klinsmann's claim that the United States needs players who "have a hunger" for the game. The pyramid upside down doesn't make it that easy.

* * * *

At the bar in Boone Saloon, watching the USMNT play Honduras in a CONCACAF Gold Cup semi-final, we struck up a conversation with a young man sitting next to us. It was apparent that he knew a lot about soccer and he was soon sharing a personal story that, with some variations we had heard countless times before. He grew up in Wilmington, North Carolina, and by the time he was nine years old, he was playing on a local club team. Comfortably upper-middle class, his parents could afford the club fees, the uniforms and equipment, the travel expenses around the state, the tournament fees, the summer soccer camps, and the time investment to play club soccer.

In his mid-teens, he was good enough to try out for a U.S. Soccer Academy team in Raleigh, 125 miles northwest of his home. He was psyched. However, when his parents calculated the cost as approximately $10,000 a year to play academy soccer, they scuttled the idea. At age 15, their son would require a hefty three-year investment prior to attending college. They already had invested thousands of dollars in his club career. The pay-off might be a college scholarship, with a chance for him to go even further. But a $30,000 investment in an uncertain soccer future just didn't seem economically rational.

Our young acquaintance continued to play elite club soccer and eventually earned a partial scholarship to a small private college in western North Carolina. The partial scholarship covered a minimal proportion of the college's $35,000 annual costs. The college's educational reputation was below average, as were the soccer opponents his college team faced. His soccer skills didn't develop and he was dissatisfied with the education he was receiving. With nine years of club soccer experience and two years of college soccer, his parents had invested more than $80,000 in his soccer future. After two years, he transferred to a public university where he is currently studying to become a high school history teacher. "I don't think that what my parents invested in me, all the money and the time, was really worth it," he concluded. "Yeah, I got a partial scholarship that covered maybe 15 percent of expenses, but it was to a mediocre academic school that wasn't really a good fit for me. So what was all that money about?"

With slight variations, this young man's story is repeated time and again in the United States. Most players start out in informal Parks and Recreation leagues with minimal participant fees. If kids demonstrate enthusiasm, athleticism, and skills, they can progress to a local club team. Registration fees at the club level accelerate considerably, as do tournament entry fees, uniform and equipment fees, and travel expenses. Time commitments for both kids and parents extend from two hours a week to dozens of hours for practice and travel. As talented kids progress through the system to more elite levels, expenses expand dramatically. As a former Olympic Development club player named Jeremy Wright explained in our documentary on youth soccer in America, "You have to have the same warm-ups (two pair in case one gets dirty), the same boots; and then there's a lot of travel. And all this takes a whole lot of money."[12]

Fully comprehending how the pay-to-play system of club soccer established such a hold on youth player development requires an understanding of transitions in the cultural landscape of U.S. soccer. In the early years of soccer in the United States, there were youth teams scattered around mostly urban, ethnic neighborhoods in cities in the northeast and upper Midwest. Many of these youth teams were connected to semi-pro and nonprofessional adult teams that dotted the sports landscape. In 1935, the U.S. Soccer Federation initiated its U-19 boys' National Junior Challenge Cup. The initial champions came from New Bedford, followed by teams from Brooklyn, Philadelphia, and Trenton. In the immediate post–World War II era, teams from St. Louis won a number of championships. Almost all of these early youth Challenge Cup titles were won by teams from areas that had a long history of soccer connected to working-class cultural milieus. Despite the presence of this U-19 boys' Cup, no systematic national youth development system existed.

The transition began in the post–World War II years as soccer's primary growth occurred at the collegiate level. Prior to that time, player development was informal and anchored primarily in the working-class, ethnic social landscape. As we point out in Chapter 9, university soccer grew dramatically after the war, just as it receded at the national level. In 1945 there were only 42 collegiate men's teams. Ten years later there were 171, and by 1970 423, 1,000 percent increase in just 25 years. By 1970, a handful of women's collegiate teams also emerged onto the scene. By 1992, that number had climbed to 348.[13] This growth was originally fueled by an influx of international students who'd grown up playing soccer, as well as the expanding number of working-class Americans, many of them GIs from urban ethnic enclaves, who were attending university for the first time. Yet there was no organized system of youth development. In other sports like football and basketball, high schools became the major feeding system for the expansion of those sports at the collegiate level. In the 1950s and 1960s, relatively few high schools fielded soccer teams. As collegiate soccer teams exploded, the need for an organized youth system to feed that growth became evident.

Although various organizations attempted to develop a comprehensive youth system, the establishment of the U.S. Youth Soccer Association in 1974 marked the first successful bid to nationalize youth soccer. Within a few years, the USYSA had registered over 100,000 players and developed an ever-widening organizational structure. For many years it was the only youth development organization officially affiliated with the U.S. Soccer Federation, the governing body of American soccer. This link established the USYSA as the pathway to higher levels of soccer. By the late 1970s and into the 1980s, it represented the dominant force in player development that fed the expansion of university soccer. Although high school soccer also grew during this period, the recruiting pipeline for university teams centered more on players from the club system. This trajectory still exists today. As one university coach told us in *Offside(s)*, "The pipeline [to the university] is from ODP (Olympic Development Program), Super-Y League, or some type of extracurricular soccer." Regarding university recruitment, another soccer coach mentioned, "It's almost like high school soccer is irrelevant."

The only way to develop the USYSA was through a pay-to-play system of parent financing. The national team and the U.S. Soccer Federation had all but disappeared from 1950 to 1990, leaving both organizations even more financially impotent than in pre-war years. In addition, the professional North American Soccer League walked a financial tightrope during its 16-year existence, struggling to maintain financial viability, which made investment in player development impossible. Corporate investment, when it existed at all in the sports landscape, supported more lucrative, money-making sports. The amateur and semi-pro leagues that functioned had no real interest or capability to develop youth programs. In other words, the system of youth development had no choice but to finance itself.

This period represents the beginning of a major shift in the social space occupied by soccer in the United States. For the first 75 years, soccer's waxing and waning fortunes were squarely located in a working-class, largely ethnic landscape. As the system shifted to a university-based sport fed by a burgeoning youth club system, however, soccer moved into the social space of middle- to upper-class lifestyles. Requiring economic capital for prolonged participation, soccer garnered the class-based, symbolic capital that made it emblematic of elite class status. Participation in the club system became a mode of class differentiation that distinguished it and its participants at the time from major American sports like baseball, basketball, and football. As Gordie Howell writes in a relatively obscure manuscript, "In the late 1960s and early 70s, the transformation of soccer from a sport played primarily by ethnics ... to one whose status was rooted in middle-class or upper-class suburbia began to develop."[14] The youth soccer boom that accompanied the expansion of university soccer created a distinctly American brand of soccer, a "suburban game, identified as a 'yuppie' and 'preppy' indulged by suburban 'soccer moms.'"[15] Not only did youth soccer require considerable material capital from parents, but it also became a kind of cultural capital that served as a symbolic marker of an elite, socioeconomic space.

With over three million registered players between the ages of 5 and 19, the USYSA today contains over 6,000 clubs organized into 55 state associations. All 50 states have an organization, and several of the more populous states (California, New York, Ohio, Pennsylvania, and Texas) are divided into two branches. The state organizations, each with an extensive professional staff and a core of volunteers, are organized into four national regions. Some 600,000 volunteers and paid staff, from administrators to coaches to referees, make the USYSA the largest member organization of U.S. soccer. The national organization is headed by a 12-member Board of Directors consisting of elected officers, four regional directors, two at-large members, two independent directors, and the immediate past president.

The tripartite division of teams into Classic, Challenge, and Premier levels of competition represents the core of the USYSA system. Large clubs usually offer teams at all three levels, while smaller clubs offer a selection of Classic and Challenge teams. In theory, each higher level is more competitive than the one preceding it, and therefore more selective. Individual teams schedule matches against other similar teams at the same level within a region, and also participate in various tournaments. Participant expenses typically escalate as a player moves up the system.

In addition to these different levels, the USYSA operates two other significant activities: the U.S. Youth Soccer National Championships and the U.S. Olympic Development Program (ODP). The USYA National Championships are the culmination of local, state and regional championships for all member clubs from U-13 to U-19. Both boy and girl state champions in each age category advance to regional championship tournaments, and the winners from the four regions then proceed to the national championships held each July. Each state also holds try-outs for the state ODP program. Usually upon invitation, players who make it at this initial level may try out for the regional, and then the national, ODP program. The national tournament and the regional and national ODP camps are the sites of most university recruitment activity. In 2013, over 600 university coaches attended the national championships held in Overland Park, Kansas.

Kansas may seem like an unlikely place to hold such an important youth tournament. Although Kansas City hosts an MLS team, the state isn't the first place that comes to mind when one thinks of soccer powerhouses. Instead, soccer enthusiasts typically turn to the urban northeast, or to Florida, Texas, and California. In fact, the entire state of Kansas has only 35 USYSA club system members. Of course, this number exceeds the eight club systems in Montana, 11 in Wyoming, and 22 in South Dakota. But Kansas's club systems pale in comparison to the 162 California clubs, 158 New York clubs, 156 Texas clubs, and 127 Florida clubs. Yet four of these Kansas clubs are located in Overland Park, a suburb of Kansas City with a population of approximately 175,000.

Actually, Overland Park is an ideal location for club soccer's premier tournament. With an average age seven years younger than the rest of the state and a median family income of $97,634, considerably higher than any other urban or suburban area, the small city displays the requisite material and symbolic qualities of "Club Soccer City, USA" (if there were such a title). In fact, the website *Livability* bestows the title of "The Number One Soccer City in America" on Overland Park.[16] In 2012, *Money Magazine* ranked it the ninth most desirable place to live in America, mentioning its "world class soccer fields" as one of its greatest assets.[17] The centerpiece is a $36 million soccer complex consisting of 12 immaculate, lighted fields covered with synthetic turf with a built-in system to control turf temperatures, team dressing rooms, concession stands, and more. *Livability* calls Overton Park "home to one of the most expensive and unique soccer complexes in the country, as well as a passionate and large base of fans."[18]

Like any growing suburb of this size, Overland Park is not socioeconomically uniform. Yet it's a suburb of largely white, upper-middle- and upper-class residents. Officially, the city's residents are 77.6 percent white, with 7.4 percent Hispanics, identified as the largest minority. When *Money Magazine* named it the ninth best place to live in the country, online reader comments were telling. One reader mentioned, "If you are raising a family, Overland Park can't be beat. Yes, it's suburbia. With that we get a great quality of life that includes great schools, parks, public safety, tons of after-school activities (i.e., sports), and homes." The reader concluded, "I make no apologies for earning the standard of living my family enjoys." Another wrote, "I grew up in Overland Park. If you're white and live in a box of TV generation one-tracked minds, you belong in this town of boring, soulless drones." He ended by saying, "I am so glad I visited the world and have an eye for the big picture 'cause life would have been terrible for me if I stayed." Another claimed that "the entire place is one big soulless strip mall ... it's the epitome of everything that's wrong with suburbia."[19]

Thomas Frank, author of *What's the Matter with Kansas?*, writes that during Overland Park's growth spurt in the 1980s and 1990s, the suburb dreamed of rivaling Kansas City without that city's problems:

> It built hotels and a convention center, hoping to siphon even more sustenance away from the gasping metropolis; it slapped up shopping malls; it constructed a new office district, complete with runty glass mini-skyscrapers at the southernmost point of settlement; and it platted out subdivisions without end—a raw, wood-shingled fortification stretching over the hills as far as the eye could see.[20]

Overland Park also became the corporate home of Sprint and its planned 3.9 million square feet of office space with 16 parking garages.

The demography of Overland Park doesn't tell the whole story, as adjacent communities are even more affluent. Just northeast of Overland Park, Mission Hills is a 2.02-square-mile, incorporated town with 3,500 residents, three country clubs—the most prestigious in the Kansas City area—and a median household income of $188,821. *Forbes* lists it as the third wealthiest municipality in the country. Originally designed as a country club development in the early twentieth century, Mission Hills changed its status in 1949 to an "incorporated town" in order to protect itself from possible encroachment from less affluent suburbs.

Frank describes Johnson County, Kansas, where Overland Park and other affluent, white-flight suburbs exist, as

> a vast suburban empire, a happy, humming confusion of freeways, shopping malls and nonstop construction; of identical cul-de-sacs and pretentious European street names and overachieving school districts and oversized houses constructed to one of four designs. By all the standards of contemporary American business civilization, it is a great success story. It is the wealthiest county in Kansas by a considerable margin, and the free-market rapture of the New Economy nineties served it well, scandals notwithstanding.[21]

Even putting stereotypes aside, this cultural landscape of America's "soccer city," would be strangely unrecognizable to pre–World War II players and fans alike. The manicured, high-tech fields set amid a suburban, affluent community of planned housing developments, country clubs, and shopping malls would seem as alien to those early players and fans as a barren Mars landscape. Yet it perfectly encapsulates the generalized cultural landscape of youth soccer in the United States today.

Teams from California dominated the USYA National Championships, winning the girls' U-13, U-14, and U-16 titles. They also won the boys' U-13, U-14, U-15, U-17 and U-18 titles. In all, eight of the 14 titles went to Californian teams representing communities like Riverside (four titles), Orange County (two titles), Santa Barbara, and Del Mar. Not since teams from Texas won seven of 12 titles in 2008 had a single state dominated tournament play.

In 1977, the boys' Olympic Development Program was initiated. A similar one for girls followed five years later. The programs sought "to identify players of the highest caliber which will lead to increased success of the U.S. national teams in the international arena." Within a short time, however, a secondary intent of grooming players for the university soccer landscape emerged. The ODP camps and tournaments quickly became major sites of university recruitment efforts, and remain so today.

Each state-level member of USYSA includes an ODP camp for top players in the state. Each state program operates according to its own guidelines, but top players either try out or are asked to participate. State-level ODP players may then be invited to join one of the four regional ODP programs. The national program organizes ODP camps and interregional tournaments held several times each year. Currently, it supports five different age groups for boys, with the youngest born since the year 2000 and the oldest since 1996. Four age groups between 1996 and 1999 make up the girls' ODP program. In 2013, ODP teams from the western and the northeast regions placed in the top seven of nine age group tournaments.

Local-level participation in the club system is expensive, although for the short term not beyond the reach of many middle-class Americans. Club participant fees, uniforms, equipment, individual player tournament fees, and travel expenses may range between $2,000 and $5,000 per year, depending on the club. However, costs escalate as a player advances through the system. Not only are participant fees more expensive, but travel expenses also increase exponentially. Most Challenge- and Classic-level teams play the majority of their matches at the local or state level, with the exception of one or two out-of-state tournaments. Because fewer clubs operate Premier-level teams, however, the travel distance for season matches and tournaments extends throughout the multi-state region. The Olympic Development Program and other high-level youth programs like Super-Y League add dramatically to the cost.

Additionally, players often attend summer camps sponsored by a host of soccer programs, from universities to professional domestic and foreign teams. The website *socceramerica* lists over 250 soccer camps offered in the United States. Most of these camps run three to five days in length, with varying costs. For example, Colgate University offers a four-day/three-night camp for $575 (overnight stay) and $405 (day camping). By comparison, the summer camp at Appalachian State University offers a bargain at $405 for a four-day/three-night stay, or $330 for a day camper. Athletic camp programs at universities have become a big business, generating much-needed revenue, summer salaries, and a more efficient use of dorm and dining facilities. A number of soccer camp businesses have also appeared on the horizon. Camp All-Star in Maine offers summer camp programs in most major sports, including soccer, at a rate of $2,999 for a two-week camp, and up to $6,999 for a six-week stay. Some of the most famous professional European teams have jumped into the summer camp business as well. FC Barcelona offers a camp for $4,295, not including airfare. Manchester United advertises a camp for $1,595, plus airfare. If a player prefers Italy, there is always the seven-day stay with AC Milan for only $1,345, plus airfare. Paris St. Germaine offers a six-day camp for $1,595, not including airfare. Selected camps even provide language instruction for an extra fee.

Club systems try to reduce the heavy financial burden on parents by acquiring sponsorships, holding fundraising events, and offering limited scholarship opportunities. Yet, even with all of these efforts, one reality remains: a long-term investment in a player's development is prohibitively expensive for most Americans.

* * * *

The local club system in our corner of southern Appalachia typifies many small-town soccer clubs. High Country Soccer Association (HCSA) was founded in 1986. In the beginning the program grew modestly, playing home matches on a variety of fields carved out of local parks. But in 2006 the association began an ambitious fund-raising campaign to finance a dedicated soccer complex. Kick-started by a significant donation from a local business family, HCSA developed a three-way partnership with Appalachian State University and the local Watauga County Parks and Recreation department. The county program donated the 10-acre tract of land, and the university provided additional construction funds. In return, the university received the rights to use the new facility as its collegiate home field, and the local Parks and Recreation leagues were allowed to use the facility for part of their fall youth soccer program.

The Ted Mackorell Soccer Complex was dedicated in November 2008. The $2 million facility included two 90 × 130 feet full-sized, artificial turf fields and additional practice fields. Grandstands accompany one of the fields, along with a fieldhouse and concession stand. By 2012, sufficient funds had been collected to virtually eliminate the construction debt and interest that HCSA accrued for the project.

Currently, HCSA sponsors three levels of informal academy programs for boys and girls ages 4–10. These levels do not participate in matches, but rather emphasize skill building, team play, and fun. Travel teams in age categories U-11–U-18 exist for both boys and girls at the Challenge and Classic levels. Over 150 local kids participate in these programs. Academy-level participation is reasonably priced at $55–$75 a season. Yearly club fees for U-11–U-14 Challenge teams amount to $814; for Classic teams, the price jumps to $1,034. Classic U-15–U-18 teams are $520 per season. The club doesn't operate these teams year-round, allowing players to play with the local Watauga High School team in either the spring or the fall. HCSA also operates an adult league. Last season the league supported eight local teams from two divisions.

Three of our own children played one season each with traveling teams. Although we didn't keep a precise log on costs at the time, we estimated the total at $1,500 per season, with travel expenses far outweighing club and uniform fees. (HCSA does offer scholarships based on need that cover up to half of individual participant fees.) Although $3,000 a year does not seem exorbitant to many, it's difficult to sustain over the years, particularly for parents with several children interested in soccer and other activities.

The local youth system is a member of the North Carolina YSA, one of the 55 state organizations that make up the USYSA. The state organization has approximately 74,000 registered players at the Recreational, Challenge, Classic, and Premier levels. The state organization is funded through a series of fees paid by each club. Each club pays an initial membership fee and annual dues, which are determined by the size of the club. A percentage of annual player participation fees also go to the state office. The state organization does not impose minimal coaching qualifications or pay on local clubs, in which many coaches are volunteers with few formal qualifications, while the larger clubs maintain full- or part-time coaches who've played or coached soccer at other levels.[22]

Officials of the NCYSA understand the socioeconomic dilemma of the club system. As the Hispanic population has mushroomed in the state, the organization has attempted to incorporate these families into the system, but with little success. The reality is that while the state and national organizations are nonprofit, they also operate on a business model. To generate sufficient money to staff and operate a vast national bureaucracy, youth programs from the local club level to the national organization must generate cash flow. The only real source of needed financing comes from the players' families, who, in essence, are customers that purchase services provided by the clubs and the various organizational levels. There is little to be gained by righting the pyramid to allow those who cannot pay to play. Instead, the emphasis is on expanding the consumption of the product—the soccer experience—through the only viable market that the system knows.

And what are the customers of the system receiving? A positive recreational experience for their children? Certainly. The development of athletic fitness? In most cases, yes. A college scholarship? Only for a select few. These recreational, fitness, and financial goals are certainly emphasized. More than anything else, however, customers typically are purchasing a class space that differentiates them from less elite social classes, providing them with the symbolic capital that reinforces their elevated status.

In their book *Offside: Soccer and American Exceptionalism,* Andrei Markovits and Steven Hellerman offer several historical reasons why soccer has remained relatively marginalized in the U.S. sports landscape.[23] The first is that soccer was effectively crowded out of prime real estate in the sports landscape by baseball, basketball, and (American) football, all American inventions. This marginalization was bolstered by the perception that soccer was not a "true" American sport at a time when issues of a homogenized national identity, accelerating power, nationalism, and exceptionalism were coming to the forefront of national character. These barriers were solidified by the absence of a coherent organizational structure that could effectively handle the competition and dissention from various constituent groups interested in promoting and controlling the sport. But while all of these reasons are significant, they don't fully explain the continued marginalization of a sport played by tens of millions of kids, organized into a vast and expensive national bureaucracy, and financed in hefty sums by millions of parents. Until U.S. soccer comes to grips with the elite social space occupied by the sport (restructuring youth access in the process), soccer will remain a sport played by millions of kids but remembered by few.

* * * *

The U.S. Men's National Team entered the 2006 World Cup in Germany with confidence. They had won the 2005 CONCAF Gold Cup and marched through regional qualifications for the World Cup, going 7–2–1 in the final round, including a 1–1 split with archrival Mexico. By December 2005, the United States had climbed to its highest FIFA ranking in history, at number eight in the world. In the five months prior to the premier world soccer event, the United States had posted a 6–2–2 showing against a series of international teams, including four straight victories against Norway, Japan, Guatemala, and Poland. They had outscored their international competitors 18–8. It mattered little that they lost to powerhouse Germany 4–1, or that most of their victories were against teams that hadn't qualified for the 2006 World Cup. The team was psyched and the U.S. media was right there with them.

The draw placed them in a competitive (but far from overwhelming) group with Czechoslovakia, Ghana, and Italy. Despite a 1–1 draw with group winner Italy, the United States was eliminated from the round of sixteen by losing its other two matches, 0–3 to the Czechs and 1–2 to Ghana. The early exit of a team believed to be the most promising American squad ever ironically produced at least one positive result: a serious re-evaluation of the U.S. system of youth development.

By 2007, leaders of the U.S. Soccer Federation decided that the present youth development system needed a dramatic overhaul. While the elaborate and diversified club system successfully fed players to university teams, youth development failed to contribute to building a strong national team. The USSF did operate national U-15–U-19 teams, but most elite players were also playing for an assorted hodgepodge of teams that included their local club as well as state and regional Premier and ODP teams. There was a growing sense that the youth system emphasized playing matches over training, and that many of those matches fielded inferior teams that produced bad habits. As USMNT assistant coach John Hackworth noted,

> On the national staff, we would talk about some habits, or talk about reactions, and where those habits and reactions get instilled. They get instilled in young players when the game doesn't really meet the demands ... we needed to have these players not only play less games, but we needed them to play meaningful games, so the competition would hold them accountable, and make them play out of their comfort zone.[24]

An additional realization was that the U.S. youth players lacked the stamina to play at a consistently high level for 90 minutes. Youth soccer at all levels allowed multiple substitutions, and players could often re-enter a game after resting for a period of time. In 2009 Thomas Rongen, the U-20 national coach, observed, "We still find players that have a very rough time getting through 90 minutes at the highest level because their bodies, physically and emotionally, are not accustomed to that."[25]

Finally, USSF and other organizations started critiquing the club to university to national team pipeline. By the time players graduated from college, they typically were past their prime, having developed bad habits in games against opponents who didn't push them enough. Even if they left college early to turn professional, players lost valuable development time.

The result of this internal critique included the establishment of the USSF's Development Academy program. Examining youth development programs in countries like Brazil, Argentina, France, Spain, and Holland, the USSF created a new strategy, adapting elements of these successful soccer countries into an American context. The emphasis of these academies would be on training rather than playing matches. Kevin Payne, DC United president and CEO, who chaired the committee that designed the academy program, notes:

> I think the biggest thing we found, something that was very consistent (in other countries) was that we had the ratio of training time to game time exactly reversed. In those countries that are so good ... for every hour of playing time, they sometimes have five or more hours of training time. We are doing the opposite.[26]

A 2005 USSF survey of the U-15 national team found that players participated in upward of 100 matches a year, but found only 10 percent actually challenging.[27]

In 2007, 64 clubs established a national system of academy teams at the U-15–U-18 levels. By 2012, that number had grown to 80 clubs. Although the teams were spread throughout the country, the system focused primarily on the already existing regions of soccer development: 13 clubs in California, nine in Texas, and eight in metropolitan New York. The decision to expand the program to the U-13/U-14 levels in 2013 added 23 more teams, mostly in urban areas of California, New York, Washington, D.C., and Florida.

In 2012, officials made a somewhat controversial decision to expand the academy program season to 10 months. Previously, elite players had participated in both club and high school soccer, alternating seasons between the two. The decision by the USSF for its academy players meant that young players would be unable to play for their high school teams. High school coaches were outraged. Although those coaches often pushed their players to play on club teams when they weren't playing for their high school team, coaches felt that the new system would rob them of their best players. Dan Woog, the boys' soccer coach at Staple High School in Westport, Connecticut, recalled an incident after his team won a conference championship. Some of the players went to a restaurant after the match and customers spontaneously gave them a standing ovation: "They're going to remember that [moment] the rest of their lives. They felt like kings. That's not going to happen in the academy."[28]

Tony Lepore, director of scouting for the academy program, notes, "We're not surprised by the reaction, and we get it; high school sports are a big part of the culture. But when it comes to elite soccer players and their development, this change is optimal." Coach Woog counters, "We should be in the business of letting kids be kids. Not forcing them into thinking they're going to be playing for Arsenal or Manchester United two years from now."[29]

The reality is that the 3,000 or so youths playing on the academy teams are a small dent in the hundreds of thousands of kids playing high school soccer. While some kids will have to make tough choices and high school teams will miss the skills of those players who do opt for the academy system, high school soccer will not disappear. The ingrained club system has for years diminished the significance of playing high school soccer; the academy system simply takes that process a step further.

The final problem the USSF faces in its academy program is the pay-to-play system. After Jürgen Klinsmann was named head coach of the USMNT in 2010, top brass encouraged sponsors to underwrite the program so that talented kids with moderate incomes could participate. The USSF developed a two-track system for finding corporate and professional team sponsors. By 2012, 44 of the 80 teams had a professional team affiliation with MLS teams, international teams, and lower-level U.S. professional teams. Twenty-four of the 80 teams are fully funded by these organizations and 16 others are funded at 50 percent of the costs. According to the Development Academy program, 150 players received scholarships in the 2011–2012 year. While these efforts have a long way to go in remedying the upside-down pyramid, they are moving in the right direction.

9

Appalachian State University Soccer in the National Fabric: A Case Study

One of the first things students notice when they walk through the main entrance to the Plemmons Student Union at Appalachian State University is a series of photo collages hanging from the wall. The 75-plus colored pictures document the school's 115-year history, from its humble beginnings in 1899 to the present, in which Appalachian, known as the Mountaineers, touts more freshmen applicants than any other state university outside UNC Chapel Hill. The five collages are grouped by years—1899–1929, 1930–1955, 1956–1980, 1981–2000, and 2000–present—and offer a wide array of photographs depicting university life, including cooking, chemistry, and modern dance classes as well as Glee Club, Female Student Society, streaking, Black Cultural Organization, and Homecoming Queen. The collages also showcase intramural games and physical activities such as croquet, snowboarding, and Ultimate Frisbee, plus more traditional intercollegiate sports like tennis, baseball, track and field, football, and basketball. Conspicuously absent from the mix is soccer.

The omission wouldn't be so glaring had soccer not established such a strong tradition at Appalachian. But it did, and like ASU's more popular revenue sports such as football and basketball, the Mountaineers garnered a national reputation that pitted its men's varsity soccer team against the University of North Carolina, Clemson University, and other established soccer powerhouses across the South. ASU qualified for the first round of the NCAA Championship Tournament 11 years after initiating its men's program in 1961. Two years later, its team was ranked twelfth in the nation. By 1980 the Mountaineers had climbed to eighth among all collegiate teams. From 1971 to 1981

Appalachian dominated regional play, compiling an unprecedented 104–32 win-loss record. After a second-place finish in 1976, it won the Southern Conference Championship six consecutive years, continuing this winning trend into the next decade.

During this time the university relied heavily on international recruits, including Emmanuel Udogu, Kingsley Esabamen, Emmanuel Igbeka, Michael Somnazu, and Thompson Usiyan from Nigeria; Keith Layne from Guyana; and David Mor from Israel. Udogu won Southern Conference Player of the Year in 1974, and Esabamen did the same in 1979. Usiyan holds the SoCon record for winning the title three separate times—in 1977, 1978, and 1980. Igbeka made the All-Conference team from 1977 to 1979. Guided by these players and dozens of others, Appalachian's program thrived, filling one side of the university's football stadium to capacity during home matches and supporting a caravan of student buses to out-of-state games. Both players and coaches alike won regional and national awards. Usiyan's seven goals and one assist during a postseason match against George Washington University on November 15, 1978, still stand as one of the top single-game scoring performances in NCAA history.

This "golden era" of Appalachian soccer influenced future generations of men's varsity soccer. It also inspired a women's soccer program that started in 1994. Since 1981, the ASU's men's team has won Southern Conference titles five times. It's finished in the top four 14 times and placed almost 100 players on All-Conference teams. Several players and coaches have been inducted into the university's Sports Hall of Fame.

So what happened? Why did a sport that drew 5,000 fans to home matches in the 1970s disappear from a university's retrospective landscape? After a record-setting 108 career goals, Thompson Usiyan is arguably the best athlete to pass through Appalachian State University. Why isn't his picture hanging on the student union wall? Where is the photograph of his teammates, who undoubtedly represent one of the earliest attempts to diversify the university both racially and internationally? Or those of the coaches, Vaughn Christian, Hank Steinbrecher, and Art Rex, who both recruited and mentored these international players through their careers? Where are the hundreds of other young men and women who've worn Appalachian soccer jerseys?

The easy answer is to blame it on accidental oversight. The person or persons responsible for assembling the photographs may have simply overlooked the obvious contribution of Appalachian soccer. Another possibility is the sheer volume of the project: there are just too many subjects to choose from when compiling a university retrospective, let alone the thousands of archival photographs that accompany them. While these scenarios seem plausible, we suspect there's a more substantive reason behind the omission. It centers on the salient invisibility of the sport in the university landscape, both yesterday and today.

* * * *

Despite its one-time national rankings, Appalachian soccer rarely received proper recognition. For the first 10 years it chalked up a pitch on the university baseball field. When it garnered accolades for its remarkable achievements in the 1970s, the team merely relocated to Kidd Brewer Stadium, carving out a niche on the football field. For the first 43 years the soccer program never operated within its own complex, despite the administration's pledge to build an on-site stadium. "Plans are already underway to improve the home of the Mountaineers in the near future," a publication from ASU's Sports Information Office declared in 2007. "As part of a $32 million athletics facilities enhancement plan, the Mountaineer soccer program will have a new on-campus facility ... in the coming years."[1] That never happened.

The university did allocate money for a new field, but the stadium was located 1.6 miles from campus. The complex included no locker rooms. During halftime at home matches, teams gathered in the end zones to discuss game strategy. In 2008, the men and women's teams relocated to their current facility, Ted Mackorell Soccer Complex in Brookshire Park. The new complex is a marked improvement over its predecessor. Still, Appalachian's teams share the facility with the High Country Soccer Association, the Watauga Hispanic league, and other organizations from the local soccer community. The new field is located exactly 3.2 miles from campus, twice as far as its predecessor.

While it's conceivable that a regional university like Appalachian wouldn't pour huge sums of money into an untested program in the 1960s, it speaks volumes when that same institution relocates a 50-year-old varsity sport off campus. Who would ever think of erecting a football stadium that far from the university? What administration would build a basketball arena three miles away? How many students would drive a car or take a bus to watch a university tennis match or a baseball game played on the other side of town? A sense of place defines a university sport's identity. When it's surrounded by a clubhouse, academic buildings, dormitories, a library, cafeterias, and thousands of students, that sport feels like a vital part of a larger community. When it's promised one thing and then handed another, it feels slighted. Pushed to the outskirts of town, it wonders how in the world it's supposed to survive.

The problem of physical location is only one of Appalachian soccer's foibles. As a non-revenue sport, the men and women's soccer teams continually fight for an adequate fiscal budget. Each year the soccer program has to bargain with 20 other varsity programs for its share of the pie. To add insult to injury, the NCAA controls the number of scholarships allotted to athletic departments. Historically, those given to soccer are disproportionately inadequate. In order not to be accused of favoritism, coaches often divide scholarships among team players. Given the piddling amount typically granted to programs at regional universities like ASU, such distribution of financial aid barely covers the cost of a player's textbooks.

Additional roadblocks get in the way, including competing with high-end revenue sports like football and basketball. The support for these sports, fixated in the university (and community) psyche for almost a century, obviously affects general interest in Appalachian's soccer program. While attendance at soccer matches 40 years ago numbered in the thousands, today's crowds total a few hundred fans at best. The fact that the first off-campus soccer field seated a mere 360 people attests to the importance the university placed on its soccer program. While the current 960-seat stadium holds almost three times as many fans, the facility doesn't allow much room for growth. There's overflow parking in adjacent lots, but only 40 parking spaces are available in front of the stadium entrance. The most dedicated fan base includes family and friends of players on the team. In 2012, the men's soccer program averaged 352 fans per home game, up from an average of 230 in 2006 at its old facility. While these numbers indicate a modest growth, they still pale in comparison to other ASU sports like football and basketball. Even non-revenue sports like baseball drew more fans.

Similar obstructions affect other university soccer programs across the country. In fact, ASU soccer represents a classic case study of the idiosyncrasies commonly associated with collegiate soccer. Despite moments of past glory, it's been habitually mired in a system that stifles positive growth, suppresses student and community interest, and diminishes its overall status in the university's sports hierarchy. Such a system translates into an almost invisible program that can't even find its photograph on a student union wall.

1960s: The Beginnings

Changing its name four times from 1899 to 1967, when it finally became Appalachian State University, ASU officially inaugurated its men's soccer program in 1961. R. W. "Red" Watkins, Appalachian's wrestling coach from 1934 to 1959, actually tried to start a men's club as early as 1936, when he recruited players from physical education classes and the football team. His team beat nearby Catawba College in two matches, inspiring Watkins and his entourage to attempt to form an intercollegiate program the following year. The administration rejected the initiative, but Watkins's early attempt stands as an interesting footnote in Appalachian soccer history, especially considering that only 80 universities in the entire country fielded soccer teams prior to World War II.

The 23 players composing the initial 1961 squad resembled anything but a modern collegiate soccer team. Pictures from *The Rhododendron*, the university's photographic yearbook, show ASU's players decked out in all-white uniforms reminiscent of the Victorian era, when teams dressed in light-colored clothing to maintain cooler body temperatures during warm summer seasons. Except for Bill Bookout's hat trick, the 1961 season proved uneventful, more akin to intramural play than to organized collegiate soccer. A photograph of the second-year team resembles a squad straight out of physical education class. Jersey numbers identifying players with specific positions apparently held little stature. In the 1962 team photograph of 32 players—actually a significant number for any team, let alone a second-year one—only one player in the first row bears a number under 52. The team appears to be wearing hand-me-down football jerseys to accompany shorts typically worn in gym. On the field the players seemed as flummoxed as they were in choosing appropriate attire. Appalachian teams managed a meager two wins against 14 losses and one tie during their second and third seasons.

Teams from subsequent years experienced similar misfortune. The 1964 squad graduated to pinstriped jerseys, black pants, and striped socks to form a new sense of identity, but they could manage only four wins against six losses and a tie on the field. Appalachian continued its losing streak during the next two seasons, posting a 5–12–3 record overall. To the team's credit, the sport generated more enthusiasm after its initial two years. As early as 1963 a student journalist commented that, despite its novelty, soccer at Appalachian State Teacher College (as it was known then) "thrilled many fans who watched the intense games."[2] By 1964, action photographs had replaced staged ones, but short descriptions underneath these pictures—"Block it boys!" and "Get it Jim!"—read more like vacuous claptrap than a general understanding of the game.[3] Despite a dismal 1966 season, a player named Howard Murphy garnered a nomination for ASU "Athlete of the Year."[4] The prediction that "next year promises to be a better season" came true in 1967, as the squad posted an impressive 8–5–0 record, its first winning season, beating North Carolina State University and local rival Davidson College. After a 1–7–2 season the following year, Appalachian closed out the decade with its second winning season, 7–5–0, including a 2–0 smashing of the University of North Carolina at Chapel Hill. Repeat victories over NC State and Davidson helped balance a lackluster, nine-season record of 27 wins, 49 losses, and 7 ties.

A more compelling story, and one that better illustrates the on-again, off-again decade, is that of Eric DeGroat, Appalachian's first varsity men's soccer coach. DeGroat held the head position from 1961 until 1969, when he retired from coaching soccer altogether. The grandson of Dutch immigrants who changed their name from DeGroot to DeGroat because Americans couldn't pronounce the family name correctly, Eric DeGroat grew up in Springfield, Massachusetts. His father wrote how-to instruction books on baseball, which the local Springfield College published during the 1930s. First called the International Young Men's Christian Association Training School, Springfield College developed a name for itself in 1891 when Professor James Naismith invented the game of basketball. The ensuing decades saw the institution cultivate one of the most innovative physical education programs in the country, offering specialized courses in sports medicine, physical therapy, and wellness physiology. DeGroat enrolled as a physical education major in the mid–1940s. He played varsity football, ran track, and wrestled. Upon graduation, he directed the high school's physical education program in nearby Washington, Connecticut, eventually assuming the role of the township's director of recreation.

While DeGroat received little formal training in soccer, his university days coincided with Springfield's undefeated soccer seasons. Led by players like All-American team captain Ted Smith, the Springfield College Pride won both the New England Championship and back-to-back National Championships in 1946 and 1947. Like DeGroat, Smith majored in physical education and epitomized Springfield's Humanics philosophy—a lifelong advocacy of Christian ethics, physicality, intellectualism, and positive social relations. A World War II veteran enrolled under the recently enacted GI Bill, Smith later used this philosophy to develop successful high school and community soccer programs in the Springfield area. We can only speculate, but as a local native DeGroat probably knew about Smith's success, and as a fellow physical education graduate of Springfield, he modeled his own coaching aesthetic on the Humanics method. By the fall of 1947 DeGroat had landed a job in Raleigh as an instructor in the Department of Physical Education at North Carolina State College, eventually renamed North Carolina State University (NCSU). Two years later he received an appointment as head soccer coach.

Similar to his situation at Appalachian State University, DeGroat initiated NCSU's first soccer program. In terms of a winning season, his six-year tenure as head coach lacked flare. From 1950 to 1955 he compiled a 17–29 win-loss record, with 10 ties. Part of the problem centered on developing a soccer program from scratch, as the sport had only begun to trickle south a few years earlier through the universities. As at ASU, DeGroat had to build a program with only a handful of players, primarily North Carolinians from the surrounding hinterland who hardly knew the game. A more compelling problem included the Atlantic Coast Conference conference to which NCSU belonged. Each year DeGroat's team faced the University of North Carolina in its first match, and typically scheduled a second game against UNC before the end of the season. On more than one occasion NCSU also faced Duke and the University of Virginia. These universities not only were better endowed but already had established soccer programs. DeGroat's team managed a 4–0 trouncing of UNC in 1953, but overall most of his 17 victories came against lesser-known teams outside the ACC.

More impressive than the 44 wins and 78 losses he compiled while coaching at NC State and ASU is the philosophy DeGroat brought to the sport. According to Stephen DeGroat, his son, Eric DeGroat preferred coaching "on a low key." He "enjoyed the game" but didn't have "the attitude that every time [his teams] played someone they were going to have to win."[5] Jim Jones, an accounting professor and tennis coach who handled scheduling and public relations for Appalachian sports when DeGroat first arrived, agreed. Soccer under DeGroat was intercollegiate, but, according to Jones, it was more like "an intramural game" in which students "played for fun." Even after Jones became athletic director and offered the soccer program a small fund to help lure out-of-state players to ASU, DeGroat refused the offer. DeGroat was a "purist" who "wanted nothing to do with recruiting," Jones remembers. More tellingly, he was a "true believer that athletics should be conducted like the Olympics.... His idea was to play with the best [he] could find on campus." As an athletic director who had his hands in both revenue and non-revenue sports, Jones saw the change coming. He informed his staff that if a coach could find a "blue chipper" player who could help attract fans to a particular sport, it was worth investing in his textbooks and defraying the cost of out-of-state tuition. It had worked in football and basketball, the two sports that divided the bulk of scholarship funds. Why couldn't it work for a sport like soccer, especially if a prospective player was willing to come? DeGroat countered that he'd work with the players "he could find in the classroom."[6]

According to Jones, DeGroat fit the mold of a "great physical education–

type person."[7] He epitomized the kind of soccer coach most schools in the 1950s and 1960s relied on, before programs around the country institutionalized coaching and turned college sports into big business. DeGroat was an educator first, but because sports typified his academic discipline, he was *expected* to coach. When he wasn't teaching or directing soccer players from the sidelines, he coached ASU's track and field team. In the winter he coached swimming. Because he was raised in New England and exposed to winter sports, he also formed and supervised ASU's first ski patrol. It's no wonder that DeGroat cultivated such a low-key approach to coaching soccer. Like other physical education teachers of the time, his plate was full.

Even if he'd brought a more competitive philosophy to the sport, DeGroat would have faced major hurdles, such as competing against revenue sports like football and basketball. Appalachian started its football program as early as 1928, playing as an independent against regional universities. Within three years it had joined the North State Conference, where it remained for the next 30 years. The football team lost all but three games its first season, but by 1930 it posted impressive wins and began attracting fans from both the university and surrounding community. Interest in the sport grew even more after Appalachian hired Kidd Brewer, who coached the Mountaineers from 1935 to 1938. He led the team to its first postseason bowl games. The most impressive season came in 1937, when Kidd's squad went undefeated, outscoring opponents 206–0. During the 1940s and 1950s the Mountaineers continued to roll, collecting three conference championships under Coach E. C. Duggins and appearing in seven postseason bowls. From 1928 to 1961 the football team played all of its home games on College Field, located on River Street near the center of campus.

The Appalachian men's basketball team started even earlier, in 1919, posting an impressive 86–33 win-loss record for its first nine seasons. While baseball still maintained its status as the country's national sport—Appalachian inaugurated its own men's varsity baseball team in 1903 four years after its founding—Mountaineer basketball drew substantial home crowds. By 1934 the university had hired its first coach, and over the next 40 years, under the direction of Flucie Stewart, Francis Hoover, Bob Light, and a handful of other coaches, the Mountaineers compiled 472 wins against 375 losses. From 1939 to 1967 Appalachian won the North State Conference championship six times. For 13 years the team played home games in the historic Broom-Kirk Gym, eventually transferring to Varsity Gym a building away. Like College Field, both facilities were located on River Street, close to the heart of campus.

DeGroat had a strike against him when he tried to establish a novelty program like soccer in the middle of the Appalachian Mountains, far removed from the sport's northeastern U.S. origins. He courted an even bigger problem in trying to implement such an unfamiliar sport in a university fully ensconced in football and basketball. But even if he had used a different approach from the puritanical "Olympic" one that relied on local talent, DeGroat still would have faced an obstacle. When Jones took over as athletic director during DeGroat's reign, football awarded 22 athletic scholarships, and basketball eight. Soccer received none.

In all fairness to Appalachian, the university interest in high-end revenue sports reflected the tendency present in the rest of the country. Football and basketball now competed with baseball as national American sports, and as the century unfolded, both sports started replacing baseball as the newest sports of interest. A photograph in Appalachian's *Rhododendron* from DeGroat's early years reveals the difficult challenge of trying to develop a new soccer program in such a competitive arena. The photograph shows an Appalachian player kicking a ball during a home match. No one is watching from the sideline.

1970s: The Golden Era

ASU's historic success the following decade didn't come overnight. The year after DeGroat stepped down, Bill Teeple took control of the team. For a brief moment it looked as if the newly appointed coach would continue to build on DeGroat's 7–5 record from the previous season. Facing East Tennessee State University in their first match, Teeple prepared Appalachian for a 10–1 trouncing, recording one of the most lopsided victories in Appalachian soccer history. However, the celebration ended there. Teeple's team lost its next three matches, including its own 10–1 slaughter at the hands of DeGroat's old alma mater, North Carolina State University. Recording its only other victory against the relatively unknown King College next match, Appalachian lost the next five straight games to finish with a 2–8 season. ASU's opponents outscored the Mountaineers 48–17. Teeple stepped down the following year.

If Bill Teeple failed to re-energize a floundering program, Vaughn Christian took Appalachian soccer to new heights. Like DeGroat, Christian had little formal soccer training during his youth. As an undergraduate at Vanderbilt University in the mid–1960s, he lettered in track and field and played baseball. Similar to his predecessors, he joined the university as a physical education instructor, intent on implementing what he'd learned in exercise science at Vanderbilt, and later as an EED graduate student in physical education at Louisiana State University. Unlike DeGroat, however, Christian arrived with a progressive vision. He'd coached for one year prior to joining his new team when he had accepted a dual teacher-coach appointment at Emory at Oxford, located outside Atlanta, Georgia. The coaching position allowed Christian an opportunity to carpool his young players to practices of the Atlanta Chiefs, one of a handful of franchises in the newly formed National Professional Soccer League (NPSL). Two years later the NPSL reorganized into the North American Soccer League (NASL), and the following season, under the leadership of Phil Woosnam, the Chiefs won the NASL Championship.

While future Atlanta teams never achieved the early success of the 1968 championship squad, the brief exposure to the Chiefs left a permanent impression on Christian. He still remembers the charisma of Coach Woosnam, who eventually left Atlanta to serve as commissioner of the NASL. No doubt the young Christian also remembered the skills of Kaizer Motaung, Everald Cummings, and Victor Crow, international players who'd joined the Atlanta franchise to help bolster performance. Each player had starred on his respective national team before moving to Atlanta. The South African Motaung finished his three-year Chiefs career with an impressive 32 goals, including 16 goals in 15 straight matches during his debut season. Through attending the Chiefs' practices and a handful of matches, as well as reading how-to books on coaching soccer, Christian learned the basic fundamentals of the game. He also understood that developing a successful soccer program meant recruiting experienced players from the national and international arena.

Unlike DeGroat, Christian jumped at the opportunity to recruit. Early on Jim Jones provided Christian with a soccer budget and reiterated his position of financing a blue-chip player. Christian remembers telephoning international contacts he'd made at Vanderbilt about prospective teammates, writing countless letters encouraging prospects to attend ASU, and driving as far as Baltimore and Miami to watch matches and to talk to prospective players. He finagled the system, recruiting players through work-study programs and with the promise of playing on artificial turf, which had just been constructed for the football team in Kidd Brewer Stadium.[8]

Remarkably, Christian produced a winning squad his first season, the same year that the university joined the Southern Conference. After a 9–0 trouncing at the hands of UNC Chapel Hill in their first match, he converted a group of "unskilled but talented" athletes into a successful soccer team.[9] Appalachian held its own in most conference matches, ending the 1971 season with six wins and five losses. Over the next several seasons Christian recruited players outside North Carolina, among them Frank Kerno, a three-time All-Conference selection from New Jersey; John "Stump" Gimenez, a two-time Southern Conference Most Valuable Player and team captain from Florida; and Fernando Ojeda, a Costa Rican–born All-Conference player, also from Florida.

Through hard work and determination, he also landed international players—Nigerians Emmanuel Igbeka and Emmanuel Udogu and Israeli David Mor among them. Igbeka won All-Conference Selections each year he played at Appalachian; Udogu, a Southern Conference Player of the Year, also earned a bid for All-American. With Mor, a Southern Conference Player of the Year, as well as Bob Hark, Mark Rozanski, Tony Suarez, Peter Gustafson, Michael Somnazu, and a host of other talented players, these Mountaineers led Appalachian to four straight Southern Conference championships. Appalachian finished second in the conference in 1976, and won a fifth Conference title the following year. Christian won Southern Conference Coach of the Year in 1974, 1975 and 1977. From 1972 to 1977 he compiled an unprecedented 55–13–3 win-loss record. His 1975 team went 12–1, beating UNC Chapel Hill and conference rival Davidson during the regular season. They lost 3–1 to a Trinidadian-led Howard University team in Appalachian's first NCAA National Tournament.

According to Jones, who became Appalachian's athletic director in 1972, Vaughn Christian was a "promoter" who "took ASU soccer to a more competitive level." In order to familiarize the student body with a lesser-known sport like soccer, Christian turned his players into "showmen."[10] He put them on the field at halftime during football games to show off their skills. He also had them play volleyball, with their feet, in between games at volleyball matches and at halftime during basketball games. The performances paid off. Soccer was "fast becoming a favorite game of ASU sport fans," a student journalist wrote in the school's 1975 edition of *Rhododendron*. That same journalist quoted Christian outlining his winning philosophy:

> The unique thing about soccer is its creativity ... I can't dictate to my players when they are on the field. It's them—their ability, creativity, and finesse that wins their games. The skill is important but it is the creativity and imagination—looking for plays and being there—that wins it.[11]

Christian's teams consistently lured thousands of students to home matches. Several photographs from *The Rhododendron* show one side of Kidd Brewer Stadium filled to capacity during Appalachian soccer games. The university also chartered buses to carry faithful fans to out-of-town games. Jones remembers how students "used to mob Christian after Appalachian victories."[12]

If Christian emphasized the importance of creativity and finesse, he also depended on gifted athletes to win games. His most talented player in the early 1970s was a striker named Emmanuel "Ike" Udogu. Raised in Warri Delta State, Nigeria, Udogu grew up playing soccer in the streets. He honed his game by kicking balls on the local recreation center's soccer fields, built by the British during colonialism. In high school Udogu was team captain and earned a reputation as one of the top players in the Delta region. While his family supported his athleticism—he was a talented tennis player as well—their "number one concern was education."[13] A gifted student, Udogu eventually moved to the United States, where he enrolled in Montreat College, a private, Christian liberal arts school located in North Carolina's Appalachian Mountains. While he wasn't studying, he played on Montreat's soccer team. Christian heard about Udogu's accomplishments on the field, drove to the school to watch him play, and recruited him to Appalachian in 1973. Udogu became the first ASU soccer player to receive a meaningful scholarship. He was also the first black to play on an Appalachian soccer team.

To Christian, Udogu was "one of the finest athletes in the state."[14] During his first season at Appalachian Udogu scored 22 goals, breaking the old school record of 19 set by team captain John Gimenez. He also contributed nine assists during his 1973 debut and helped lead his team to a second conference championship. Udogu's next year was even more impressive. He broke his old record by 10 goals and earned honors as the Southern Conference Player of the Year, Appalachian soccer's first. He also was the only Southern Conference player named to the All-South soccer team, selected by university coaches throughout the South. After the end-of-year tallies, he received the most prestigious nod for All-American. He "was like poetry in motion," Christian remembers, and when playing beside teammates like David Mor, an Olympian forward from Israel who scored 27 goals that same season, he was difficult to stop.[15] During his senior year Udogu led the Mountaineers to a 12–1 season and first-place finish in the conference. In 1986, he became the first person associated with ASU's soccer program to be elected to the university's Hall of Fame.

Udogu not only helped establish student interest in soccer but also set in motion the recruitment of other international players, including fellow Nigerians. By far the most important recruit, and arguably the best player to ever wear an Appalachian jersey, was Thompson Usiyan. Raised in Nigeria's Delta State like Udogu, Usiyan made the Nigerian Olympic squad in 1976 after proving his talent on a government-sponsored municipal team. After opening-day ceremonies in Montreal, Nigeria joined 28 other nations, most of them African, in boycotting the Olympics over a South African apartheid incident. As an 18-year-old, Usiyan spoke to Nigerian commissioners about remaining in North America to pursue an education and to play soccer. Clemson and Howard University recruited him, but he chose to attend ASU, following in the footsteps of another Nigerian already playing for the Mountaineers named Michael Somnazu. Usiyan also was impressed by Vaughn Christian's persistence. According to Usiyan, the Appalachian soccer coach wrote him a letter almost every other week, trying to persuade the young Nigerian to attend ASU.[16] His decision to join the Mountaineers proved to be the most rewarding one in Appalachian soccer history.

Usiyan played at ASU from 1977 to 1980, setting more Appalachian, Southern Conference, and NCAA records than any other Mountaineer player. He accomplished these feats in three and a half seasons, sitting out most of the 1979 season with a knee injury. He's still the only soccer player in Southern Conference history to win Player of the Year honors three separate times. He scored 22 goals in his first season and helped lead the Mountaineers to an 11–2–1 season. He topped this mark the following year with 34 goals, including an amazing seven goals and one assist against George Washington University in an NCAA tournament game. This performance still stands as the second most goals by a single player in an NCAA match. Appalachian finished the season 10–1–2, losing to Clemson by a score of 2–1 in overtime during the NCAA tournament. Usiyan finished his career in 1980 with an unprecedented conference record 46 goals (2.71 goals per game). The Mountaineers posted 14 wins that season, including a 3–2 victory against nationally ranked Clemson University, at home. Usiyan set NCAA records for Career Goals Leader (109), Career Scoring Leader (255 points), and Season Scoring Leader (108 points). In 1989, he became the second Mountaineer soccer player to be inducted into Appalachian's Hall of Fame.

Even after a successful 15-year professional career, including leading the United Soccer League (USL) in scoring in 1984, Usiyan remains humble about his collegiate accomplishments. "I was good because we had other good players," he remembered in an interview. "We had Esabamen, Igbeka, Somnazu, and [Mark] Schwartz ... I was a good finisher.... They'd work on getting me the ball and I'd try to kick it in."[17] Although Usiyan did play with a number of accomplished players—Esabamen scored 18 goals in 1979, while Schwartz made 20 in 1981—few people would deny the national caliber of Usiyan's play. No one remembers his remarkable performances better than Hank Steinbrecher, Appalachian's fourth soccer coach.

After an unprecedented seven-season, 71–22–4 record (.753 pct.) as head coach, Vaughn Christian stepped down to return to the classroom. He turned over the reins to Steinbrecher. Unlike Christian, Steinbrecher grew up playing competitive soccer during his youth. In the 1960s he honed his skills in the German American Soccer League in New York, and then he played as a collegiate starter at Davis & Elkins College in Elkin, West Virginia. He played semi-professional soccer in Connecticut before taking a job in North Carolina at Warren Wilson College, where he coached from 1973 to 1978. Steinbrecher also refereed local collegiate matches, where he got to know Vaughn Christian. If the opportunity arose, he took his team to Appalachian to scrimmage. When the coaching position at Appalachian opened up, Steinbrecher jumped at the chance.

"I inherited one of the best teams in the United States," Steinbrecher reminisced in a telephone interview. "I was lucky." Unlike DeGroat a decade before, Steinbrecher played to win. Whenever his team stepped on the field, "it was a war." The most effective way to win battles was to turn to Usiyan. Steinbrecher can't find enough praise for the star forward: "Thompson Usiyan was the first guy at practice and the last player to leave.... He was brilliant ... I never saw a more gifted player at that age." As an experienced player-coach, Steinbrecher was still young enough to train with his team. He remembers that Usiyan "came by you like a NASCAR car, but you never heard him."[18]

While he witnessed Usiyan's seven-goal performance against George Washington University, Steinbrecher's most memorable moment came when Appalachian beat George Washington University during an NCAA playoff match. The Mountaineers were down a goal, with only a few minutes left to play. Appalachian scored, and then immediately stole the ball from GWU. A pass went to Usiyan, who carried the ball the length of the field, outmaneuvering every player on the George Washington team. He scored a last-second goal to give Appalachian the victory. During his three-year tenure at Appalachian's helm, Steinbrecher compiled a 33–10–2 record, garnering three conference championships and two NCAA post-season appearances. The Mountaineer coach would be the first to admit that Usyian helped pave the way.

Steinbrecher also knew the importance of team play and recognized that no matter the caliber of an individual performance, it took 11 players to win a soccer match. He praises a number of Usiyan's teammates—Mark Schwartz and Keith Layne among them—and emphasizes that his international connection went beyond Nigerian borders. "I jumped on what Vaughn built," Steinbrecher told us, but he also traveled in other directions to recruit. He remembers flying to Guyana to land Layne, and he signed another player from

Guyana living in New York. One of his players also came from Chile. "We had guys from everywhere ... South America, South Florida, England, the Caribbean."[19] In fact, Steinbrecher recalls players from 17 different nationalities playing during his tenure. On his most accomplished team from 1980, which saw seven Mountaineers make the All-Conference team, only three of 18 players came from North Carolina.

One of the most difficult challenges for Steinbrecher was managing such a diverse group of players. He experienced language clashes while trying to coordinate multiple distinct personalities. George Duprey, one of several players from Miami, remembers that "Coach ... taught us a lot about brotherhood."[20] Despite his achievements on and off the field, Steinbrecher faced an insufficient budget. "I read the other day that the University of San Francisco—they're ranked No. 1 now—has a travel budget of $17,000," he stated in a 1980 newspaper article. "Our whole program doesn't get that much!"[21] Steinbrecher remembers traveling with his teams to out-of-state matches and using all-you-can-eat salad bars for 99 cents to keep his players full. "Every coach will say you never have enough support," he concluded.[22]

The dynasties that Vaughn Christian and Hank Steinbrecher built in the 1970s were the envy of schools across the country. By the end of 1980 the Mountaineers had climbed to a Number 8 national ranking in the NCAA first division. They had managed showings in the Top 20 since 1971, when Christian turned Appalachian's program into a legitimate varsity sport. ASU held top honors in the Southern Conference in seven of the last eight years of the decade. Incredibly, this success apparently wasn't enough. By the end of Steinbrecher's third season, the university administration initiated plans to downsize the soccer program and turn its support to high-end revenue sports, even though Christian and Steinbrecher had led the soccer team to seven straight seasons without a conference loss. "They started talking to me about reducing scholarships [to three], at a time when we were outdrawing the football team," Steinbrecher recalled in an interview. Disillusioned with the lack of support, he left ASU for a head coaching position at Boston University. Looking back on his Appalachian coaching days, Steinbrecher commented, assuredly, "I think ASU had a goldmine and they wasted it."[23]

1980s–Present: Into the Club System

Art Rex coached the Mountaineer team from 1981 to 1997, longer than any other coach in ASU history. During his first year he continued the unbeaten conference streak started by his predecessors, which gave ASU eight straight years with a combined 49–0–2 conference record. During his 17-year tenure he recorded more victories than any other Appalachian soccer coach, guiding his team to four Southern Conference titles. He also received Southern Conference Coach of the Year honors in 1984, 1985, and 1989. A Department of Athletics publication from 1996 lists additional achievements under his leadership: "30 Mountaineers ... received All-Southern Conference honors 61 times, seven players ... selected to the All-South squad on 10 occasions, four players ... tabbed Southern Conference Player of the Year six times, 12 players ... made the Southern Conference Player of the Year six times, 12 players ... made the Southern Conference All-Tournament list 19 times, and one received All-Tournament MVP laurels."[24] These honors alone place Rex in a distinguished category by himself.

Rex came to ASU in 1979 as an MA student in geography. He also expressed an interest in an assistant coaching position under Steinbrecher, whom he knew from previous years in competitive soccer. Rex coached under Steinbrecher for two seasons. Like his New York predecessor, he had enjoyed a successful career as a youth player. He honed his skills in and around Pittsburgh, playing in high school and for a club team sponsored by a local bar. A 1977 Slippery Rock University graduate, he also captained his collegiate soccer team for two seasons. As a forward for the SRU Rockets, he set a number of records, including most goals in a game (six, against his father's alma mater, Geneva College), most season goals, and most career goals. He played professionally for three seasons in the ASL and MISL. One of those years he worked on his graduate degree during the fall semester, and then joined the four-month professional season the following spring. Rex knew the game well, and when Steinbrecher stepped down he willingly accepted the head coaching position.

With 147 wins under his leadership, Rex coached several memorable players. By the time he left the Mountaineers in 1982, Mark Schwartz, who played under Rex during his tenure as both an assistant and a head coach, finished his career with 54 goals, second only to Thompson Usiyan. Schwartz ended second behind Usiyan in season goals, season shots, and career shots as well. Rex coached other record holders—Scott Anderson, John Nedd, Robert Wilcher, David Terry, and Carlos Lee among them. Like Schwartz, Anderson won Southern Conference Player of the Year in 1983. Nedd, from Trinidad, took similar honors the next two years. Lee earned the award in 1989. Nedd was inducted into Appalachian's Hall of Fame in 2000; Schwartz followed four years later. Wilcher, who won All-Conference honors from 1982 to 1985, was inducted into the Hall of Fame in 2006. Andy Salandy was another Rex standout, becoming the only player to be named MVP of the Southern Conference Tournament (in 1990). Brian Jillings, Mark Hemphill, Tim Ross, Christian Tam, Todd Johnson, Art Patsch, Ray Wells, Ryan Anderson, Paul Stahlschmidt, and Kevin Turner are just a few of the other talented players who played on successful teams under Rex.

The longer Rex coached, however, the more he saw Appalachian soccer change. If the athletic department "talked" to Steinbrecher about reducing soccer scholarships, it fully implemented those changes during Rex's career. In the course of his tenure as head coach, Rex's teams averaged 3.5–4.5 scholarships a year. The reductions couldn't have come at a more inopportune time. By the late 1980s the youth soccer craze that had started the decade before finally caught up with the university system. Subsequently, more and more schools across the country started funding soccer programs, which meant that under-subsidized programs like ASU's couldn't compete for the most talented players. At the same time, the NCAA started clamping down on international recruits. More than one nationally ranked team, including two that ASU faced during its Golden Era, fielded squads almost exclusively made up of foreign players. As a way to discourage recruiting players born outside the United States, the NCAA slapped one-year probations on any university that signed an international player over 20 years of age. In addition, the "Nigerian connection" Christian implemented and that Rex had enjoyed as an assistant coach under Steinbrecher virtually dried up, as the Nigerian government stopped subsidizing its best players. Rex turned to Trinidad and Tobago for talented prospects, but eventually players from this and other countries started signing contracts with European teams whose professional leagues had developed into highly competitive and lucrative enterprises.

Rex wouldn't settle for second- or third-place conference teams, however. "I wanted to win [the conference even if it took] every four or five years," he recalled in an interview.[25] In the 1980s he achieved that goal, and more. During his first year his team went 10–6, winning the Southern Conference championship. Despite a lackluster second season, his squad captured another conference title in 1982. The Mountaineers repeated back-to-back championships in 1984 and 1985, posting 27 wins. His last title came in 1989, when his team went 12–8 overall. As time passed, though, Rex realized the difficult challenges he faced: "I didn't mind building a program, but we just didn't have the money to sustain it like an Akron or a Wake Forest or a Chapel Hill." Ranked fourth among Southern Conference coaches in "Most Overall Wins," Rex recognized that after 17 years he could no longer "affect change." In 1997, facing a fifth-place finish in the conference and a university that didn't "see soccer as a priority," he handed in his resignation.[26]

Since Rex stepped down, ASU has hired six different coaches. Paul Stahlschmidt, one of Rex's players from the 1990s, lasted the longest. T. J. Kostecky, whose team posted a 13–8 record the year after Rex resigned, won Southern Conference Coach of the Year during his first season. He left the next year. Aidan Heaney, who coached from 1999 to 2000, received the same award in his second season. Dave Golan took over from Heaney, posting 23 wins against 13 losses and a tie before leaving after his second year. Stahlschmidt, who went through several rebuilding seasons, placed six players on All-Conference teams his first three years. He stepped down in 2008, when Shaun Pendleton, a native of Sheffield, England, took control. Pendleton compiled a 27–26–4 record before his tragic death, at the outset of his fourth season, in 2011. Matt Nelson, who had assisted at Appalachian since 2008, replaced Pendleton. As of 2014 he's still head coach, posting an impressive 10–5–4 record the year he took the helm. Nelson received a Southern Conference Coach of the Year award in 2011, rallying the Mountaineers to a 7–0–4 winning streak, their longest since Usiyan started for Appalachian in 1978. From 1998 to 2011 these coaches compiled a 133–112 win-loss record.

The background of each coach highlights the requisite credentials that are expected at the collegiate level today. Kostecky came to ASU from Pfeiffer College, where he compiled a 46–27–5 record. He captured two Carolina Conference titles and was twice named Carolinas Conference Coach of the Year. Born in Newcastle, England, Heaney played collegiate ball in Charlotte, leading the 49ers to a first-time NCAA tournament in 1991. He played in the USISL for two years before signing with the New England Revolution of the MSL, from 1996 to 1997. After assistant coaching stints at UNC Chapel Hill and Penn State University, he transferred to ASU. Dave Golan played for the University of South Carolina Gamecocks (1984–1988) before coaching as an assistant for six years at his alma mater. Stahlschmidt played for Appalachian in the early 1990s, and then took an assistant coaching position at Pfeiffer College. After two years he was appointed head coach at Belmont Abbey, where his teams posted over 50 wins and captured a conference championship. Before taking over from Stahlschmidt, Pendleton coached 22 seasons at Lynn University in Boca Raton, Florida, where his teams chalked up an unprecedented 347–79–18 record. Pendleton also starred as a collegiate player at Akron and played four seasons in the American Indoor Soccer Association before turning to coaching. Nelson played goalkeeper at Lynn under Pendleton. He holds university records in most starts, wins, shutouts, and saves. He also played professionally after graduating from college in 2000 and was selected as a USL First Division All-Star in 2006.

In other words, coaching a university team in this day and age of modern soccer is far removed from Vaughn Christian's time, when a physical education teacher with limited experience could successfully manage a varsity soccer team. For the last three decades college coaches have had to earn their appointments, with hard-fought, proven records. The more playing experience, the better, and without coaching more than a handful of successful competitive teams, one's chances of getting hired have already started to fade.

Credentials don't mean a hill of beans without adequate university and community support, however. As we pointed out in the previous chapter, part of the blame for the general disinterest in university soccer falls on the club system that typically nurtures today's collegiate players. The exclusive, closed system that defines so many club programs has failed to make inroads into the larger community. There is rarely a solid fan base for club teams outside of family and close friends. If the student population of a university such as Appalachian is not part of this relatively small support group, and it rarely is, it makes sense that the vast majority of students would hardly care about attending a university soccer match.

But as Hank Steinbrecher points out, rarely does a university coach feel that he has enough support. The university is also at fault, especially the higher-up, administrative powers that control finances. In an interview Art Rex mentioned that it's pointless "to be bitter" about the lack of university support. "It's a business decision," he argued. ASU chose to support football and basketball and not make soccer "a priority" sport. He also asked, "Would I like to see a 3,000-seat covered stadium out there [Ted Mackorell Soccer Complex] instead of 960 seats? Absolutely. If you had 3,000 seats, you would have to build a much bigger parking lot."[27] A bigger parking lot translates into more cars, and ultimately thousands of additional fans.

Because the university shares its current facility, Rex believes that ASU should build better "synergy" with the local community. He stressed that the university must find a way "to get the kids and all the local teams [they play on] to come to the games."[28] In a university program that still considers soccer a "minor" sport, synergy may well be the answer. It might be a long time coming, though. A few years ago the university finished constructing a major food court in the heart of campus, capable of feeding thousands of ASU students. For ambience, the interior designer superimposed hundreds of ASU photographs on the cafeteria walls. Once again, not one of them highlights Appalachian soccer.

* * * *

The roller-coaster ride of Appalachian's soccer program reflects the many ups and downs of collegiate soccer in the more than six decades since the end of World War II. The war had actually reduced the number of collegiate teams from a pre-war high of 80 in 1940 to 42 teams in 1945. As we mentioned in an earlier chapter, thanks to the GI Bill, the growing university enrollment that cut across socioeconomic class lines, and the influx of international students, the number of university teams grew steadily in the late 1940s and throughout the 1950s. The official introduction of men's soccer at Appalachian in 1961 coincided with the national leap in the number of university soccer programs.

Appalachian's first coaches typified coaches of their day. Some coaches of major soccer programs in the 1950s and 1960s were foreign-born ex-professionals, such as Jimmy Mills at Haverford, Bill Jeffrey at Penn State, and Gus Donoghue at the University of San Francisco. Others, including Charley Scott at Penn, Pete Leanness at Temple, and Whitey Burnham at Dartmouth, had played on the few university teams that existed before and immediately after the war. But most college coaches, like Appalachian's DeGroat and Christian, had no playing experience. Mickey Cochran, who took the coaching position at Johns Hopkins in 1953, remembers that "most of us were physical education majors. We took classes in the various sports.... We learned the game by coaching it. When I was at Hopkins, I had to coach track, soccer, and freshman baseball, all because I was a physical education major." Cochran and Len Oliver, a star for Temple's powerhouse squad in the early 1950s who'd developed his skills in Philadelphia's ethnic leagues and high school, recall that because most coaches lacked soccer experience, "a college team's fortunes would ebb and flow based on its [players'] talent. Coaching often had very little to do with the success of the teams."[29] Such was the situation of ASU's early coaches.

Players in those early years came from varied backgrounds that characterized the changing landscape of university campuses. Many of the strongest programs in the 1950s and early 1960s drew on players who'd developed in urban ethnic soccer clubs. Teams from Temple, Penn State, and West Chester drew on the soccer tradition of working-class neighborhoods in and around Philadelphia, while St. Louis University recruited first-generation students from that city's strong tradition of soccer in ethnic clubs and high schools. Seton Hall, Brooklyn College, and City College of New York recruited heavily from the ethnic neighborhoods in New Jersey and New York. Coaches often called these "Sunday players," since most of the ethnic club teams played their matches on Sundays.[30] While most university teams played 10–12 matches per season, university players from ethnic club backgrounds often played another 40–50 matches a year, giving them a decided advantage over other players.

Other productive university programs relied on international students. In the 1950s, the highly successful University of San Francisco fielded teams made up almost entirely of foreign players. The same was true of UCLA. As we point out in Chapter 5, the explosion in international students after World War II included many students who'd played both informally and formally in their home countries. With the relative dearth of home-grown talent available to universities, most competitive programs sought at least one or two international student athletes to serve as the nucleus of the team. This was Christian's strategy at Appalachian in the 1970s. It worked beautifully.

Two other sources of talent were available in those early years of university soccer. One of these was players coming out of prep schools who went on to play at elite private colleges that often had better soccer programs than large universities. Tom Fox, an outstanding player for Williams College in the late 1950s and early 1960s, remembers, "None of us played soccer until prep school in New England. We never played soccer on Sunday or club soccer. We only knew a highly physical kick-and-run game ... an aggressive, in-your-face style."[31] Dick Packer, a prep school product from the suburbs of Philadelphia who starred for Penn State in the 1950s, noted, "We didn't have the exquisite skills of the urban guys who grew up with the game in the streets, but we had guts, determination and a hard-nosed grind-them-down spirit."[32] Small private colleges like Wheaton, Springfield College (DeGroat's alma mater), and Williams College thrived in those early years with prep school players.

As we pointed out at the beginning of this chapter, ASU's source of talent in the formative years of the early 1960s was similar to that of other small universities entering the world of collegiate soccer: athletic individuals who had little or no experience with soccer, but whose athleticism allowed them to develop into reasonably competent players. Even by 1971, when Christian assumed coaching duties, the team still relied on these athletic individuals, mostly from the football team, who'd never played soccer.

With little access to recruits from urban, ethnic leagues or prep school players who chose to attend elite universities, ASU in the 1970s moved in the only direction it could to build a competitive soccer program: a nucleus of international players. With a small but significant financial boost from the university, Christian recruited those few outstanding international players who would transform a ragtag team from a small state university located in the hinterlands of rural Appalachia into a nationally ranked team competing equally with more established teams in the country.

As that core of international players grew, ASU eventually made its way into the NCAA playoffs. Those playoffs officially began in 1959. They were dominated for more than a decade by a home-grown squad from St. Louis University that had recruited players from the long-standing city leagues and high school teams that had a deep history. St. Louis won four of the first five national championships and a total of 10 (they were co-champions with Michigan State in 1967) of the initial 15. From 1959 through 1974, they failed to make it to the finals only three times—in 1964, 1966, and 1968.[33]

Other national championship teams from that era evidenced a mix of home-grown talent from urban ethnic leagues and international players. San Francisco (1966) and Howard (1971, 1974) fielded teams heavily stacked with international players. When ASU played in its first NCAA championship series in 1975, it lost to the reigning champs from Howard and their mainly Trinidadian players.

While San Francisco dominated in the mid- to late 1970s, winning the championship four times between 1975 and 1980, university soccer began to change in the next decade, as major universities with lucrative athletic budgets and modern facilities began to catch up with programs in smaller universities. The initial products of the pay-to-play club system were increasingly coming of age as recruits in the expanding university soccer scene. Major sports universities like Indiana, Clemson, UCLA, and Duke won championships in the 1980s. The 1990s saw Virginia, which won four consecutive titles from 1991 to 1994, emerge as a powerhouse, alongside the University of Wisconsin.[34]

More recently, no single college team has dominated NCAA play. In the past 14 years, 11 different teams have won the championship. Only Indiana (2003, 2004, and 2012) and North Carolina (2001, 2011) have repeated in the championship bracket.[35]

Since the advent of Title 9 in 1974, which requires relative equity between women's and men's collegiate athletics, soccer has grown into a major women's sport on campuses across the United States. In 1982, the first year of the NCAA women's soccer championships, only 77 collegiate women's teams competed in the entire country. A decade later that number had grown to 348. The University of North Carolina has dominated women's soccer from the beginning of collegiate play. They won the first three championships and 13 of the next 16 through the new millennium. They won nine championships in a row between 1986 and 1994. Since 2001, UNC's dominance has diminished slightly, as they've won *only* 5 of 13 championships. The only other universities to repeat as champions in 32 years of women's play are Portland (2002, 2005) and Notre Dame (2004, 2010). In all, UNC has won 21 of 32 championships.[36]

ASU's varsity women's team, which began competing in 1994, has never achieved the notoriety of the men's team, especially those from its golden era of the 1970s and early 1980s. The women have racked up only seven winning seasons in 20 years, compiling a total record of 148–193–39. Their most successful years were 2003–2007, when they compiled a 51–36–9 record, with winning teams in four out of five of those years. Despite the overall performance, attendance figures have increased slightly over the years. The women's program averaged 311 in match attendance in 2012, compared to a meager 132 in 2006.[37]

Ben Popoola coached the Lady Mountaineers during that stretch. A Nigerian who'd performed for five years on his country's national team, Popoola played collegiate soccer at Clemson University in the late 1970s. He won Outstanding Player honors in the Atlantic Coast Conference in 1977. Ironically, Popoola played for the Clemson team that twice eliminated ASU's men's team from the NCAA tournament in 1977 and 1978. After graduating in 1979, he played in the waning years of the North American Soccer League with Kansas City, Chicago, Cleveland, and Memphis. He also coached the Nigerian U-19 national team at the 2003 Women's World Championships in Canada.

Since Popoola's Appalachian tenure (1997–2008), the women's team has been unable to attract a coach with similar stellar credentials as a player. Sarah Strickland, the current coach, played collegiate soccer at George Mason University, leading them to two NCAA tournament appearances in the late 1990s. Before becoming head coach at ASU, she served brief stints as assistant coach at Troy State, Auburn, and Mississippi State University. Although her overall record is 29–34–12, her team managed back-to-back winning seasons in 2012 and 2013. Drawing its players from within the state and nationally, Appalachian's women's team guarantees a competitive match with whomever it plays.

* * * *

Like other university programs, the men's and women's soccer teams of ASU have struggled for the past three decades against high-end revenue sports that bring big bucks and publicity to universities across the nation. This struggle ballooned dramatically when ASU's football team won three straight national FCS championships (2005–2007). Along the way Appalachian also beat Michigan, a perennial FBS powerhouse ranked fifth in the nation at the time. ASU collected $300,000 for the game, a cover story in *Sports Illustrated,* and a major push from alumni to move up to FBS football. In the fall of 2014, the latter goal became a reality.

The seemingly endless struggle continues. Yet the current men's head coach, Matt Nelson, remains optimistic, choosing to see the silver lining in even slight signs of increasing university support. Nelson points to "about a 20 percent increase in funds for scholarships over the past few years" and attendance of more than 600 per home match in 2013. He feels that ASU's administration is committed to a successful soccer program. But with only 6.4 scholarships in 2013, recruiting top players is difficult. Because scholarships for in-state students go further, most recruiting occurs through the four North Carolina academy programs. ASU's emphasis on recruiting a core of international players, which began in the 1970s, continues. However, as Nelson admits, "The best international recruits go to the major programs." Still, the large pool of quality players in other countries means that ASU can sign its share of international recruits. Nelson's seven recruits for the 2014 season include two players from Australia and France.

Despite the optimism, obstacles still remain: too few scholarships; life in the shadow of football; tough recruiting in competition with major soccer programs; an apathetic fan base; and a stadium more than three miles from campus. To add insult to injury, the nearest bus stop to the soccer complex is more than a thousand yards away.

10

From Boone to Siler City: Case Studies in Latino Soccer

In one of those rare moments of serendipity, Appalachian State University selected a book for its 2007 freshman summer reading program about a successful North Carolina high school soccer team made up of Hispanic players. The selection of *A Home on the Field* (2006) by journalist Paul Cuadros, who also coached the team, created a campus and community-wide discussion on the transformations and struggles resulting from Latino immigration into the United States. Initially the influx of immigrants to the small town of Siler City had created racist reactions and anti-immigration demonstrations; outside agitator and white supremacist David Duke had attended rallies organized by local residents to protest the number of Hispanics moving into the area to work in the chicken-processing industry. As a guest of honor at ASU in 2007, Cuadros spoke eloquently about the positive role that high school soccer had played in Siler City, not only for the Latino boys and their families but also for the entire community. He described how Siler City had been through an "anger stage," and then stated that the town transcended initial hostilities and rallied behind the soccer team's success. "The soccer team's victory in the state championship helped people in the town understand and realize that this community and these kids are just like any other kids at the high school," Cuadros remembered. Winning the championship match helped old-time residents "identify with that group."[1]

The visit by Cuadros to Boone coincided with the documentary video we were making on youth soccer called *Offside(s): Soccer in Small-Town America*. We jumped at the opportunity to participate. We volunteered to lead discussion groups on the book, to introduce Cuadros at various campus events, and to show him around the community. When we had him alone we pummeled him with questions, knowing that during our three years of coaching at the Parks and Recreation level, we had coached not one Hispanic. We wondered why Hispanics were not a bigger part of the cultural landscape of U.S. soccer, and why there were separate leagues for Latinos and other groups from local communities. We asked why Hispanics typically did not participate in Parks and Recreation soccer programs even though they were recruited to join across the state. Cuadros and his book resonated with our attempts to understand the larger social dynamics of soccer in the Boone community. We clung to his story.

Actually, we knew that our coaching experience didn't accurately reflect the dramatic growth of the local Latino population. As North Carolinians, we were well aware of the demographic shifts taking place in our state, including those in the Appalachian region in which we live. Because of our interests in ethnicity, as well as cultural studies and related academic subjects, we took note of the number of Latinos moving into the area. In Mecklenburg County, which includes Charlotte, the state's largest city, 7,000 Hispanics reported living there in 1990. By 2000, that number had climbed to 45,000, a 570 percent growth rate.[2] Similar growth had occurred in smaller cities and towns across the state, where workers found employment in construction and the food processing industry. Siler City reflects this change, with Hispanics representing less than 40 percent of the town's total population in 2000. Ten years later this same group represented almost 50 percent of the total.[3] In 2000, Boone's Watauga County reported almost as many Latinos living in the area as African Americans—in a state that had reported a 22 percent black population a decade earlier. By the next census Hispanics outnumbered blacks in our county two to one.[4] According to a recent North Carolina state government publication, the immigrant population from or rooted in Latin America "grew by 943 percent from 1990 to 2010." As of 2010, Latinos, the vast majority of whom are rooted in Mexico, comprised 8.4 percent of the state's population.[5]

We also knew that such growth didn't occur in a vacuum. Social activities accompany these demographic shifts, often defining how immigrant groups assimilate into other communities and cultures. For Hispanics living in North Carolina and the rest of the country, soccer is by far the most popular cultural activity. "Soccer affiliation easily represents the largest demographic participation in voluntary associations by Latinas and Latinos," sports historian Juan Javier Pescador writes in "Soccer (Fútbol) in the Americas." "Latin Americans and U.S.-born Latinos participate in the sport on a regular basis and have made it not only an integral part of their recreational activities and leisure behavior but also a singular feature of the Latina/o popular culture and experience in the United States."[6] This "singular feature" manifested itself on a large scale in North Carolina when the Mexican national team played Iceland in a friendly on March 24, 2010, in Charlotte's Bank of America stadium. A sold-out crowd of over 63,000 fans decorated the stadium with thousands of Mexican flags and the green, red, and white colors of *El Tri*. Cuadros identified similar enthusiasm in *A Home on the Field,* describing time and again how Latinos across the state spend hours playing and watching the sport. He reiterated this passion for soccer when he spoke at ASU.

After Cuadros left Appalachian, we continued to probe. We read other authors writing about soccer and immigration. We talked to local and state officials about recent immigration trends, and which government offices in North Carolina helped Latinos to more effectively transition into new environments, socially as well as culturally. We spoke to a variety of people, both Latino and non–Latino, asking questions and looking for answers. Not surprisingly, we discovered what many researchers across the United States learn about population shifts, Latinos, and a love for soccer: the answers to our numerous questions could be found in our own backyard.

Liga de Fútbol: La Michoacána

Alfredo Álvarez was born in Los Angeles, California, in 1973. When he was seven years old he moved with his family to Degollado, located in the southwestern Mexican state of Jalisco, where his parents were born. A decade later, at the invitation of a friend, Alfredo returned to the United States to work in a Mexican restaurant. This time he relocated to the South, settling in the Appalachian Mountains in Boone, North Carolina. He worked his way up through the business and eventually became co-owner. Twenty years later he's still in the area, with a wife and three kids. He's also a partner in five Mexican restaurants in Boone and the surrounding area.

Like so many others rooted in Mexico who moved north during the 1990s, Alfredo brought his passion for soccer (or *fútbol,* as it's known throughout Latin America) with him to the United States. The first couple of years he couldn't find a local league in which to play. To satisfy his craving for the sport, he traveled 50 miles to Taylorsville on weekends to join pick-up games. Later he transferred to an actual league in nearby Morganton, which drew players from local hatcheries, processing plants, and feed mills owned by Case Farms. The giant chicken conglomerate employed a number of Guatemalan and Mexican immigrants, who teamed up against each other on the soccer field to display their national pride. By 2002, comfortably settled in Boone and starting a family, Alfredo led a push to start a league closer to home. But with little spare time on his hands, he turned to brothers Gerardo and Manuel Alcaraz, who'd moved into the area 13 years earlier from the Mexican state of Michoacán, to plan and organize it. With Alfredo and a handful of other friends, they started their own league—La Michoacána.

In the mid–1990s, the Latino population in Boone still hadn't taken off the way it had in Charlotte and other metropolitan areas. Hispanics in Watauga County and the surrounding area had been limited primarily to working in the Christmas tree industry, which discouraged new immigrants from moving west into the mountains. By the start of the new millennium, however, when the university and local community started to grow, more and more Mexican families joined fathers, husbands, and friends living in Boone. Latinos soon established a noticeable presence in the small Appalachian town. Yet even then, while workers found new employment in construction, furniture factories, and various service jobs, the expanding Latino population in Watauga County couldn't field its own league. Alfredo and his friends recruited two all–Hispanic teams from Boone, including one from his own restaurant, Los Arcoiris, but they had to recruit players from Jefferson, Newland, and other nearby communities to form a competitive league.

At first glance, the early years of La Michoacána don't seem too impressive. Only six teams competed during the first season. They played most of their matches on Sundays, starting in the early morning. For a soccer pitch, they converted a dusty football field located on the lower level of a county elementary school. Because it included only one section of aluminum bleachers (located at the far end of the pitch), fans typically sat on a hillside overlooking the field. There was no shade to protect them from the glaring sun. To add to the inconvenience, players and fans shared a parking lot with a local church that rented school space for Sunday morning services. For a competitive soccer league, the arrangements weren't exactly pristine.

A closer look at the league, however, reveals that over time La Michoacána evolved into a highly functional and successful soccer organization. Each match showcased a referee and two linesmen, talented players and teams, and a dedicated following. Within a few years the league supported twice-a-year seasons—at the time one of the most competitive soccer venues in Boone outside university soccer. The first season started in early spring and continued into mid-summer. After a short break, a second season began and ran through fall. Each season consisted of 13 games, played by as many as 14 teams from the area. Each team included 18 players, almost all of them Latino. Typically the players ranged in age from 18 to 40. The first eight places in the standings determined who would participate in end-of-season tournaments. The winner of each seasonal tournament played for the league championship at the start of the following spring season. While most competing squads came from Boone, Newland, and Morganton, the tournaments grew, eventually expanding to outlying cities such as Greensboro, Winston-Salem, and Charlotte. Within a few years the tournaments attracted players from the other side of the state, including Wilmington, seven hours away.

Shortly after Cuadros's visit to Appalachian State University, we started attending local Sunday morning matches. We'd finished filming Parks and Recreation soccer for our documentary as well as most of the club, high school, and university soccer months before, but we still needed footage from Latino teams to fully document local soccer venues. After receiving permission from coaches to film our first match—one coach needed a little coaxing, since a few of his players were still undocumented—we settled in to shoot. It didn't take long to discover that Cuadros's "home on the field" metaphor applied to La Michoacána as much as it did to the younger, all–Latino high school team from Siler City. League teams dressed in familiar uniforms reminiscent of Mexico's national team, brandishing names of restaurants, construction companies, and other sponsors that employed them. They also wielded colorful logos of favorite club teams like Las Chivas and Cruz Azul from Mexico's professional league, reminding players of allegiances to their native homeland. Most players arrived hours before scheduled matches to mingle, cheer on friends' teams, or scout opponents they would face later that day. Fans turned out as well, in droves—mothers holding babies; wives and girlfriends shouting encouragement from the sidelines; sons, daughters, and other family members and friends applauding goals as players ran up and down the field. In between matches players and fans socialized, swapping tales about family and friends, especially those still living in Mexico. Everyone also made their way to the mobile food stand run by league organizers to feast on shredded pork tacos, guacamole, homemade salsas, and soft drinks. The music blaring from nearby cars, trucks, and vans added to an environment more akin to a street festival than a weekly soccer match.

Actually, the atmosphere surrounding La Michoacána matches is typical of hundreds of other Hispanic soccer communities across the United States, including a highly active one in Hickory, an hour southeast of Boone. We learned about Hickory's competitive soccer league one evening when we stumbled upon a regional newspaper published in Spanish. Abel García, an avid soccer player and owner of Hickory's WCXN 1170 a.m. radio station, edited the 10-page weekly. Supported by advertisements catering to the Latino community, it carried local soccer stories, published up-to-date statistics for Latino soccer leagues, and touted achievements of talented fútbol players from Mexico and Central American countries. Because we were still shooting our video and found ourselves intrigued by Abel's story, we drove down the mountain to film another league. The local fútbol venue we found in Hickory was even more vigorous than that in Boone. Teams from Greensboro, Raleigh, Winston-Salem, Charlotte, Statesville, Boone, Morganton, and Lincolnton regularly competed on various fields throughout the year. We learned that 18 teams in the community play every two hours (typically on a Saturday or a Sunday) from 7:00 a.m. to 7:00 p.m. We also discovered that soccer was so ingrained in Hickory that the city had become a center for Latino soccer in western North Carolina. The focal point of that center was Abel's radio station. Every Friday afternoon, Abel positioned himself behind suspended microphones and other state-of-the-art sound equipment to broadcast scores for local soccer matches as well as those in Mexico and other countries in Latin America.

According to Marie Price and Courtney Whitworth, "immigrant-run leagues" like La Michoacána and its Hickory neighbor "selectively link immigrants ... with their communities of origin."[7] These leagues "create a cultural space that is familiar, entertaining, practical, inexpensive, transnational ... where immigrants gather to reaffirm their sense of identity and belonging."[8] For both players and fans, they offer the memory of a distant land in a familiar language everyone can understand. As we witnessed, they also "link people with similar levels of resources and information," providing a system that might prolong, or even discourage, cultural and social assimilation while also strengthening the ability to "survive."[9] Because a league like La Michoacána, as well as larger organizations found in bigger cities, commonly field teams comprising of players from the same Mexican or Central American state, if not the same village or town, an even greater sense of bonding can manifest itself on the playing field. As Price and Whitworth point out, the soccer league satisfies "the human desire for status," which drops considerably when Latin American immigrants are ostracized in public, as is often the case, or relegated to undesirable jobs. The distinction received in scoring a goal, blocking a kick, or playing on a team with a shared cultural identity takes on even greater meaning, providing a social standing "that validates one's life as significant and meaningful to others."[10]

The Los Arcoiris teams that Alfredo first sponsored demonstrate the importance of identifying with relatives and friends rooted in a distant land. The first year he formed his restaurant team—practically the entire squad was from the state of Jalisco—Alfredo not only footed the required $300 league registration fee but also bought each player's uniform. The benevolent gesture paid off. Of the 20 league tournaments held from 2002 to 2012, Los Arcoiris won 10. The trophy case in the foyer of Alfredo's Boone restaurant attests to the team's success. Sixteen trophies adorn the entrance, including the multi-tiered La Michoacán Torneo de Copa, from 2005. The four-tiered Campeón de Liga trophy from 2012 is so big that it won't fit inside the trophy case. Alfredo, however, merely shrugs off his contribution to his team's success. He attributes the restaurant wins to "cultural passion," proclaiming that "soccer is like a religion for Hispanics." A little faith for Los Arcoiris "went a long way," he explained.[11] While one might attribute Los Arcoiris's success to soccer fervor, raw talent, and skill, an equally persuasive argument centers on the willingness to perform well for a fellow "brother" from Jalisco like Alfredo who contributes to the collective good.

Alfredo also remembers that the more the Hispanic league grew, the more his team's composition changed. Little by little, non–Latino soccer aficionados started attending La Michoacána matches. The more these fans showed up, the more they wanted to play. Because of Los Arcoiris's reputation, several of the best players matriculated to Alfredo's team. Soon Los Arcoiris consisted of former university players, local league coaches, and a handful of individuals with MLS and semi-professional experience. When Alfredo "stacked" his team with old soccer friends from Wilmington for end-of-season tournaments—a practice not uncommon across the state in a number of leagues—Los Arcoiris dominated league play.[12]

Success inevitably breeds more competition, however. Eventually a group of Latinos from the local area branched out and formed a new league. They lured away as many as six teams from La Michoacána, leaving six teams in the original league. According to Alfredo, the same time that it started showing interest in developing a women's league, La Michoacána had run its course. After ten years it finally came to an end.[13]

But as any die-hard Latino soccer player knows, religion does not die easily. An aging Alfredo and a handful of players from his early teams continue to play in the newly formed Mountaineer League. As Alfredo explains, two of the league teams consist entirely of "Americans."[14] The rest of the league is predominantly of Latino origin. Alfredo's new team, Degollado (named after his actual hometown in Jalisco), is still mixed, with Latinos and non–Latino whites primarily from the United States. Gone are the days of dusty, makeshift fields—the new league plays in the Ted Mackorell Soccer Complex, shared by Appalachian State University and local club teams. The food stand

and smell of pork tacos wafting through the air have also disappeared. Enthusiastic Hispanic crowds still attend matches, but they blend in more with other Boone residents who share the fields. Although Latinos may long for the festive atmosphere of bygone days, this blending of cultures reflects a positive change. While the old Michoacána league was relegated to Sunday matches played on unaccommodating pitches, the more integrated Mountaineer League can now be seen playing successive games on state-of-the-art artificial turf, under the lights, on almost any seasonal Friday night.

Unfortunately, this soccer passion never filtered down to the Parks and Recreation Youth League while we were coaching. Each season we worked with other members from the community to recruit local Hispanic kids into the league. We even set up a booth one summer morning with a P&R administrator, advertising, in Spanish, free cleats and shin guards and a registration fee waiver, but to little avail. Alfredo's oldest daughter did play for three years in a Parks and Recreation league with one of our own children; later, that same daughter played on another team with the daughter of our colleague friend. Also, after we finished coaching, two of our daughters played in a gender-mixed Parks and Recreation league beside (or behind) a sensational Latino forward named Antonio, but these players were the exception. We knew that members of La Michoacána had talented children because we filmed them playing on the sidelines during league matches. We also accepted that, given the challenging variables—an obvious language barrier, identifying with another homeland, distrust and occasional fear of the local community, to name just a few—assimilating into other cultures takes time, even when it involves fútbol and a soccer-loving tradition associated with so many Latinos.

* * * *

As we soon learned, the local Latino soccer scene in Boone and the surrounding area was just the tip of the iceberg. Once Paul Cuadros finished speaking at ASU, we continued to follow his story. We learned that many of the social and cultural dynamics that characterized La Michoacána also defined Latino soccer in Siler City. In his book Cuadros describes how Mexican-born workers who labored during the week in chicken-processing plants in Siler City played aggressive, uncompromising soccer each Saturday and Sunday throughout the county. They eventually formed their own private league (La Liga) and held Sunday matches in an open space in Bray Park near the center of town. Like the one in Boone, the field they played on was rundown. Cuadros describes the brown, barren field as unlevel, with no conveniences such as restrooms and bleachers to accommodate fans.[15] It didn't seem to matter which side of the state Latinos lived on: for first-generation immigrants at the start of the new millennium, soccer conditions were noticeably substandard.

La Liga in Siler City and the surrounding communities was much bigger than the Latino league in Boone. Started in the 1990s, it included 20 times more teams than La Michoacána. The players numbered in the thousands. The ranks swelled so much over the next couple of years that organizers divided the league into three divisions. Division one displayed the best talent, and division three the most disorderly. Cuadros describes the third tier as "junky soccer," in which "players routinely tackled from behind, bringing talented players down and injuring them."[16] Tempers flared and referees broke up fights. League officials eventually had to hire local law enforcement to secure the grounds.

As he chronicles in his book, however, Cuadros was more interested in the younger generation of players in search of a field. When he arrived in Siler City, one of the first things he noticed was the lack of public facilities for Latino youth soccer. Kids played pick-up matches in backyards or nearby vacant lots, without coaches or referees. Because he'd played soccer in Michigan with his father and brothers, and eventually became captain of his high school soccer team, Cuadros knew the game well. Before long he'd initiated a community-based, intermediate level Challenge soccer team comprising Latino and white teens. This experience motivated him to help establish a high school soccer team, and in a matter of months he was appointed head coach of Siler City's Jordan Matthews Jets. Because Cuadros's Jets were closer in age to the players we coached on our own youth teams, they provided a more plausible comparison for our soccer documentary. We decided to film them.

Cuadros arrived in Siler City in 1999, five years after the North Atlantic Free Trade Agreement (NAFTA) went into effect. According to most reports, the agreement endorsed by the United States, Canada, and Mexico benefited corporate interests but devastated other areas of the work force, particularly Mexican farmers. By the end of the decade thousands of laborers had started migrating to the United States, searching for employment in construction, agriculture, and other food-related industries. Because of its prosperous chicken-processing plants, rural communities like Siler City attracted hundreds of displaced Mexican workers. On the one hand, these new arrivals provided "a shot in the arm to Siler City," translating "into new business growth and opportunity" in an economically depressed area of the state.[17] On the other, they also presented a culture shock to a predominantly white, southern community set in its ways and fearful of change. Long-established citizens of Siler City openly demonstrated against the shifting demographics, displaying racist placards like "La Raza GO HOME" and "This is OUR LAND!" at City Hall.[18] Angry, provocative rallies isolated the two communities and left many immigrants feeling unwelcome and afraid.

Cuadros could empathize with such isolation. The first child of a Peruvian family to be born in the United States, he grew up in predominantly white Ann Arbor, Michigan, in the 1960s. In *A Home on the Field* he writes that he "never felt like [he] fit in anywhere.[19] He adds that he'd "never been embraced as a true American" and bemoaned how many times he'd been asked "whether [he spoke] English or if [he was] a citizen."[20] He overcame such racist remarks and eventually earned a college degree. He knew that he wanted to write for a living and enrolled in a graduate program in journalism. As a writer, he felt he could address marginalized groups in the United States. By 1999, he'd won a fellowship to explore the reticent movement of Latinos filtering into the South, particularly Mexican laborers who ended up in rural communities like Siler City working in the food-processing industry. He eventually moved there.

Cuadros's book follows two basic narratives. The first one chronicles the seemingly unending battles Latinos faced with long-time Siler City residents, law enforcement, and a public school system unwilling to change. He relates personal tales of Latino families to help develop his story, among them harrowing anecdotes of children crossing the U.S./Mexican border and escaping violence and poverty in Chicago and other big cities before moving south. He critiques what he witnessed upon his own arrival in Siler City, including an angry demonstration led by David Duke, who spouted malevolence against local food-processing industries and then stuffed his face with fried chicken at a local Golden Corral restaurant, leading Cuadros to denounce him as "an opportunist." He concludes his immigration commentary on a somber note, pointing out that over the last decade and a half the Latino journey into the United States has left many Americans feeling resentful and insensitive. If demographics "is destiny," as he writes in his epilogue, "then Latino immigrants will one day be accepted. But we are far from that day."[21]

The second narrative is interwoven into the first and traces the Jordan Matthews Jets soccer team over three seasons. In the section called "First Season," Cuadros recalls the difficulty of winning administrative approval to start a soccer program and battling both the school's football coaching staff and the local community for a place to play. Both Cuadros and his players faced racist incidents at the high school. One day in the head football coach's office Cuadros read a caption below a photograph of someone throwing a soccer ball: "El Lowmano. You not throw the soccer ball, you keeck it, eh?"[22] Insults were even more humiliating on the soccer field when Cuadros took his team to out-of-town games. Opposing players hurled racist epithets, attempting to provoke Jets players by calling them wetbacks and telling them to return to Mexico. The opposing teams' fans were just as bad, shouting at referees to give the Jets a green card instead of a yellow card when the team committed a foul. Cuadros encouraged his players to capitalize on the insults by scoring more goals. The strategy worked. The Jets turned in a remarkable performance during their first year, winning eight straight matches and posting three consecutive shutouts. They made it to the state playoffs before being eliminated 1–0 in a crushing defeat in the second round. They finished the year with an impressive 15–3 record overall.

Cuadros had always argued that, given the chance to perform, Siler City's Latino youth would prove they could play. The first season had drawn lots of attention and legitimized the new varsity soccer program. Still, Cuadros recognized that his players needed to improve. They were too influenced by the rough, *cascarita* play that characterized La Liga. Despite their record, the Jets lacked discipline and teamwork and needed to learn how to better control the ball. Even though he coached a handful of first-year players the preceding summer in a public league, Cuadros's Jets lost their second season opener. They lost their next match as well. Fearful that his team was sinking into disharmony, he finally implemented a 4–4–2 system that would better utilize the midfield. The change paid off. After a 6–0 trouncing of South Davidson High, which Cuadros described as verbally abusive and the most indignant game his team had ever played in, the Jets finished second in the conference. For the second year in a row they advanced to the state playoffs, losing a close match in the quarter-finals to Albermarle High. Despite the loss, the Jets had finally discovered how to play as a team.[23]

Americans have always loved success stories. Few in the soccer world can match the one of the Jordan Matthews Jets during their third season of play. Once again, the team had to put up with the usual racist comments, this time from a white referee. Before the Jets squared off against Albermarle High in their first conference game, the referee called each team to the field to discuss fair play. Glancing at the Jets, he asked, "Where are the Americans?" When no one from Cuadros's team cracked a smile, the referee tried to save face, asking, "Do you all understand English?"[24] Perhaps these questions provided the spark the Jets needed. They not only slaughtered their conference rivals 8–1 but also rolled through the season. During their final regular match they trounced their nemesis, South Davidson High, 6–0. Surprisingly, this time after the match the two teams shook hands, congratulating each other on good play. In fact, near the end of the third season a lot more had changed. During the quarter-finals, the Jets beat a North Monroe team that also included several Latino players. Other schools around the state were experiencing similar demographic transformations and utilizing the talent they found as a result. Probably the most notable change occurred during the final match of the state tournament, when the Jets beat the first-ranked team in the division, the Lejeune Devil Pups, 2–0 for the championship. As Cuadros glanced at the stands, he noticed a big difference from the Jets' first season of play:

> Siler City had really turned out for the big game. There were black, white, and brown students in the bleachers. Teachers came to support their kids. Latino advocates, employers, and anyone who came into contact with Latinos in town had also bought tickets.

"Win or lose," Cuadros reflected, "we had at least gotten the town to be of one mind about one thing."[25]

When we started filming the Jordan Matthews Jets two years later, Siler City's cultural hybridity had almost run its course. The sleepy downtown accommodated as many *tiendas* as it did long-time, established businesses. The town's favorite restaurants for both Latinos and other residents served standard Mexican cuisine. In the streets, stores, and playgrounds, one heard Spanish as much as English. A mural painted on the side of a downtown building revealed just how much Siler City had changed. In the picture a white man behind the counter of a hardware store is helping a black woman read from a catalog. Another white man on a ladder is retrieving goods for a Latina woman. Her daughter is talking to a young white girl, the latter displaying a wide, toothy smile.

We first traveled to Siler City in August, when the Jets' women's team was about to embark on its own season. (Cuadros had been coaching the women's team for the same number of years that he'd coached the men's team, including when the Jets won the state championship. Because there was too much soccer ground to cover in a three-year period, he chose to chronicle only the men's team in *A Home on the Field.*) From the outset we noticed that the Lady Jets were more mixed than the men's team, including a handful of non–Hispanics (three of them starters) as well as Hispanics who'd grown up with the fútbol fever of their families and cultural background. The team started out strong, posting a 4–1 record early in the season. By midseason, however, they were struggling, playing teams with girls who'd come up through the ranks of club soccer. Even though they'd dropped to a 6–6 record during one of our visits, they still managed to make the state playoffs, advancing through the second round. The last match we filmed was the quarter-finals game against perennial powerhouse Bishop McGuiness High, a private suburban school with a steep tuition and a roster of club players. The contrast with the Jordan Matthews Jets couldn't have been greater. Their field was immaculate and the fans turned out in great numbers. The Jets lost that match, to a team that eventually played in the state final. Despite the loss, Cuadros knew that his players had triumphed. Like the men's team, the women's team proved that competing in a high-profile club system was not always necessary to field a successful high school soccer program.

Reflecting on the success of the women's team and its relationship to our own soccer story, we decided to film the Siler City men's team the next fall. Some of the seniors on this team had been freshmen the year the Jets won the state championship and they were anxious for a repeat. The team also included non–Latino freshmen who, for the first time, found their majority status reversed. At a barbeque Cuadros sponsored for his team, we asked a non–Latino freshman what it was like to play on a team of mostly Latinos. Surrounded by his teammates, he joked that it was "odd" and "scary sometimes" because when they switched over to Spanish, he couldn't tell if "they were talking about [him] or not." One of the most positive things he told us was that his experience had convinced him that he "wanted to learn Spanish."[26]

The Jets' men's team surprised even their most ardent supporters that season, defying preseason predictions by advancing, once again, to the state playoffs. Like the women's team before them, they lost to a more powerful and club-based Bishop McGuiness team. They fought hard, and the emotion they expressed at the end of the game captured their journey both on and off the soccer field. They ended the season with their trademark cry: "Who are the Jets? We are! Who are the Jets? We are! One, two, three, let's go Jets!"[27] It rang even louder because they cried out in English.

Finished with our Siler City filming as well as our ritual jaunts to La Michoacána and Mountaineer league matches, we were left with a new set of questions. We wondered how the continuing wave of immigration into the state (and country) might impact the soccer landscape. We asked: Will talented Latino players who sometimes come from families without adequate financial means continue to be excluded from player development opportunities? Will U.S. soccer suffer as a result? Will more Latino kids feel welcomed into a cultural landscape populated predominantly by white professional families?

The answers to these questions depend upon the ability of American soccer to return the upside-down pyramid to its proper architectural form. American soccer was conceived in ethnic communities populated by immigrants who arrived on this country's shores with hopes and dreams similar to those carried today by recent immigrants. Many modern immigrants are even more immersed in the world of soccer than their nineteenth-century counterparts. As Klinsmann said in his 2010 remarks during the World Cup, the future of American soccer in no small way depends on reaching out to new citizens like Latinos who live and breathe soccer.[28]

The Latino leagues that are flourishing throughout the country are vivid evidence of this largely untapped soccer fever. The huge crowds of fans that turn out for matches played by the Mexican national team on U.S. soil are even more evidence, as are the efforts of people like Paul Cuadros to integrate Hispanic youth into high school soccer. The MLS Sueño programs sponsored by U.S. soccer help as well.

While the leagues and attendance at Mexican national team matches serve as significant social spaces for the articulation of cultural identity and pride, they remain marginal to the cultural space currently occupied by American soccer. None of these efforts will turn the tide until the pyramid is turned right side up. In a country that still suffers from the diseases of racism and the paranoia of cultural difference, this won't be easy. It may be just a matter of time, but that time could be a lot shorter if the system of youth development becomes genuinely accessible.

On a hopeful note, one of our Appalachian colleagues recently mentioned that her 10-year-old daughter's Parks and Recreation youth soccer team included four Latina players. Maybe the tide really is starting to change, at least in the Appalachian region. For the rest of the state, only time will tell. But one thing is certain: Latino soccer, with all of its tradition, competitiveness, and fervor, is here to stay.

11

Professional and National Soccer in the United States Today

After more than six years in the English Premier League, Clint Dempsey decided to return to Major League Soccer (MLS). Only 30 years of age, Dempsey left England with 57 goals, the most ever made by an American playing in the Premier League and matching the combined total of the next three Premier players from the United States. He ranks sixtieth on the all-time Premier League scorers' list, with only six years of play, and seventh on the list of goals scored by non–Europeans playing in England.[1] Had he played out his career in England, Dempsey undoubtedly would have moved up in those rankings. Instead, he left to join the Seattle Sounders FC in the United States. Even to American soccer fans, the move was enigmatic.

Why would the most successful American to play abroad choose to downsize to the MLS? Why would a player who once aspired to play in the Champions League with Arsenal or Manchester United move to the Seattle Sounders FC? Even the most feverish MLS fans don't consider the league the pinnacle of soccer accomplishments. Top players in this country and abroad rarely dream of playing in the MLS unless they are staring down the end of their careers. The international soccer giants associated with the MLS arrived in the United States after long, successful careers in Europe or Latin America. David Beckham came to the LA Galaxy after a 15-year career with Manchester United and Real Madrid. Thierry Henry, who still plays for the New York Red Bulls, arrived after 12 years with Arsenal and Barcelona, having scored 209 goals in 334 appearances. Robbie Keane joined the LA Galaxy after playing more than 14 years in Europe, the last 10 with Tottenham Hotspur and Liverpool. Juan Pablo Angel played in Colombia and Argentina for eight years, and then in the English Premier League for seven more before joining the New York Red Bulls. These players moved to the MLS to wind down their careers in style, with paychecks commensurate with their accomplishments. Conversely, top American players who first sign with Major League Soccer typically aspire to hone their skills for a few years before moving to Europe for bigger paychecks and more competitive soccer.

USMNT coach Jürgen Klinsmann expressed the conventional wisdom when he found out that Dempsey was moving back to the MLS: "We all hope that, by going back to the MLS, [Dempsey's] own level is not dropping, because he is going from the [Premier League], one of the best in the world, into a league which is trying to improve each year."[2]

On one level, personal reasons contributed to Dempsey's decision to play closer to home. As he explained in a *Sports Illustrated* interview in August 2013, "It's kind of been that thing in my life, trying to go and do your career, being a little more selfish in that regard, but also trying to be around your family too. I saw my grandparents getting older and I just want to be around my family more.... So family was a big thing."[3] But Dempsey also explained that he wanted to return to the United States in his prime, when he could still make an impact in professional American soccer. The British style of play had benefited his overall development as a player, but Dempsey felt the "one-and-two-touch, never-lose-the-ball" English strategy stifled the creativity he'd learned as a youngster.[4]

Furthermore, Dempsey recognized that the MLS he'd participated in from 2004 to 2007 didn't compare to the MLS of today. Formed in 1996, the MLS struggled financially during its early years, unable to attract top players from abroad. Today, the quality of competition is much higher, the financial status of the league stronger, and the pay scale on the rise. Omar Gonzalez, a stalwart of the USMNT defense, provides a recent success story. Gonzalez left the University of Maryland after the LA Galaxy drafted him in 2009. He originally thought he'd play MLS soccer for a few years, refining his game, and then move to Europe for more competitive play. Five years later he's still playing with the Galaxy, recently signing a hefty increase above his $283,000 annual salary. Gonzalez applauds the higher pay and strong competition, commenting in a recent interview that the MLS is "making huge strides."[5] Even Cristiano Ronaldo, who ranks with Lionel Messi as one of the top players in the world today, recently stated that he, too, wants to play in the MLS someday.[6] Dempsey's jump to Major League Soccer, in other words, isn't the jump into oblivion it might have been five or six years ago. His purported $25 million multiyear contract attests to an evolving financial security in the MLS. It also supports the theory that professional soccer in the United States is finally attracting a broader range of players more capable of higher levels of play.

Of course, this wasn't always the case in professional U.S. soccer. After the collapse of the North American Soccer League (NASL) in 1983, the United States lacked a truly viable, professional league. While the semi-professional leagues that had dotted the soccer landscape for decades continued to play, the NASL went underground, developing a "professional" league out of the public's sight. As other major sports continued their upward climb, propelled significantly by expanding television coverage and media hype, professional soccer in the United States once more faded into a seemingly permanent sunset.

Several events in the 1990s produced a new dawn for American soccer, however. One event that ushered in a significant change was the first FIFA-sponsored Women's World Cup, held in Guangdong, China, in 1991. American women led the charge. Women's soccer in the United States had grown steadily through both the club system initiated in the 1970s and the expansion of women's collegiate sports following the implementation of Title IX. Organized women's soccer in most other countries languished behind, since there were few similar initiatives to support female participation. By 1991, however, other countries had bolstered a sufficient number of women's leagues, and enough national teams had organized in different regions of the world to justify an international women's competition. FIFA invited 12 national teams to participate in the Cup—the United States, Sweden, Denmark, Norway, Germany, Italy, Brazil, China PR, Japan, Chinese Taipei, Nigeria, and New Zealand.

The USWNT marched through the first Women's World Cup by winning all six of its matches and outscoring its opponents 25–5. Michelle Akers won the Golden Shoe Award with 10 goals—five in one match against Chinese Taipei—and teammate Carin Jennings earned the Golden Ball Award as the tournament's outstanding player. With the USMNT still languishing in obscurity, the women's dominance of international soccer propelled the USWNT and soccer back into the sports landscape.

The second occurrence in the 1990s that illuminated professional soccer was the United States hosting the 1994 Men's World Cup. As part of an agreement with FIFA to host the Cup, the USSF agreed to implement a top-tier professional league. By most accounts the U.S. World Cup was an unabashed success. Played in nine venues spanning the country, the American-sponsored event shared a substantial portion of the U.S. media limelight that summer. At times, it seemed that other national sports barely existed. Although the

United States drew a relatively easy group with Romania, Switzerland, and Colombia, it staggered through the group stage with a 1–1–1 record, placing third, only slightly ahead of Colombia. One of four best third-place teams to make it to the knock-out stage, the USMNT lost its first match to eventual Cup winner Brazil, 1–0. Despite the team's less-than-spectacular performance overall, soccer filled television airwaves in an unprecedented fashion. Additionally, the tournament was the best-attended World Cup in its 64-year history. Average attendance for matches reached 69,000; total attendance was almost 3.5 million. The numbers still stand as records today. By all measures, the United States had demonstrated both an organizational capacity and a sufficient soccer fan base to impress FIFA officials.[7]

The rise of the USWNT and the successful staging of the World Cup in the United States provided the necessary impetus to reinvigorate a professional American soccer league. Although representatives from 10 teams had met in 1993 and committed to starting a new league, the 1994 World Cup made professional soccer a reality. These events demonstrated to potential investors a sufficient interest to warrant the financial risks involved in underwriting a new league.

The first MLS season began in the spring of 1996 with 10 franchises. Over the next five years the league expanded to 12 teams but eventually contracted back to 10, reportedly losing $250 million in the process.[8] By 2005, the league returned to expansion mode, steadily increasing to its present configuration of 19 teams, which includes three Canadian clubs based in Toronto, Vancouver, and Montreal. Recently the MLS committed to adding a club in New York City called New York City FC. A partnership between the New York Yankees baseball organization and Manchester City of the English Premier League paid the $100 million expansion fee. Plans include building a soccer-specific stadium in Queens, with a seating capacity of 25,000.[9] Orlando has also vied for acceptance into the league, although there has been no official commitment. Remembering the burden created in the NASL by unchecked expansion, the MLS has been appropriately cautious.

The MLS has also made considerable progress in building soccer-specific stadiums. The league started out with eight of the ten original teams playing in oversized football stadiums, which accentuated the relatively sparse attendance at soccer matches. Although 20,000 fans per match might make a team financially viable, sitting among 60,000 empty seats is far from ideal. In addition, football stadiums don't allow for proper dimensions of the soccer pitch. Temporary homes are never good for professional sports. What's needed is a permanent stadium that people can identify with, one where 20,000 fans packed shoulder-to-shoulder can feel like they're twice their size. In 1999, the Columbus Crew of Columbus, Ohio, opened the league's first stadium dedicated to soccer. Six additional teams constructed soccer-specific stadiums from 2003 to 2008. By 2009 a majority of MLS teams were playing in their own stadiums. Today, 14 of 19 teams play in soccer-specific stadiums, and several more stadiums are either under construction or in the planning stages.[10] These stadiums allow the MLS to control parking, concessions, and use for outdoor concerts and other sporting events. Such stadiums eliminate rental fees, reflecting a sound, long-term business practice.

MLS has expanded its sponsorship program and media contracts as part of its financial strategy. Today, 15 teams have sold jersey sponsorships—a well-worn practice of other international leagues—for sums ranging from $2.5 to $5 million per team. Representative sponsors include Corona (Chivas USA), Alaska Airlines (Portland), Barbasol (Columbus), and Bank of Montreal (Toronto and Montreal). Teams wear corporate logos on both the front and the back of their jerseys. For additional revenue, the league signed a $150 million deal with Adidas to help sponsor team uniforms and to use their equipment.[11]

From the outset, MLS signed limited agreements with ESPN, ESPN2, and ABC for coverage of matches. In 2006, the league achieved greater media security by signing an eight-year agreement with ESPN, which guaranteed MLS a significant profit over a number of years. The league also maintained separate agreements with other media giants, including Fox Soccer. In 2011, MLS signed a three-year deal with NBC Sports to televise 40 matches a year. Individual clubs have joined the fray by signing their own media contracts. For instance, the LA Galaxy reached a 10-year, $55 million deal in 2011 with Time Warner Cable.

Deep-pocketed financiers invested substantial sums in teams with hopes of turning an eventual profit. The LA Galaxy reported the first club profit in 2003; FC Dallas followed in 2005. Today a majority of league clubs are either making a profit or on the verge of turning one. A November 2013 *Forbes* article reported that 10 of the league's 19 teams earned an operating profit in 2012, while two broke even and seven chalked up losses. *Forbes* also valued the league's average franchise at $104 million. The $175 million value of the Seattle Sounders FC topped the list.[12]

Attendance figures in the league have leveled off over the past few years. They reached an all-time high in 2012, dropping slightly in 2013. Average attendance in 2013 ranged from a low of 8,366 at Chivas USA home matches to a high of 44,038 for a game played by the Seattle Sounders FC. The average for all league games in a 34-match schedule was 18,807 fans. Montreal, Kansas City, Portland, and San Jose averaged more than 100 percent stadium capacity.[13]

Although total MLS attendance of six million fans fails to measure up to the total attendance of MLB, NFL, and NBA events, attendance numbers are difficult to compare. For example, Major League Baseball sponsors 30 teams that play 162 league games each. The 74 million fans in attendance are thus spread out over 2,430 games. Average attendance for MLB games peaks at 30,453. Similarly, the NBA consists of 30 teams, each team playing an 82-game regular season schedule. Average attendance for the NBA is 13,886 per game. Viewed in this light, average attendance at MLS matches is reasonably healthy.[14]

Compared to professional leagues in other countries, MLS average attendance is not too far off the mark. Japan's J League averages 17,226, while Argentina's Primera Division pulls in 18,165. France's Ligue 1 attracts 19,261 per match, while Italy's Serie A averages 23,459. MLS averages are right in line with these more established leagues.[15]

MLS was designed both to provide a professional outlet for quality American players and to furnish a reasonably high level of soccer for the enjoyment of fans. In the early years of the league, top-level players from the USMNT like Alexi Lalas, Tony Meola, and Eric Wynalda received handsome contracts. A modest number of international players did as well, among them Mexico's Jorge Campos and Colombia's Carlos Valderrama. In 2007, the MLS initiated changes that internationalized the league. First, MLS raised the cap for international players, creating an incentive for more international recruiting. Second, the league created the Designated Player Rule, which allows clubs to sign better players from the United States and abroad by not counting full salaries against league-enforced team salary caps. This rule is also known as the Beckham Rule, because David Beckham became the first international superstar to sign under the new agreement, with a reported $6.5 million guarantee per year. The LA Galaxy signed Beckham; the New York Red Bulls followed suit with Colombian Juan Pablo Angel, and the Chicago Fire had Mexican Cuauhtémoc Blanco.

The salary cap per team in 2007 topped out at $2.1 million. An agreement in 2010 raised it to $2.55 million, with an automatic 5 percent increase each year, making it over $3 million today. Each team was initially allocated one slot for a designated player, with the opportunity to sign a second. Only the initial $300,000–$400,000 of the player's salary counts against a team's salary cap. This program has allowed teams to manage salary budgets while the same time recruiting additional top-level players.

Today, MLS is one of the most diverse soccer leagues in the world. Approximately 600 players suit up in the MLS; over 220 are international players as defined by their place of birth. Currently players come from over 60 countries. Almost 40 percent of foreign-born players hail from six countries: Colombia, Brazil, Canada, Argentina, France, and England. In the 17-year history of the MLS, players from 104 countries outside of the United States have appeared on league rosters. While the number of international players constitutes about 35 percent of team rosters, these players often dominate quality playing time. The 2013 All-Star squad started six American players and five international players, while the 2011 and 2012 teams each started seven international players. The 2010 starting team consisted of eight international players. Over the past eight years, 43 Americans and 45 international players have started for the MLS All-Star squads.[16]

While salary caps have helped tighten expenditures—a lesson learned from the NASL's failure—they have also restricted Major League Soccer from recruiting quality players who opt for more lucrative salaries in other professional leagues. Until the creation of the Designated Player Rule, top American players also went abroad, attracted not only by higher salaries but also by better-quality soccer. Players like Clint Dempsey and Jozi Altidore are cases in point. Moreover, over-the-hill stars from abroad could still make more money playing on their home turf than they could in the MLS.

The Designated Player Rule has been effective, but it hasn't solved the problem of holding down salary expenses while also raising the level of play. Only nine MLS players make over $1 million a year: Clint Dempsey ($5 m) and Landon Donovan ($2.5 m) from the United States; Robbie Keane ($4.3 m) from Ireland; Thierry Henry ($4.3 m) from France; Tim Cahill ($3.6 m) from Australia; Marco Di Vaio ($1.9m) from Italy; Obafemi Martins ($1.7 m) from Nigeria; Dan Koevermans ($1.6m) from the Netherlands; and Kenny Miller ($1.1 m) from Scotland. Despite these millionaire salaries, however, average annual pay in the MLS is less than $150,000. The median salary of all MLS players is $100,000. Approximately 25 percent of roster players make less than $50,000 a year.[17]

While such figures are respectable, they are paltry indeed when compared to salaries in other U.S. sports, or to soccer salaries elsewhere in the world. The average salary in the NBA is $5.1 million; the MLB, $3.3 million; and the NFL, $1.9 million.[18] In other words, the average NBA salary surpasses the highest-paid MLS player, while the average MLB salary surpasses all but four MLS players. The average NFL player makes more than 99 percent of MLS players.

Similar discrepancies appear when comparing MLS salaries to those of players in other countries. FC Barcelona players average $8.7 million a year. Real Madrid salaries average a slightly lower $7.8 million, while Manchester City players make an average of $7.4 million. Thus the general salaries for players on these teams far exceed the highest-paid MLS player.[19]

These salary differentials point to a major problem for American professional soccer. As long as top players in the United States and other countries around the world command salaries exponentially higher than MLS clubs are able to pay, those players will continue to play abroad. Added to the financial benefits are the myriad benefits of playing more skillful soccer.

Despite the positive strides American professional soccer has made, it still has a long way to go in catching up to the rest of the world.

* * * *

The USWNT's victory in the 1999 World Cup—their second championship in three attempts—provided the necessary incentive to form a women's professional soccer league. Hosted by the United States, the Cup set a number of records, including 1.1 million total fans and an average attendance of 37,319 in 32 matches. The U.S. team drew consistently large crowds in its six matches on the way to the championship. Over 400,000 fans attended USWNT matches played at venues in New York, Chicago, Boston, Washington, San Francisco, and Los Angeles.

The USWNT marched through the tournament undefeated. Winning all three of their matches in the group stage and outscoring Denmark, Nigeria, and Korea DPR 13–1, they prepared to face a powerful German team in the first round of the knockout stage. Before a crowd of 54,642 in Washington, D.C., Germany took a 1–0 lead in the fifth minute when Brandi Chastain scored an own goal. The U.S. women battled back but trailed 2–1 at halftime. Chastain made up for her early mistake by scoring an equalizer in the forty-ninth minute. Seventeen minutes later Joy Fawcett scored another goal and the U.S. team held on for a 3–2 victory. The United States next faced Brazil, recognized as the most improved team in the tournament. Before a record crowd of 73,123 in San Francisco, the USWNT prevailed 2–0 to make it to the final. They faced a China PR team that had decimated five opponents by a combined score of 19–2. The new match shattered the attendance record set in San Francisco days earlier, when the largest crowd ever to watch a sporting event played by women—90,185 people—jammed into Rose Bowl Stadium. Regulation play ended in a 0–0 draw. After 30 minutes of overtime, neither team scored a goal. Moving to the first ever penalty kick shootout of a men's or women's World Cup final, both teams made their initial two shots. On China's third attempt, U.S. goalie Briana Scurry made a diving save to stop a goal. With penalty kicks eventually tied at four apiece, Brandi Chastain placed a final kick that gave the USWNT a hard-fought victory.[20]

Record attendance figures and media coverage convinced investors of the viability of a women's professional soccer league. By 2001 the Women's United Soccer League began play, but the optimism that had surrounded the 1999 euphoria dissipated quickly. After three mediocre seasons, the WUSL folded, with little fanfare. With the men's professional league gaining traction, the idea of a women's league remained in the background. When the American women took the gold medal at the 2007 Olympics, optimism surfaced once again in the guise of Women's Professional Soccer. The new league showcased seven teams, opening its first season in 2009. Each team received three Olympians from the 2007 American team and drafted up to four international players. An enthusiastic crowd of 14,000 fans watched the Los Angeles Sol beat the Washington Freedom 2–0 in the initial match.

As in the earlier attempt to develop a women's professional soccer league, attendance at the WPS matches declined precipitously. By the third season the league had dropped to six teams, with only three original clubs surviving. Attendance surged temporarily after the United States played (and lost) a dramatic match to Japan in the 2011 World Cup final. Also, a match between Western New York Flash and magicJack in Rochester—USWNT star Abby Wambach's hometown—set another WPS attendance record. One match wasn't enough to turn finances around, however, and by the start of the 2012 season the league announced that it was disbanding.

For some time investors had been working with the U.S. Soccer Federation to create a more viable plan. After the cancellation of the WPS's fourth season, officials announced the reorganization of the league into the National Women's Soccer League. Eight teams committed to the new organization in the spring of 2013. They would play a 22-match schedule spread out over six months. The U.S. Soccer Federation worked out an agreement with both the Canadian Soccer Association and the Federación de Mexicana Fútbol to underwrite the salaries of national team members who would play in the league. Under the new agreement, the United States would pay the salaries of 24 national team members, Canada 16, and Mexico 12–18. Organizers hoped that playing professionally in such a league would improve the level of play of all three national teams. Initially, each team was allocated three American national players and two each from the Canadian and Mexican national teams. Each team received two additional slots that could be filled by other international players. The remainder of team rosters would be filled by American players who were not members of the national team.

In the first season the Western New York Flash won the regular season title. The top four teams in the league then played a final tournament at the end of the season. FC Kansas City, the Portland Thorns FC, and the Sky Blue FC of Piscataway, New Jersey, joined the Flash in a single elimination tournament. Portland came away with the trophy in a final 2–0 win over the Flash.

Attendance for all NWSL matches averaged a disappointing 4,271 fans. Sadly, a more than respectable 13,000-person attendance average at Portland Thorns matches actually inflated the low league average. Blue Sky FC averaged a meager 1,677 fans.[21] Without salary subsidies from the three national soccer associations, financial losses would have made the league unsustainable.

Even with the subsidies, the league remains shaky. In a recent interview league, Director Cheryl Bailey revealed that salaries for NWSL players range from $6,000 to $30,000 for a six-month season.[22] While it's uncertain how many players receive top dollar, it's highly likely that even national players receive substandard pay. Although national team players are also paid by their respective soccer associations to play on the national teams, most NWSL players do not receive extra compensation. Such poor wages call into question whether the NWSL is a true "professional" league.

To complicate matters, women's professional leagues in other countries compete with the NWSL. Because many of the teams in these leagues are closely affiliated with established men's teams, their financial situation is more stable. Such stability enables these teams to offer higher salaries to prospective players. There's a distinct possibility that many American stars will be lured by these higher salaries, deserting the NWSL for greener pastures. A recent case in point is Megan Rapinoe, an established midfield star on the USWNT. In January 2013 she signed with Olympique Lyonnais, the strongest team in the French women's league. Lyonnais has won seven straight league titles and is vying for its third straight European Cup championship. Rapinoe moved to Lyon and is reportedly paid $14,000 a month.[23] This figure tops what most NWSL players receive for an entire season. Rapinoe also joined the Seattle Reign of the NWSL for 12 of 22 matches after she finished playing for Lyonnais. How many other top U.S. players—who arguably are among the best women players in the world—will opt for these international leagues as they gain prestige and experience? Where will such an exodus leave professional women's soccer in the United States?

* * * *

While playing professional soccer is a goal of almost every top-level American player, it's not the only goal. In many ways, playing professionally takes a back seat to playing for the U.S. national team. The FIFA World Cup is still the crown jewel of international soccer, and the USMNT has now qualified for seven straight tournaments. Equally impressive, the USWNT has won two of the six women's World Cups and placed second or third in the other four. While soccer in the United States doesn't share the same intense relationship with national identity that it does in most of the rest of the world, the national teams are perceived internationally as the primary emblem of the sport in this country.

As we've mentioned in previous chapters, the USMNT finished third in a 13-team field in the first FIFA World Cup, held in Uruguay in 1930. Back then the Cup lacked the international prominence it has today, but 1930 still stands as a high-water mark for an American squad. Despite a U.S. victory over England in the group stage, the first post–World War II World Cup in 1950 witnessed the rapid elimination of the United States. Paradoxically, while soccer became entrenched in universities, the NASL, and the youth club soccer movement, the USMNT performed a rapid disappearing act, failing to qualify for nine consecutive World Cups. When qualification finally came in 1990, 40 years after the previous U.S. appearance, national team soccer occupied less than a square foot in the U.S. sports landscape.

In 1990, Mexico and Costa Rica were considered the top teams in the Confederation of North, Central American, and Caribbean Association Football, better known by its acronym CONCACAF. Mexico, however, had been disqualified from the World Cup qualifying rounds for using overaged players in the 1988 Olympics. This elimination opened the door for the U.S. squad. Despite this break, U.S. qualification came down to a final match against a surprising Trinidad and Tobago team. The two teams had played to a 1–1 draw in their first qualifying match when Trinidad and Tobago scored an equalizer in the eighty-eighth minute of the game. Going into the final match, the United States had nine points; T&T trailed close behind at eight. The United States needed a draw to sustain its one-point lead. Midfielder Paul Caligiuri scored in the thirtieth minute of play. The lead held through a furious ending for a 1–0 U.S. victory. The United States proudly headed for the 1990 World Cup in Italy. Finally, they'd broken a 40-year drought.

In the group stage the United States was placed with Italy, Czechoslovakia, and Austria. On June 10, 1990, the USMNT entered the World Cup pitch in Florence as a decided underdog. Their first match was a disaster, as the Czechs took a 3–0, early second-half lead. Although Paul Caligiuri scored the first U.S. World Cup goal in 40 years to cut the lead to 3–1, the Czechs went on to claim a humiliating 5–1 victory. The Americans played better in their next two group stage matches, but they lost both: 1–0 to Italy and 2–1 to Austria. Ten days after arriving in Italy, they flew home.[24]

In 1989 FIFA awarded the 1994 World Cup to the United States. High-caliber international soccer had miraculously arrived in America. As the host, the USMNT received an automatic berth in the tournament. It was grouped with Switzerland, Romania, and Colombia. The initial match pitting the United States against Switzerland was held in the Silverdome in Pontiac, Michigan. A capacity crowd of 73,425 witnessed the first World Cup match played on American soil, and in an indoor stadium to boot. The United States played well and held the Swiss to a 1–1 draw. Colombia followed the Swiss. A sell-out crowd of 93,869 turned out to watch the United States play at the Rose Bowl, marking the largest single-game attendance in American soccer history. In the thirty-fifth minute of play, Colombian defender Andrés Escobar deflected a U.S. pass to score an own goal, putting the United States ahead 1–0. Forward Earnie Stewart added a second goal in the fifty-second minute, and the Americans held on for a 2–1 victory. With a victory and a draw, the United States needed a win against Romania to win its group stage. Unfortunately, jitters got the best of the United States, and they fell 1–0, placing them third in their group behind Romania and Switzerland. Four third-place finishers were selected to move on to the knockout stage. Fortunately, the United States advanced alongside Argentina, Belgium, and Italy.[25]

As fate would have it, the United States drew powerhouse Brazil. The USMNT battled mightily but lost to a better team, 1–0. Brazil went on to win the tournament in a penalty shootout against Italy.

Despite its elimination, the United States had advanced to the World Cup knockout stage for the first time since 1930. The team had played consistently well, and the overall success of hosting the country's first World Cup added to the sense of victory. Post-tournament activity ended tragically, however. Andrés Escobar, the Colombian defender who'd scored the own goal in the match against the United States, was found murdered in a bar parking lot shortly after his return home to Medellín. Accounts vary, but it's widely believed that the killing was in retaliation for Escobar's own goal. Humberto Castro Muñoz was arrested, tried, and convicted of the murder. A chauffeur bodyguard for the Medellín cartel, whose top echelon had bet heavily on Colombian soccer, Muñoz served 11 years of a lengthy prison term.[26]

Despite the tragedy, the USMNT had inched its way out of the shadowy decades in which it had languished so long. It's an exaggeration to say that the

United States had caught soccer fever, but by a number of accounts, the temperature was starting to rise.

By the 1998 World Cup, anticipation ran high for the USMNT. Relative success in 1994 sparked a sense of optimism in the team. Moreover, the 1998 tournament expanded from 24 to 32 teams, making U.S. qualification more likely. The United States qualified during CONCACAF play and landed in a group with Germany, Yugoslavia, and Iran. While Germany was a force to be reckoned with, the remaining countries in the draw seemed vulnerable. The United States landed a fourteenth seed while Yugoslavia, in the midst of a fracturing war, drew twenty-first. Iran was seeded dead last. For the United States, making it to the knockout round once again appeared likely.

As expected, Germany ran the deck at the group stage, beating the USMNT 2–0 along the way. Unfortunately, the two victories that the Americans anticipated never came. They lost both matches: 2–1 to Iran and 1–0 to Yugoslavia. Once again they flew home, their rise in world soccer cut short. France beat Germany 3–0 to win the 1998 World Cup.[27]

In 2002 the bluster that followed the 1994 World Cup had worn thin. The USMNT regrouped, however, winning the CONCACAF Gold Cup by beating Costa Rica in the final, 2–0. The victory marked its second championship, and the team found its way into the next World Cup held in Korea and Japan. As in 1998, the United States received a fair draw in the group stage, sharing the pitch with Portugal, Poland, and South Korea. FIFA ranked Portugal fifth in the world, but Poland and South Korea shared some of the lowest rankings in the 32-team tournament.

In the topsy-turvy world of international soccer, the unexpected often happens. With a goal by John O'Brien in the fourth minute of play complemented by an own goal made by Portugal in the twenty-ninth minute, the Americans built a commanding 3–0 lead over their more commanding opponent after just 36 minutes of play. Caught off-guard, Portugal responded, as expected from a top-ranked team, pulling within 3–2 with 19 minutes left to play. But the United States fought hard and secured an unprecedented win. The USMNT was within reach of its best finish since 1930. As so often happened in past years, however, the team played tentatively in the next two matches. They tied South Korea 1–1 and lost to Poland 3–1. Nevertheless, the Americans finished second in their group and advanced to the round of sixteen.[28]

They faced CONCACAF nemesis Mexico in their first match. The United States recovered its swagger and defeated its neighbor by a convincing 2–0 score. The team now entered the coveted quarter-finals, a space they hadn't reached since 1930. Unfortunately, they faced a strong German team. The

USMNT played well but lost (albeit narrowly, 1–0) to a more powerful German team. Germany reached the finals but lost to Brazil 2–0.[29]

The USMNT continued its roll. They won the CONCACAF Gold Cup in 2005, beating Panama on penalty kicks after a scoreless draw. Anticipating a repeat of the success of 2002, they hoped to reach the semi-finals in the 2006 World Cup. Once again the draw for the group stage provided hope. They drew a strong Italian team, seeded among the top seven teams. But the remainder of the group—Ghana and the Czech Republic—seemed vulnerable. The initial match against the Czech Republic set the tone, as they crushed the United States 3–0. Luckily, the United States managed a 1–1 draw against Italy. A victory over Ghana, ranked forty-eighth in the world by FIFA, would guarantee advancing to the knockout round. The Ghanaian team was also fighting to survive, having lost to Italy while defeating the Czech Republic. Ghana ultimately prevailed by a score of 2–1, and the Americans went home. Inconsistent play characteristically plagued the USMNT. They tied the eventual winner of the tournament, but lost to two teams they should have beaten. The pattern of playing reasonably well against tough opponents but wilting when faced with weaker ones became a melancholy mantra. The mystery of the USMNT's roller-coaster ride would continue.[30]

We described the 2010 World Cup hosted by South Africa in Chapter 1. For the United States, the result in this tournament was more of the same. To their credit, the USMNT qualified for their sixth straight World Cup. In the group stage they faced one superior team, England, and two weaker teams, Algeria and Slovenia. Once again the path to the final sixteen looked clear. Play started out well, as the United States battled England to a 1–1 draw. As one of the top seven seeds in the tournament, England was expected to win that match. For the United States, recording a draw seemed as good as a win. In the next match their optimism waned as Slovenia registered a 2–2 tie. The United States needed a victory against Algeria, which they barely achieved with a 1–0 win. Surprisingly, they tied England for the group lead, both teams turning in lackluster performances.[31]

In the first round they faced Ghana, their nemesis from 2006. They lost the rematch 2–1 and boarded an airplane home. Although they'd reached the knockout round once again, their overall performance on the field drew criticism. ESPN commentator Jürgen Klinsmann's observation that the Americans weren't "hungry" enough was an oversimplification, but his reference to the upside-down pyramid hit the nail right on the head. After the draw with England, which should have infused their next games with confidence and determination, the USMNT turned cautious instead.

Once he took over the USMNT coaching reins in 2011, Klinsmann kick-started the reforms that had begun a few years earlier. In addition to introducing changes in the youth development system, the new coach examined the makeup of the team's roster. Previous national teams had comprised players who'd come up mainly through the traditional route—university to professional or semi-professional U.S. soccer. Klinsmann set out to change that design.

In his first call-up for the USMNT camp preparing for qualification matches in the build-up to the 2014 World Cup, Klinsmann enlisted 29 players. Only nine of these came from the MLS. The majority of players from the MLS group had also played at least one year on a university team. The other members had honed their skills playing in either Europe or Mexico. Most from the group had no university experience. The final 2013 men's roster included seven MLS players and 12 players who currently play in Europe or Mexico. Out of the 19 on the roster, only seven played university soccer.

Klinsmann's intensions are clear. While there has not yet been time to right the upside down U.S. pyramid, his experiments with the USMNT's roster take a closer look at players with more diverse player development backgrounds: fewer players with university and MLS-only experience and more players who by-passed university soccer and who have international professional experience.

In contrast, the 1994 USMNT's World Cup team consisted of 22 players, 17 of whom had come up through the traditional university route. The five members of the team who'd followed alternate routes were born outside the United States, but by 1994 all were American citizens: Thomas Dooley (Germany), Fernando Clavijo (Uruguay), Frank Klopas (Greece), Hugo Pérez (El Salvador) and Earnie Stewart (Netherlands). Four of these players had played professionally outside the United States, but most of that experience was limited.

While these changes may be interpreted as cosmetic, they also reflect two basic insights. The first recognizes that playing abroad against stiffer competition on an international stage improves the quality of play—both the nuts and bolts of the game and the intangible "feel" for the game. The second acknowledges that playing at the university level may actually inhibit player development. The years 18–22 are a critical time for player development. Considering that not more than a handful of college matches are sufficiently competitive, precious time may be wasted playing university soccer. Furthermore, compared to the high-level play in other parts of the world, season schedules and training time are often limited in American university soccer. The long-range impact of these changes on the national men's team remains to be seen.

* * * *

Unlike the men's team, the USWNT has been incredibly successful. For the past five years, they've occupied the top spot in FIFA's rankings. They have consistently dominated international competitions. They have no peers in the CONCACAF region and very few in the world.

The national women's team was formed in the 1980s. Its domination of world soccer began with the first women's World Cup held in Guangdong, China, in 1991. Twelve national teams participated. The American squad made it through the group stage undefeated, with victories over Sweden, Brazil, and Japan. The knockout round started with a 7–0 stampede over Chinese Taipei, followed by a convincing 5–2 victory over Germany. The final was the team's most difficult match, which they eventually won over Norway 2–1. Overall, the Americans outscored their opponents 25–5. The USWNT broke on top of the international soccer stage with a bang.

The second women's World Cup was staged in Sweden. The American squad had its string of six straight victories marred in the opening match against China PR, but managed a furiously played 3–3 draw. They had an easier time in their next group matches, dispatching Denmark 2–0 and Australia 4–1. Moving into the knockout round, they easily took care of Japan 4–0. Paired in the quarter-finals against Norway, the team they had defeated in the 1991 final, the United States gave up a goal just 10 minutes into the match. The Norwegian defense was merciless for the rest of the game, which ended in a 1–0 defeat for the Americans. Norway went on to blank Germany in the final, 2–0. In their six matches the champions outscored their opponents 23–1. The Norwegians dominated the Cup even more than the Americans had four years earlier.

The United States hosted the 1999 women's World Cup. On the heels of hosting the 1994 men's Cup, the U.S. Soccer Federation outdid itself. Total attendance far outpaced the previous two women's World Cups, and the final between the United States and China PR drew the largest crowd ever to watch a women's soccer match: 93,185. Attendance averaged 37,319 for the total 32 tournament matches. In comparison, the largest crowd in Sweden to watch the 1995 World Cup was 17,158, when Norway played Germany. Total attendance for the Swedish-hosted World Cup was 112,334 for 26 matches, barely surpassing the attendance of the 1999 final.

Once again the United States swept through the tournament, winning all six of its matches and outscoring opponents 18–3. They beat a rising German team 3–2 in the quarter-finals, and a Brazilian team 2–0 in the semi-finals. The final with China PR was a bruiser, ending in a 0–0 draw. The USWNT won in a tense penalty kick shootout. With its second World Cup title in three tries, the USWNT appeared nearly invincible. Behind the scenes, however, the rest of the world was finally catching up.

FIFA selected China PR to host the 2003 women's World Cup. Five months before the start of the tournament, however, China tragically experienced an outbreak of Severe Acute Respiratory Syndrome, or SARS, which resulted in over a thousand deaths. FIFA decided to change the location of the tournament to the United States. Reasoning that the United States was the most likely country to be able to organize the tournament on such short notice, the USSF agreed to the challenge. At the time, the professional Women's United Soccer League was struggling, and the Federation hoped that the World Cup might ignite enough interest to save it.

Due to the short planning time, there were limited available stadiums. Many larger stadiums that had been used in the 1999 Cup were already scheduled for NFL and university football. In the end, the USSF located six places to play. The Lincoln Financial Field, home of the NFL Philadelphia Eagles, was the largest, with a seating capacity of 69,500. Most of the other venues had seating capacities of just over 20,000. Attendance at this tournament was destined to be a fraction of the 1999 total.

The USWNT swept through the group stage, easily dispatching Sweden, Nigeria, and North Korea. They managed a 1–0 victory over an always competitive Norwegian squad in the quarter-finals. But the German team that had succumbed to the United States in the quarter-finals of the previous Cup obliterated the Americans 3–0. Germany went on to win the tournament, beating Sweden 2–1 in the final, joining the United States and Norway as international champions.

When organizers moved the 2003 tournament to the United States, FIFA had promised China that it would host the 2007 tournament. North Korea surprised the heavily favored U.S. team in its opening match, taking the USWNT to a 2–2 draw. Quickly recovering, the Americans marched through their other two group matches against Sweden and Nigeria without giving up a goal. The shutouts continued, with a 3–0 trouncing of England in the quarter-finals. The United States then faced Brazil in the semi-finals, having last faced the Brazilians in the 1999 World Cup semi-finals. The USWNT had prevailed in that match 2–0. This time things changed. Brazil touted one of its upcoming stars, Marta Vieira de Silva, better known as "Marta" on the playing field. The previous year, FIFA had recognized Marta, at age 20, as Player of the Year. Now, at 21, she'd scored five goals in Brazil's first six matches. On her way to winning the tournament's Golden Boot and Golden Ball awards, Marta added two goals against the American team, decimating the USWNT 4–0. Despite her team's 2–0 loss to Germany in the finals, Marta was named 2007 FIFA Outstanding Player, the second in a string of five consecutive selections as the world's best woman player.

Germany, winner of the previous two World Cups, hosted the most recent women's World Cup in 2011. Germany and Brazil joined the United States in an elite group of favorites. The U.S. team won its first two group matches over North Korea 2–0 and Colombia (appearing in its first World Cup) 3–0, but Sweden surprised the United States in its final match, beating the Americans 2–1. With two wins under its belt, the team continued its unbroken streak of qualifying for the knockout stage. The other two superpowers, Germany and Brazil, advanced unscathed. Germany then played Japan, which showcased its diminutive rising star, Homare Sawa. Japan had collected victories over less than impressive squads from New Zealand and Mexico, but lost 2–0 to England in the group stage. The battle with Germany ended in a 0–0 draw, but eight minutes into overtime, Japan scored, holding on for a 1–0 victory over the reigning world champions. They would face Sweden in the semi-finals.

The USWNT drew Marta's Brazil in the quarter-finals. The Americans received a gift when Brazil scored an own goal in the second minute of play. Marta scored an equalizer in the sixty-eighth minute and regulation play ended in a 1–1 draw. The Brazilians looked like they would defeat the Americans again when Marta scored a second time in the first two minutes of overtime. In a frantic finish, Abby Wambach tied the score at 120+2 minutes, seconds before the final whistle. The United States won the penalty kick shootout, surviving to meet France in the semi-finals.

With both Germany and Brazil defeated, the path to a third title looked good for the United States. They beat France 3–1, while Japan continued its Cinderella story against Sweden with an identical score.

The final proved a defensive battle, with both goalies playing spectacularly. The United States scored first at the sixty-ninth minute, and it appeared that this single goal would be enough to win the match. But with only nine minutes left, Japan found an opening and scored, tying the match 1–1. Regulation play ended, and once again the Americans scored first in overtime, taking the lead at the 104-minute mark. With the match winding down to its final minutes, Sawa continued her tournament magic by scoring a goal at the 117-

minute mark. Overtime ended in a 2–2 draw. In disbelief at the Japanese comeback, the Americans blew the penalty kick shootout, and Japan was crowned champion. Sawa replaced Marta as the winner of both the Golden Ball and the Golden Boot awards.

* * * *

An important question remains: If Jürgen Klinsmann is right about the primary cause of the USMNT's uneven progress in international competition, why has the same system of development worked for the USWNT? In other words, if the problem revolves around structuring the pyramid upside down, relegating American soccer to a relatively closed, elite class structure, why has this system failed for the men but succeeded for the women?

The answer lies in the relatively recent time scale of women's international soccer. As we pointed out in the earlier chapters, international soccer was an exclusively male space for more than a century. Not until the 1980s did women's national teams begin to organize effectively. American women received a jump-start with the growth of university soccer and the youth club system in the 1960s and 1970s. By the time of the first women's World Cup in 1991, the combination of university and club soccer had produced players in the United States who'd come up through years of experience in that system. That they had to pay to play and gain experience in university competition didn't seem to matter. That is, they were part of an organized system of development long before such systems existed for women in other countries around the globe. Almost every member of U.S. women's national teams from 1991 onward has developed through a similar pipeline. It's as true today as it was in the beginning.

The men are a different story. Turning the pyramid upside down has been detrimental to the men's team's ability to consistently compete at the international level. While creating a system of youth development that fed the expanding university soccer landscape, the relatively exclusive class space occupied by men's soccer has limited the pool of potential players. At the same time, it has produced a cadre of players whose experience with international competition comes too late.

Conclusion

As we've mentioned throughout this book, *American Soccer: History, Culture, Class* was inspired by a documentary video we made on youth soccer called *Offside(s): Soccer in Small-Town America.* That project started in 2005 as a simple home movie of our children playing Parks and Recreation soccer in Boone, North Carolina. By the time we finished filming three years later, it had turned into an introspective study of three fathers–turned–soccer coaches as well as an extended discourse on five soccer venues in our local community. It also chronicled the journey of two Latino high school soccer teams on the other side of the state. We added a parenthetical "s" to the first word in the documentary's title to call attention to the number of ways one might interpret "Offside"—not only in the more conventional sense of a penalty but also in the numerous examples of players, coaches, officials, parents, and fans who cross social, physical, and emotional boundaries that impact soccer in negative ways.

If the documentary offers a negative look at various facets of American youth soccer, it also highlights the kinds of success stories typically found in the game. In fact, we never would have made the documentary had we not experienced something more profound than a run-of-the-mill, Saturday morning youth soccer match. As we mention in Chapter 7, we volunteered to coach our daughters' first soccer team as much out of practicality as a desire to instruct nine- and ten-year-old girls on the soccer field. With six children playing soccer on four different teams, we knew we'd be shuffling kids back and forth to practices and games while also jockeying jobs and fulfilling other family commitments. We surmised that coaching a group of nine- and ten-year-old children (even if two out of three coaches were inexperienced and couldn't determine if a player was offside) would make daily life less burdensome. Little did we know that during that first season, we'd gain as much satisfaction out of coaching as our daughters and other teammates would by playing soccer.

We coached and filmed our daughters' teams over three consecutive years, dividing the documentary into three distinct seasons. Because the idea for the video came near the end of the first season—after we'd posted nine consecutive wins—we had little actual footage of our first-year team. In order to balance the length of the first season with the second and third seasons, we explored the history of soccer in our local community, which dates back to 1961, when Appalachian State University first started its men's varsity soccer program. By the early 1970s the university had given the local Parks and Recreation complex used soccer equipment and instructed county officials on how to launch their own youth league; shortly afterward, the county's high school started its own varsity team. By the 1990s, the newly emerging Latino population in Boone and the surrounding area had introduced another soccer league and organized community matches on local elementary school football fields. In the first 20 minutes of the 56-minute documentary, we discuss the evolution of these soccer venues, including Appalachian's 1970s golden era that influenced so many generations of community league players. We finish the first part of the documentary with clips from our end-of-year trophy party, which captures the positive chemistry of a group of nine- and ten-year-old girls who overcame a general unfamiliarity with the game and produced a near-perfect, 11–0–1 first-year season.

The critique changes in the second and third parts of the documentary. Because a newly evolving club soccer league lured away four of our first-year players, the composition of our second-year team changed. We, too, became a different breed of coaches. On the one hand, we felt cheated by the encroachment of the club soccer system. This was *our* team, we grouched silently; we'd put the time and energy into molding a successful group, even if our reasons for coaching were somewhat self-centered. To have a better-financed organization promise our players matching uniforms and name-brand athletic bags (all at a noticeable financial cost) as well as more intense competition (at this level, a slight exaggeration) didn't seem fair. On the other hand, we reflected too much on glory days from the past and became obsessed with winning. Ultimately, we lost sight of the "recreation" side of Parks and Recreation soccer. In the second part of the documentary we include a montage of us screaming at our players from the sidelines—they were only nine years old!—pondering whether we had become the kind of win-at-any-cost parents we'd learned to dislike. We also show clips of our girls falling apart on the playing field as they blamed each other for missed opportunities instead of working as a team. The footage is telling: we lost the majority of games that season and finished near the bottom of the league.

We never recaptured the spirit of our first season, but the third section of the documentary captures how we made a conscious effort to worry less about winning and to simply have fun. As for playing like a unified, competitive team, the gesture paid off: the girls won more games than they lost. The last third of the video also demonstrates how making the documentary had started to trump our role as soccer coaches. Three years after our initial debut, we'd become more interested in the wider cultural landscape of local soccer. The main difference we noticed by the end of our final season was that our team rarely mirrored the changing demographics in our local community. As we point out in Chapter 10, by the time we started coaching soccer, the Latino population in our Appalachian community had grown significantly. Made up primarily of white, middle- and upper-middle-class kids, our team never witnessed this growth on a Parks and Recreation soccer field. As observers of the sport, we had to travel to Siler City on the other side of the state to fully grasp how Latinos played out in the larger arena of youth soccer. In the end, we realized that as long as these young players were given an equal chance on the playing field (including in a predominantly white community that felt threatened by recent immigration), they, too, could succeed.

We finished the documentary in 2009 and showed it at academic conferences and in film festivals in a number of states. The following year, while listening to ESPN commentators discussing the U.S. Men's National Team's implosion during the World Cup, we discovered Jürgen Klinsmann's metaphor of an upside-down pyramid. His criticism of American families' obsession with athletic scholarships, the pay-to-play club system, and the failure to significantly integrate Latinos into the fabric of American soccer struck us as similar to our own observations in the documentary. Klinsmann's figurative depiction of a soccer system structurally out of sync with the rest of the world's, in other words, reflected our multiple interpretations of "offside."

The offside application that resonated with us the most, and one that demonstrates the irony of Klinsmann's metaphor, is our own role as misguided coaches. It could be argued that beyond spending quality time with our daughters and getting to know some of their friends, we had little business being on a soccer field. We remember one match when we screamed at a referee for not calling offside against three opposing players. In front of several dozen parents, he politely told us that he couldn't call an offside penalty during a "throw in." We recall another moment when a Parks and Recreation administrator reprimanded us for uttering the "f word" five times during a soccer match. We also once received a red card for leaving the coach's box. As fathers–turned–soccer coaches, we "stepped offside" more than we care to remember.

Lots of fans and officials challenged the conventional wisdom of organized youth soccer, however. In fact, our antics were tame compared to some of the emotional outbursts we witnessed during our research. Parents kicked chalk lines in disgust when they disagreed with a referee's call. They, too, used offensive language, especially when criticizing their own children's performance on the playing field. They hurled even worse insults at opposing teams. While researching *Offside(s)*, we learned about a Charlotte mother who screamed at her son's team, "YOU'RE NOT GOING TO LET A BUNCH OF REDNECKS FROM BOONE BEAT YOU, ARE YOU?" While we never witnessed the overt racism Paul Cuadros describes in *Home on the Field,* we noticed time and again when filming his Jordan Matthews Jets that stadium bleachers were still segregated, with Latinos typically on one end and whites on the other. In addition, the kind of insensitive referee Cuadros identifies in his book found its way into the Parks and Recreation league in which we coached. One male referee in particular was issued a restraining order for shouting licentious remarks at a female coach he didn't like.

The more we studied Klinsmann's commentary on American soccer, the more questions we asked. If the structural pyramid of developmental soccer in this country was upside down, how did it work in other countries? What provided other soccer powers like Germany and newly emerging soccer countries like Japan the proper foundation for producing successful national teams? Had the United States always had its structural pyramid upside down? How could it have established a network of leagues in the 1890s and early 1900s without a sound structure in place? Or in the 1920s, when professional teams produced enough prominent players to lead the United States to a third-place finish in the 1930 World Cup? Wouldn't the 1970s have to have been somewhat structurally sound in order to produce such a successful team as the New York Cosmos? What about our own experience as both participants in and observers of the sport? Could our local soccer scene serve as a case study of Klinsmann's critique? These queries were the beginning of this book.

American Soccer: History, Culture, Class sets up a quasi-theoretical model in the first chapter that focuses on the importance of class in soccer today. The bottom line is that it takes lots of money to play American soccer, and the firmly entrenched club system and university programs that serve as gateways to higher levels of play unfairly discriminate against lower socioeconomic groups. Soccer-loving Latinos, particularly recent immigrants, feel this discernment the most. Immigrant populations from Latin America find that they're not only often relegated to menial employment, and thus unable to afford prescribed routes to competitive soccer, but also confronted by an indifferent (and sometimes racist) public unwilling to assimilate them into mainstream culture.

Because of the steep financial costs of player development through the club system, soccer is symbolically located in a middle-to-upper-class cultural milieu. As such, the sport is not only played by youth and financed by parents but also often consumed as a commodity that signifies class status. In this way, both the material and symbolic capital of soccer inhibit its complete integration into the American sports landscape. Beyond youth from lower socioeconomic backgrounds being generally financially prevented from development opportunities, those youths who do progress through the system rarely become life-long, passionate fans, since playing soccer is often a transient product consumed as a class marker. This class thread, symbolized by Klinsmann's upside-down pyramid, runs through this book.

We also argue that at various times in the history of U.S. soccer, the pyramid was properly constructed, with a solid foundation that naturally (and indiscriminately) fed into higher levels of amateur and professional soccer. Chapters 3–6 chronicle American soccer's roller-coaster journey, showing that for the first 70 years the shadow of class rarely defined successful soccer. This changed when television commercialized the sport, when American universities institutionalized varsity soccer, and when club soccer took over youth development. With these changes, Klinsmann's metaphor becomes more relevant and reflects many of the problems associated with American soccer today. Through personal narratives, the latter half of the book analyzes soccer at the community level and demonstrates the connection between the local and the national. Ultimately our stories are the same stories found all over the United States. According to Klinsmann's reasoning, however, soccer at the men's national level won't change until our personal stories change.

Again we're left with questions. What happens if all the fathers (and mothers) coaching soccer are replaced by more experienced coaches who really do know the game? What happens if the entire pay-to-play youth development system is turned upside down, so that less emphasis is placed on competitive soccer, matching uniforms, multiple out-of-town tournaments, and winning, and more on learning basic fundamentals of the game? Would the face of developmental soccer truly change if U.S. soccer successfully institutionalizes academy programs across the country, more akin to the kinds of systems in place around the globe? What would happen if American universities dismantled their entire soccer scholarship programs and focused instead on professional organizations sponsoring youth players, the way it's done in Europe and South America? Would their technical skills and sense of the game improve through year-round training? How would the sport pan out if immigrant populations once again were assimilated into the American soccer fabric, at all levels?

In the end, it all depends on how one measures "success." Is that measure to be found in the success of the national teams? Or is it in popular and financially viable professional leagues? Perhaps it's in tens of millions of loyal fans who make gate and television revenue sufficient to move the sport into the rarified air of big-money sports? Or maybe it's found in Latinos creating social spaces of their own that both reflect and ameliorate problems of adjustment in a country that does not fully accept them? Or perhaps it's in the gender equity of the sport? Or in millions of youths exercising and having fun playing soccer?

Regardless of how success is defined, the fact remains that soccer occupies a limited space in the American sports landscape, defined by both material and symbolic dimensions of class. From an ethical standpoint, this shouldn't be the case. A land of opportunity needs to build paths of equal access wherever and whenever it can. And from a practical standpoint, equal access will improve the caliber of play at all levels, gradually moving the sport from an obscure corner of the field to the center of the pitch.

Only time will tell if the upside-down pyramid of American soccer can turn right side up. There are signs that an increasing number of soccer enthusiasts recognize the problem, including those in charge of U.S. soccer. The tell-tale sign of the possible shift in the architecture of American soccer may well be the USMNT's play in the upcoming World Cup in Brazil. Klinsmann's at the helm of the team, although his appointment as head coach in 2010 hasn't provided the time and space to completely overhaul player development. Thinking about a pyramid pointing toward the sky instead of in the ground is a much-needed start, though.

Afterword: 2014 World Cup

Two nights before the USMNT's 2014 World Cup opening match in Natal, Brazil, first-time team member John Brooks had a dream. The United States was playing Ghana, its nemesis in the preceding two World Cups. The score was tied as the clock moved inevitably toward the end of regulation play. At the 80th minute, Brooks headed a corner kick into the net for what turned out to be the winning goal. Because Brooks was not scheduled to start the actual match and had no idea whether he would even enter as a substitute, the dream seemed particularly surreal. Although he mentioned it to several of his teammates, no one, including the 21-year-old Brooks, saw the dream as anything but a nighttime fantasy of an excited player in his first World Cup.

On June 16, the Americans actually squared off against the Ghanaian national team in Natal, the northeastern seaside city. The game marked the American team's initial match in what many in the soccer world were calling "the Group of Death," although several other groups were equally intimidating. The U.S. was matched in Group G against Germany, Portugal, and Ghana. Germany and Portugal were considered among the best teams in the world, and Ghana, although not officially ranked above the United States, had eliminated the Americans from the past two World Cups by identical 2–1 scores. Few experts predicted survival for the U.S. team, especially if they lost in their opening rendezvous with Ghana.

As the match began, no one could have predicted what was about to happen. The 39,780 spectators in the Estadio das Danas had barely settled into their seats when Clint Dempsey took a pass from Jermaine Jones thirty yards from the goal. Dempsey made a beautiful run, which culminated in a move that left a Ghanaian defender spinning on his heels. Dempsey's powerful shot bounced off the right post into the net for a 1–0 lead. Only 29 seconds had elapsed in the match. Dempsey's unexpected goal ranks as the fifth fastest goal scored in World Cup history. It happened so quickly that most fans around the world witnessed the miraculous play, for the first time, on instant replay. The stadium crowd seemed momentarily stunned, uncertain about what had just transpired. Then, within milliseconds, the section of the stadium filled with red, white, and blue exploded. Back home in the United States, a record 24 million television viewers went wild.

Over the next 20 minutes the euphoria slowly evaporated, as Ghana began to control the pace of the match and create havoc in the American midfield. In the 23rd minute, Jozy Altidore made a promising run down the left side when he suddenly collapsed with a hamstring injury that removed him from the game. The unexpected departure demoralized an increasingly disorganized United States team. Despite an early 1–0 lead, things didn't look promising. Ghana controlled the ball more than 60 percent of the 45-minute half, and the U.S. offense looked amoebic after Dempsey's initial heroics. The American team's back defensive line staved off attack after attack, and the USMNT breathed a sigh of relief as they departed the pitch at halftime with a slight lead.

At the beginning of the second half, Coach Jürgen Klinnsman substituted John Brooks, the dreamer, for injured defender Matt Besler. Unbeknownst at the time, it was the only action Brooks would see the entire World Cup. Perhaps Klinsmann knew about Brooks's dream and was superstitious enough to insert the young player in case the Ghanaians tied the match. Knowing Klinsmann's characteristic understanding of soccer, he undoubtedly had a more rational reason for the substitution.

As the actual 80th minute of the match passed with the United States holding onto a precarious 1–0 lead, Brooks and fellow players privy to his dream hoped there would be no need for end-of-the-match heroics. But moments later, in the 82nd minute of play, a nightmarish Ghana goal tied the score. The pressure was on. Without Altidore, and in spite of Brooks's nighttime musing, the chances of another American goal seemed highly remote.

Yet the tie set the stage for one of the most remarkable achievements of the U.S. national team. Within five minutes American midfielder Graham Zusi let sail a corner kick toward Ghana's goal. In the right place at the right time, a towering 6'4" Brooks deftly headed the ball into the back of the net. The United States held onto the lead, and their eventual 2–1 victory bolstered their hope of surviving the group stage. Coincidence or not, the unexpected goal fulfilled Brooks's dream. It also satisfied the dreams of some 24 million U.S. fans.

Brooks typifies some of the significant changes that Klinsmann instituted in the final U.S. World Cup roster. The son of a U.S. serviceman and a German mother, he was born and raised in Berlin. Rising through the youth development program of his hometown team, Hertha BSC, he joined their reserve team at age 17 then the regular Hertha squad a year later. Holding dual German-American citizenship, he played for both the German and the U.S. U-20 teams before Klinsmann called him up to the USMNT roster in the summer of 2013.

Actually the 2014 World Cup American team contained seven players who grew up outside of the United States, learning their soccer through very different development programs than their U.S. counterpart. Five of these players developed through the German system, and one each came from Norway and Iceland. While some might see the five German-American players as evidence of a Klinsmann bias, others see it as a smart move to both improve the team and to express faith in a different national model of player development. While recent U.S. squads have included two to three players with dual citizenship who learned their soccer skills abroad, Klinsmann made an extra effort to recruit such players. He recently stated that such efforts will continue. "We are looking for Americans around the world, no matter what background they have," he told BBC News. "It's all part of globalization."[1]

Additionally, for the first time since 1990 when the United States broke the 50-year drought in World Cup qualification, the USMNT fielded a minority of players who played university soccer. Twelve of the players on the roster never set foot on a university pitch. In contrast, from 1990–2010 approximately 75–80 percent of the USMNT members came through the traditional club to university pipeline. Fourteen members of the roster spent most of their professional lives playing abroad rather than in the MLS. Even more telling were the players who comprised the core of the 2014 team. Of the six players who started all of the team's matches, five never played university soccer and all six were professionals whose primary experience came from abroad. The starting 11 against Ghana included seven players without university experience and eight who had spent most of their professional playing outside the United States.

These changes in the roster reflect Klinsmann's emphasis on diversifying the soccer backgrounds of U.S. players. They also indicate the slow but steady growth in the quality of American players. As soccer regains a foothold in the American sports landscape, more high quality players are emerging at an earlier age, which allows them to forego the university experience and turn professional. Klinsmann's focus on such players indicates a strategy of selecting players who have managed to invest the crucial 18–22 age years at the professional level rather than the university one.

After defeating Ghana the USMNT squared off against Portugal. With the international Player of the Year, Cristiano Renaldo, and a roster stacked with European professionals, the Portuguese presented a formidable foe. Coming off an uncharacteristically poor performance in their first group match by losing to Germany 4–1, Portugal was looking for revenge. The United States needed at least a draw to have a chance of moving forward in the tournament. An unlikely victory would insure an advance into the round of sixteen.

Portugal played aggressively from the outset. Within five minutes of the match, they scored. Without the powerful striker Altidore, the United States offense struggled. Twenty minutes into the second half and still trailing 1–0, another German American—Jermaine Jones—launched a rocket from more than 25 yards out, eluding the Portuguese keeper. Suddenly the score was tied. The pace of the match heightened as both teams struggled for a much needed victory. At the 72nd minute Klinsmann substituted DeAndre Yedlin, an untested 20-year-old who played two years at Akron University and professionally with Seattle in the MLS. He was the first signee of the Seattle club to come through their development program.

Yedlin's speed and energy ignited the American team. With less than ten minutes left in the match, Yedlin made a lightning fast run into the corner and launched a cross that ricocheted from Michael Bradley to Zusi, who tapped the ball to Dempsey for a go-ahead goal. Unbelievably, the U.S. led Portugal 2–1. The USMNT smelled victory against one of the best teams in the world. But the miracle never happened. With only 30 seconds left in the match, Renaldo launched a perfect cross that found Silvestre Varela with a header for the tying goal. What moments before seemed like a certain victory, ended in a tie. In a way it was what the Americans had hoped for, since a tie kept them alive. Yet within seconds of a victory that would have assured them a place in the final round, the draw seemed like a loss in more ways than one.

Their last match pitted the USMNT against powerhouse Germany, who after destroying Portugal survived a 2–2 draw with Ghana. The Germans controlled the match, but the U.S. defense held the more powerful Europeans to a single goal. Portugal defeated Ghana 2–1 in their final match, but the Americans accomplished their objective of gaining the round of sixteen on goal differentials, finishing second to Germany in such a competitive group. It was the first time the American team made the round of sixteen in two successive World Cups.

The first round opponent in the knockout round featured Belgium, a country of approximately 11 million people living in a territory roughly the size of Massachusetts. The only other time the two countries had met in a World Cup was in 1930, with the U.S. winning 3–0 on its way to a third place finish. The highest finish for Belgium came in 1986 when they finished fourth. They were no strangers to the round of sixteen.

Belgium had won all three of their group games, although they had not been tested with stiff competition. Nevertheless more than a handful of soccer experts picked the small European country as a sleeper that could go far in the quarterfinals, and perhaps even advance to the semi-finals. Having survived the competition in Group G, the U.S. team under Klinsmann felt optimistic about their chances.

After 90+ minutes of competitive play, the two teams remained at a 0–0 standstill. That was all about to change in the first few minutes of overtime. Within three minutes, Belgium scored the first goal of the match, followed 12 minutes later by a second goal. Because Belgium's defense had yielded only one goal in its previous 375 minutes of competition, a 2–0 lead appeared insurmountable. But Klinsmann had one more improbable wild-card up his sleeve. He inserted 19 year-old German-American Julien Green into the line-up. Green had grown up in Berlin and come through Bayern Munich's youth development program. After playing in 23 matches and scoring 15 goals on Bayern's development team, he signed a contract with the top division club and made his start fall 2013. In the spring of 2014, he chose to play for the United States rather than Germany, making his debut in a friendly against Mexico in April of that year.

Just two minutes after Belgium's second goal, Bradley lofted a perfect pass over the Belgium defense and Green flicked it out of the air past the Belgium goalie. It was his first touch in the match, making him the youngest U.S. player to score a goal in a World Cup. With just over 13 minutes left in overtime, the United States tried desperately to level the score, but Belgium ended up prevailing 2–1. The USMNT suffered a heartbreaking finish but had proven to the world that they too could compete on the international stage.

If the American team squandered the opportunity to reach the quarterfinals as they had in 2002, there was plenty of reason for optimism. The USMNT qualified for the World Cup for the seventh consecutive time. Despite dire predictions, the team survived the deadly G group that comprised some of the top players in the world. They broke the spell of Ghana defeats. They outplayed Portugal, coming within seconds of a victory. The Americans held the powerful German team that went on to win the World Cup to a single goal. After 90 minutes of fierce competition, they played the Belgium team to a 0–0 draw. In four grueling matches their opponents outscored them by a single goal. In addition, three of the five German-Americans recruited by Klinsmann scored goals. Youthful John Brooks, DeAndre Yedlin, and Julien Green set an enthusiastic tone for the team's future. A record 24.7 million television viewers in the United States watched the U.S.-Portugal match, more viewers than any single 2013 World Series game or the 2014 NBA finals. For the second straight World Cup, American stations televised all 64 World Cup matches.

Yet no one could deny that the USMNT performance left something to be desired. What most consider one of the greatest sports nations in the world failed to advance any further than they had in 1994, 2002, or 2010 when they also reached the final sixteen. The team's ball control, passing accuracy, technical abilities, and speed often suffered against their opponents'. In the final analysis the USMNT showed that they are certainly one of the top 20 national teams in the world. Are they one of the top 15? Maybe. Are they one of the top ten? Not yet.

The question of the team's continued progress is still unanswered. Klinsmann's strategy and player selection appears to have produced positive steps forward. In three short years under his stewardship, the team has posted an impressive 32–13–9 won-lost-tied record. While some of their opponents lacked world-class team play, in 2012 the USMNT beat Italy for the first time by a score of 1–0. The following year they beat Germany 4–3. They led CONCACAF qualifying for the World Cup. In 2013 they won the region's Gold Cup Championship, their first time since 2007. They marched over the opposition with a goal differential of 20–4 in six matches. Still, how does one truly measure their progress in the 2014 World Cup?

In their book *Soccernomics,* Simon Kuper and Stefan Szymanski maintain that three statistical variables predict a national team's success: a country's population, its per capita income, and its experience with the sport.[2] Given these dynamics the authors predict that China, Japan and the United States—"the three largest economies in the world"—will emerge as international soccer powers in the not-too-distant future.[3] These countries currently lag behind soccer superpowers, they argue, because they lack relative soccer experience. Wealthy populations should enable them to catch up over time, however. While this "inexperience" may be true for China and Japan, it's certainly less true for the United States. As we point out in Chapters 3–6, soccer has a long-standing history in the United States.

The complicating issue in the prognosis one finds in *Soccernomics* revolves around defining what constitutes "experience." Americans have been playing competitive soccer since the 1880s. They attempted to form the third professional league in the world in the 1890s. They were among the first countries to join FIFA in the early 20th century. They operated a relatively successful professional league for more than a dozen years in the 1920s and 1930s. The USMNT finished third in the first FIFA World Cup in 1930. In the 1970s, the NASL professional league attracted some of the biggest players in world soccer. This chronology certainly displays more than a smidgen of experience. In the final analysis we need to return to the pyramid upside down.

In the world of human societies there is rarely, if ever, anything akin to pristine experience. In most contemporary societies the complicated cultural matrix through which experience is defined includes socioeconomic class structures that shape life opportunities and life-styles, both materially and symbolically. Prior to World War II, Americans who played at the highest levels of soccer in the United States learned their skills and knowledge of the game in the way that the rest of the world did—informally in streets, on play grounds, and in a myriad of amateur and semi-pro leagues that displayed the pyramid right-side-up. Access to the sport was not prohibited by the inability of parents to pay for the "privilege" of playing the sport. The claim that prior to World War II the sport was a foreign sport played by immigrants is erroneous and certainly curious in a country comprised almost entirely of immigrants and their descendants. That this early American experience with soccer is marginalized indicates more about certain contemporary sociopolitical views than it does about historical reality.

As we have suggested, the growth of collegiate soccer and the pay-to-play youth development system in post-war America transformed the cultural space occupied by the sport. Access to player development pipelines transferred to those who could afford the long-term investment, and the sport quickly became materially and symbolically identified with middle to upper class life opportunities and lifestyles. Ever since, the pyramid has teetered on what was supposed to be its apex. Until the cultural space for both players and fans is broadened, soccer will remain marginal. There are signs that player development trajectories are loosening and expanding. Jürgen Klinsmann recognizes the problem, and he seems committed to solving it. Only time will tell.

A final element to this story is the finale of the World Cup. Germany defeated Argentina 1–0 for its fourth championship and its first first-place finish since 1990. They marched through the competition with six wins and one tie, outscoring the opposition 18–4. In the semi-finals they destroyed five-time winner Brazil by a World Cup record 7–1. As German coach Joachim Löw observed after the final, "We started this project ten years ago and what has happened today is the result of many years' work, starting with Jürgen Klinsmann."[4] Löw was alluding to the transformation of the German youth development system that began after Germany's failures in the 1998 World Cup. We describe these changes in Chapter 2. The young stars of the 2014 German squad developed through that new system. And with almost a third of the squad 23 years of age or younger, led by Mario Götze who scored the winning goal against Argentina, the German future looks bright.

Ultimately John Brooks's dream came true. It resulted from individual hard work and the revamped German development system that allowed him to flourish. If the United States can right the upside-down pyramid, creating a similar system of more open access then Brooks's dream might be realized, in one form or another, by countless American soccer players. Because Jürgen Klinsmann helped engineer the player development transformation in his native Germany, one can only hope that he can accomplish the same thing in the United States. As fathers-turned soccer coaches whose journey led them into the depths of American soccer, we could then join tens of millions of ardent American soccer fans in celebration. It would be a celebration of both the dream of equal access and of the United States one day winning the World Cup.

Chapter Notes

Chapter 1

1. sports.yahoo.com/news/clinton-hops-u-soccer-bandwagon-204400660-spt.html.
2. Clemente A. Lisi, *A History of the World Cup, 1930–2010* (Lanham, MD: Scarecrow Press, 2011), 297.
3. www.sbnation.com/2010/7/2/1549267/klinsmanns-thoughts-on-u-s-soccers.
4. Ibid.
5. Ibid.
6. abcnews.go.com/WN/abc-world-news-poll-us-middle-class-concerns/story?id=10088470.
7. Michael Hout, "How Class Works in Popular Conception," Working Paper (Berkeley, CA: Survey Research Center, 2007), 11.
8. homepages.sover.net/~spectrum/womensoverview.html.
9. David L. Andrews, "Contextualizing Suburban Soccer: Consumer Culture, Lifestyle Differentiation, and Suburban America," in *Football Culture: Local Contests, Global Visions*, edited by Gerry P.T. Finn and Richard Giulianotti (Portland, OR: Frank Cass, 2000), 31–53.
10. Franklin Foer, *How Soccer Explains the World: An Unlikely Theory of Globalization* (New York: HarperCollins, 2004), 296.
11. D. Zwick and David Andrews, "The Suburban Soccer Field: Sport and the Culture of Privilege in Contemporary America," in *Football Cultures and Identity*, edited by G. Armstrong and R. Giulianotti (New York: Palgrave Macmillan, 1999), 211–22.
12. www.migrationpolicy.org/pubs/MexCentAmimmigrants.pdf.
13. www.nytimes.com/2010/05/07/sports/soccer/07soccer.html.

Chapter 2

1. articles.latimes.com/1990-03-27/sports/sp-219_1_east-german.
2. www.uefa.com/memberassociations/association=ger/news/newsid=1564918.html.
3. isleofholland.com/read/sports/14-classic-johan-cruyff-quotes-explained.
4. community.seattletimes.nwsource.com/archive/?date=19900401&slug=1064097.
5. Ibid.
6. articles.chicagotribune.com/1990-07-09/sports/9002270544_1_edgardo-codesal-argentina-mario-zagalo.
7. static.bundesliga.de/media/native/autosync/dfl_leistungszentren2011_gb.pdf.
8. www.goal.com/en-us/news/1679/us-national-tem/2012/03/05/2947800/klinsmann-believes-pickup-and-playground-soccer-is-key-to.
9. Ibid.
10. sportsillustrated.cnn.com/2010/soccer/world-cup-2010/writers/raphael_honigstein/07/01/germany.reinvention/index.html.
11. static.bundesliga.de/media/native/autosync/dfl_leistungszentren2011_gb.pdf.
12. Ibid.
13. Ibid.
14. www.cuhk.edu.hk/jas/staff/benng/publications/anime1.pdf.
15. Paul Gravett, *Manga: 60 Years of Japanese Comics* (New York: Harper Design, 2004).
16. Frederick Schodt, *Dreamland Japan: Writings on Modern Manga* (Berkeley, CA: Stone Bridge, 1996).
17. Mark McWilliams, ed., *Japanese Visual Culture: Explorations in the World of Manga and Anime* (New York: East Gate Books, 2008), 8.
18. Ibid., 36.

19. Brent Wilson, "Becoming Japanese: Manga, Children's Drawings, and the Construction of National Character," *Visual Arts Research* 25, no. 2 (1999): 48–60.
20. www.fifa.com/classicfootball/players/do-you-remember/newsid=1080926/index.html.
21. www.asianfootballfeast.com/?portfolio=j-league-3.
22. www.j-league.or.jp/aboutj/pdf/2013/aboutj_eng.pdf.
23. jleague.co.uk/2012/07/09/gates-in-the-j-league-a-cause-for-concern-part-2.
24. www.tjf.or.jp/eng/content/japaneseculture/32soccer.htm.
25. edition.cnn.com/2005/WORLD/asiapcf/10/18/talkasia.nakata.script.

Chapter 3

1. www.coatsandclark200years.com/pdf/timeline.pdf.
2. Thomas Dunmore and Scott Murray, *Soccer for Dummies* (Hoboken, NJ: John Wiley and Sons, 2013), 22.
3. www.thefa.com/Competitions/FACompetitions/TheFACup/History/historyofthefacup.
4. David Wangerin, *Soccer in a Football World* (Philadelphia: Temple University Press, 2006), 27.
5. Maldwyn Jones, *Destination America* (New York: Holt, Rinehart and Winston, 1976), 107.
6. Roger Allaway, *Rangers, Rovers and Spindles: Soccer, Immigration and Textiles in New England and New Jersey* (Haworth, NJ: St. Johann Press, 2005), xii.
7. Allaway, *Rangers*, 35.
8. Ibid., 36.
9. Ibid., 37.
10. Ibid.
11. Ibid., 17.
12. Ibid., 43.
13. teachushistory.org/nineteenth-century-immigration/resources/duden-recommends-immigrating.
14. Allaway, *Rangers*, 43.
15. Dave Lange, *Soccer Made in St. Louis: A History of the Game in America's First Soccer City* (St. Louis: Reedy Press, 2011).
16. scarletknights.com/football/history/first-game.asp.
17. Wangerin, *Soccer*, 24.
18. homepages.sover.net/~spectrum/alpf.html.
19. Allaway, *Rangers*, 46.
20. Ibid., 47.
21. David Wangerin, *Distant Corners* (Philadelphia: Temple University Press, 2011), 8.
22. Ibid., 12–13.
23. Ibid., 9–11.
24. Wangerin, *Soccer*, 23.
25. query.nytimes.com/mem/archive-free/pdf?res=9D07E5DE143DE733A2575AC1A9669D946497D6CF.
26. "President Eliot on Football," *The School Journal*, Vol. 70 (New York: United Education Company, 1905), 188.
27. Wangerin, *Distant*, 18.
28. Ibid., 20.
29. Allaway, *Rangers*, 50–51.
30. Wangerin, *Soccer*, 33.
31. Wangerin, *Distant*, 43–44.
32. homepages.sover.net/~spectrum/year/1914.html.
33. Ibid.
34. Wangerin, *Soccer*, 37.
35. Ibid., 41–42.
36. Ibid., 42–43.
37. query.nytimes.com/mem/archive-free/pdf?res=9402E6DF103FE432A25753C1A9639C946195D6CF.

Chapter 4

1. homepages.sover.net/~spectrum/hist1.html.
2. David Wangerin, *Distant Corners* (Philadelphia: Temple University Press, 2011), 70–71.
3. Ibid., 71.
4. Ibid.
5. David Wangerin, *Soccer in a Football World* (Philadelphia: Temple University Press, 2006), 49.
6. Ibid., 72.
7. homepages.sover.net/~spectrum/year/1923.html; Wangerin, *Soccer in a Football World*, 53–54; Wangerin, *Distant*, 73.
8. Wangerin, *Distant*, 74.
9. homepages.sover.net/~spectrum/year/1925.html.
10. homepages.sover.net/~spectrum/year/1926.html.
11. Colin Jose, *American Soccer League, 1921–1931* (Lanham, MD: Scarecrow Press, 1998), 17.
12. Wangerin, *Soccer*, 53.
13. Ibid.
14. Jose, *American Soccer*, 329.
15. Ibid., 54.

16. Ibid., 67.
17. Ibid., 102–3.
18. Ibid., 470, 472, 494.
19. Wangerin, *Soccer*, 58.
20. Ibid., 57–58.
21. Ibid., 45.
22. Jose, *American Soccer*, 467, 472, 488.
23. Wangerin, *Soccer*, 60.
24. Jose, *American Soccer*, 26, 49.
25. Ibid., 67.
26. Ibid., 448.
27. Colin Jose, *North American Soccer League Encyclopedia* (Haworth, NJ: St. Johann Press, 2003), 49.
28. homepages.sover.net/~spectrum/year/1926.html.
29. Ibid.
30. homepages.sover.net/~spectrum/year/1927.html.
31. homepages.sover.net/~spectrum/year/1928.html.
32. Jose, *American Soccer*, 532.
33. homepages.sover.net/~spectrum/gonsalves.html.
34. Jose, *American Soccer*, 202, 230, 248.
35. homepages.sover.net/~spectrum/year/1930.html.
36. Wangerin, *Soccer*, 92; Jose, *American Soccer*, 475, 484.
37. Clemente A. Lisi, *A History of the World Cup, 1930–2010* (Lanham, MD: Scarecrow Press, 2011), 9–17.
38. Ibid., 17.
39. Jose, *American Soccer*, 471.
40. Lisi, *History*, 18.
41. homepages.sover.net/~spectrum/year/1930.html.
42. homepages.sover.net/~spectrum/year/1928.html.
43. Wangerin, *Distant*, 82.
44. Jose, *American Soccer*, 230.
45. homepages.sover.net/~spectrum/year/1932.html.
46. www.baseball-reference.com/leagues/MLB/1929-misc.shtml; www.baseball-reference.com/leagues/MLB/1932-misc.shtml; www.baseball-reference.com/leagues/MLB/1933-misc.shtml.
47. Jose, *American Soccer*, ix.

Chapter 5

1. www.historyorb.com/deaths/date/1951.
2. David Wangerin, *Soccer in a Football World* (Philadelphia: Temple University Press, 2006), 51.
3. www.nytimes.com/2009/12/10/sports/soccer/10soccer.html.
4. Clemente A. Lisi, *A History of the World Cup, 1930–2010* (Lanham, MD: Scarecrow Press, 2011), 38.
5. homepages.sover.net/~spectrum/year/1950.html.
6. www.nytimes.com/2009/12/10/sports/soccer/10soccer.html.
7. www.telegraph.co.uk/sport/football/teams/usa/7821735/England-v-USA-Fabio-Capellos-men-need-to-fear-lesson-of-Belo-Horizonte.html.
8. Lisi, *History*, 49–51.
9. www.nytimes.com/2009/12/10/sports/soccer/10soccer.html.
10. Lisi, *History*, 52.
11. Ibid.
12. www.nytimes.com/2009/12/10/sports/soccer/10soccer.html.
13. www.independent.co.uk/news/obituaries/harry-keough-footballer-who-helped-beat-England-6945646.html.
14. www.nytimes.com/2009/12/10/sports/soccer/10soccer.html.
15. Wangerin, *Soccer*, 112–14.
16. Lisi, *History*, 54.
17. Ibid.
18. www.nytimes.com/2009/12/10/sports/soccer/10soccer.html.
19. Wangerin, *Soccer*, 114.
20. www.nytimes.com/2009/12/10/sports/soccer/10soccer.html.
21. homepages.sover.net/~spectrum/collegepostwar.html.
22. homepages.sover.net/~spectrum/collegecount.html.
23. Ibid.
24. Wangerin, *Soccer*, 102.
25. homepages.sover.net/~spectrum/collegepostwar.html.
26. Ibid.
27. www.tvb.org/media/file/TV_Basics.pdf.
28. www.museum.tv/eotv/sportsandte.htm.
29. Ibid.
30. www.jfredmacdonald.com/onutv/sportstv.htm.
31. Wangerin, *Soccer*, 122.
32. Ibid., 123.
33. Ibid.
34. Clive Toye, *A Kick in the Grass* (Haworth, NJ: St. Johann Press, 2006), 6.
35. Ibid.
36. Wangerin, *Soccer*, 124–25.

37. Ibid., 125.
38. Toye, *Kick*, 8.
39. Wangerin, *Soccer*, 132.
40. Jack Gould, "TV: Soccer Makes Its Network Debut," *New York Times*, April 17, 1967.
41. Wangerin, *Soccer*, 133.
42. Ibid., 138.
43. Colin Jose, *North American Soccer League Encyclopedia* (Haworth, NJ: St. Johann Press, 2003), 384.
44. Wangerin, *Soccer*, 152.
45. homepages.sover.net/~spectrum/year/1973.html.
46. Jose, *North American*, 385–87.

Chapter 6

1. espn.go.com/classic/biography/s/Pele.html.
2. Clive Toye, *A Kick in the Grass* (Haworth, NJ: St. Johann Press, 2006), 49–53.
3. David Wangerin, *Soccer in a Football World* (Philadelphia: Temple University Press, 2006), 169.
4. Toye, *Kick*, 93.
5. Wangerin, *Soccer*, 169.
6. Ibid., 170.
7. Toye, *Kick*, 90.
8. sportsillustrated.cnn.com/vault/article/magazine/MAG1094961/index.
9. Colin Jose, *North American Soccer League Encyclopedia* (Haworth, NJ: St. Johann Press, 2003), 231, 387.
10. Wangerin, *Soccer*, 176.
11. www.nytimes.com/2012/04/03/sports/soccer/giorgio-chinaglia-italian-star-and-the-cosmos-leader-dies-at-65.html?_r=0.
12. Wangerin, *Soccer*, 182.
13. Ibid., 184.
14. goalwa.wordpress.com/2013/03/27/original-sounders-soccer-bowl-77-memories-remain-in-technicolor.
15. si.com/vault/article/magazine/MAG1092771/index.
16. Wangerin, *Soccer*, 181.
17. homepages.sover.net/~spectrum/nasl hist.html.
18. Wangerin, *Soccer*, 184–85.
19. Ibid., 186.
20. Toye, *Kick*, 153.
21. Ibid.
22. Jose, *North American*, 388–89.
23. Ibid., 49, 182, 299.
24. homepages.sover.net/~spectrum/nasl/nasl-standings.html.
25. Wangerin, *Soccer*, 191.
26. Ibid., 190.
27. Jose, *North American*, 49, 389.
28. David Wangerin, *Distant Corners* (Philadelphia: Temple University Press, 2011), 230.
29. Wangerin, *Soccer*, 199.
30. Ibid.
31. Ibid., 200.
32. Ibid.
33. Jose, *North American*, 49.
34. si.com/vault/article/magazine/MAG1123797/index.
35. Ibid.
36. Ibid.
37. Ibid.
38. Jose, *North American*, 49.
39. Ibid., 381.
40. Wangerin, *Soccer*, 211.
41. Ibid., 209.
42. Ibid., 211.
43. Jose, *North American*, 392.
44. Ibid., 49.
45. Ibid., 381.
46. Wangerin, *Soccer*, 215.
47. Ibid.
48. Jose, *North American*, 382.
49. Toye, *Kick*, 153.
50. Ibid., 165.
51. Ibid., 166–67.
52. Ibid., 167.
53. Ibid., 169
54. Wangerin, *Soccer*, 209.
55. Toye, *Kick*, 31.

Chapter 7

1. Tom Watt, *A Beautiful Game* (New York: HarperOne, 2010), 158.
2. Ibid., 91.
3. Ibid., 20.
4. Ibid., 172.
5. www.nps.gov/thro/historyculture/theodore-roosevelt-quotes.htm.
6. Ibid.
7. Alfred La Gasse and Walter E. Cook, *History of Parks and Recreation* (Arlington, VA: National Recreation and Park Association, 1974), 12.
8. Ibid., 15.
9. Ibid., 26–29.
10. www.nrpa.org.
11. www.wataugacounty.org/main/App_Pages/Dept/ParksRec/Forms/Parks_and_Rec_Master_Plan_2010-2019.pdf.

Chapter 8

1. sportsillustrated.cnn.com/soccer/news/20130812/clint-dempsey-seattle-sounders-mls-interview.
2. www.mlssoccer.com/news/article/2013/06/02/jurgen-klinsmann-gushes-over-clint-dempsey-one-best-players-usmnt-history.
3. www.espnfc.com/columns/story?id=370300&&cc=5901.
4. Ibid.
5. Ibid.
6. www.theguardian.com/football/2007/nov/24/newsstory.fulham.
7. sportsillustrated.cnn.com/2010/soccer/world-cup-2010/writers/melissa_segura/06/09/dempsey/1.html.
8. Ibid.
9. Ibid.
10. si.com/vault/article/magazine/MAG1169764/index.
11. Ibid.
12. Bruce Dick, Andrés Fisher, and Gregory Reck, dirs., *Offside(s): Soccer in Small-Town America* (Boone, NC, 2009), DVD.
13. homepages.sover.net/~spectrum/collegecount.html.
14. homepages.sover.net/~spectrum/mcdonald.html.
15. Ibid.
16. livability.com/top-10/top-10-soccer-cities.
17. money.cnn.com/magazines/moneymag/best-places/2012.
18. livability.com/top-10/top-10-soccer-cities.
19. money.cnn.com/magazines/moneymag/best-places/2012.
20. Thomas Frank, "Lie Down for America," *Harper's Magazine* (April 2004): 43.
21. Ibid.
22. www.ncsoccer.org.
23. Andrei Markovits and Steven Hellerman, *Offside: Soccer and American Exceptionalism* (Princeton, NJ: Princeton University Press, 2001).
24. soccernet.espn.go.com/columns/story?id=614020&cc=5901.
25. Ibid.
26. soccernet.espn.go.com/print?id=616267&type=story&cc=5901.
27. soccernet.espn.go.com/columns/story?id=614020&cc=5901.
28. www.nytimes.com/2012/03/04/sports/soccer/soccers-all-year-model-forces-high-school-players-to-choose.html.
29. Ibid.

Chapter 9

1. *2007 Appalachian Men's Soccer* (Boone, NC: Appalachian State University Sports Information Office), 12.
2. *The Rhododendron* (Boone, NC: Appalachian State University, 1963), 174–75.
3. *The Rhododendron* (Boone, NC: Appalachian State University, 1964), 178–79.
4. *The Rhododendron* (Boone, NC: Appalachian State University, 1966), 90–91.
5. Steve DeGroat, telephone interview with Bruce Allen Dick, July 15, 2013.
6. Jim Jones, interview by Bruce Allen Dick and Gregory G. Reck, Boone, North Carolina, June 6, 2012.
7. Ibid.
8. Vaughn Christian, interview by Bruce Allen Dick and Gregory G. Reck, Boone, North Carolina, June 6, 2012.
9. Ibid.
10. Jim Jones, interview.
11. *The Rhododendron* (Boone, NC: Appalachian State University, 1975), 152.
12. Jim Jones, interview.
13. Emmanuel Udogu, interview by Bruce Allen Dick and Gregory G. Reck, Boone, North Carolina, May 14, 2013.
14. Vaughn Christian, interview.
15. Ibid.
16. Thompson Usiyan, telephone interview with Bruce Allen Dick and Gregory G. Reck, July 7, 2012.
17. Ibid.
18. Hank Steinbrecher, telephone interview with Bruce Allen Dick, July 31, 2013.
19. Ibid.
20. J. D. Reed, "It's Happy Days at Appy," *Sports Illustrated*, November 10, 1980, sportsillustrated.cnn.com/vault/article/magazine/MAG1123938/index.
21. Ibid.
22. Hank Steinbrecher, telephone interview.
23. Ibid.
24. *1996 Appalachian Men's Soccer* (Boone, NC: Appalachian State University Sports Information Office), 7.
25. Art Rex, interview by Bruce Allen Dick, Boone, North Carolina, July 29, 2013.
26. Ibid.
27. Ibid.
28. Ibid.
29. homepages.sover.net/~spectrum/collegepostwar.
30. Ibid.

31. Ibid.
32. Ibid.
33. www.ncaa.com/history/soccer-men/d1.
34. Ibid.
35. Ibid.
36. www.ncaa.com/history/soccer-women/d1.
37. *Women's Soccer Media Guide* (Boone, NC: Appalachian State University, 2013), 36.

Chapter 10

1. Ken Peacock and Paul Cuadros, "Soccer's Power to Transform" (presentation), *Appalachian Perspective*, Appalachian State University, Boone, North Carolina, October 2007.
2. "The New Latino South: The Context and Consequences of Rapid Population Growth," Pew Hispanic Center (2005): 4.
3. John Chesser, "Hispanics in N.C.: Big Numbers in Small Towns," UNC Charlotte Urban Institute (2012): 2, ui.uncc.edu/story/hispanic-latino-population-north-carolina-cities-census.
4. "Population of Watauga County, North Carolina: Census 2010 and 2000 Interactive Map, Demographics, Statistics, Graphs, Quick Facts" (2010): 2, censusviewer.com/county/NC/Watauga.
5. Gabriela Zabala and Steven Mann, "Demographic Trends of Hispanics/Latinos in North Carolina," Office of the Governor (2010): 10, 12.
6. Juan Javier Pescador, "Soccer (Fútbol) in the Americas," in *Oxford Bibliographies in Latino Studies*, Ilan Stavans, editor in chief (Spring 2013).
7. Marie Price and Courtney Whitworth, "Soccer and Latino Cultural Space: Metropolitan Washington Fútbol Leagues," in *Hispanic Spaces, Latino Places*, edited by Daniel D. Arreola (Austin: University of Texas Press, 2004), 168.
8. Ibid.
9. Ibid., 171.
10. Ibid., 185.
11. Alfredo Álvarez, interview by Bruce Allen Dick, Los Arcoiris Restaurant, Boone, North Carolina, June 25, 2012.
12. Ibid.
13. Ibid.
14. Ibid.
15. Paul Cuadros, *A Home on the Field: How One Championship Team Inspires Hope for the Revival of Small Town America* (New York: Rayo, 2006), 34.
16. Cuadros, *Home*, 150.
17. Ibid., ix.
18. Ibid., 150–51.
19. Ibid., 22.
20. Ibid., 56.
21. Ibid., 55, 267.
22. Ibid., 95.
23. Ibid., 171.
24. Ibid., 212.
25. Ibid., 250.
26. Bruce Dick, Andrés Fisher, and Gregory Reck, dirs., *Offside(s): Soccer in Small-Town America* (Boone, NC, 2009), DVD.
27. Ibid.
28. www.sbnation.com/2010/7/2/1549267/klinsmanns-thoughts-on-u-s-soccers.

Chapter 11

1. www.theguardian.com/football/the-shin-guardian-blog/2013/aug/07/clint-dempsey-tottenham-hotspur-seattle-sounders.
2. www.nytimes.com/2014/01/10/sports/soccer/deals-show-mls-no-longer-an-after-thought.html.
3. sportsillustrated.cnn.com/soccer/news/20130812/clint-dempsey-seattle-sounders-mls-interview.
4. Ibid.
5. www.nytimes.com/2014/01/10/sports/soccer/deals-show-mls-no-longer-an-afterthought.html.
6. www.mlssoccer.com/blog/post/2012/08/03/was-cristiano-ronaldo-flirting-mls.
7. Clemente A. Lisi, *A History of the World Cup, 1930–2010* (Lanham, MD: Scarecrow Press, 2011), 254–57.
8. www.nytimes.com/2005/11/11/sports/soccer/11soccer.html.
9. sportsillustrated.cnn.com/soccer/news/20130521/mls-expansion-team-new-york-city-fc.ap.
10. en.wikipedia.org/wiki/List_of_Major_League_Soccer_Stadiums.
11. www.nytimes.com/2005/11/11/sports/soccer/11soccer.html.
12. www.forbes.com/sites/chrissmith/2013/11/20/major-league-soccers-most-valuable-teams.
13. mlsattendance.blogspot.com.
14. www.baseball-reference.com/leagues/MLB/2013-misc.shtml; espn.go.com/nba/attendance/_/year/2013.
15. www.worldfootball.net.
16. www.mlssoccer.com/players; www.mlssoccer.com/history/allstar.

17. www.mlsplayers.org/salary_info.html.
18. sports.yahoo.com/nba/news?slug=ycn-10423863.
19. soccermommanual.com/soccer-salaries-how-much-do-soocer-players-make.
20. www.fifa.com/tournaments/archive/tournament=103/edition-4644/overview.html.
21. equalizersoccer.com/2013/08/20/nwsl-attendance-watch-week-19.
22. equalizersoccer.com/2013/04/11/nwsl-salaries-national-womens-soccer-league.
23. www.nytimes.com/2013/04/11/sports/soccer/megan-rapinoe-does-it-her-way-in-us-and-in-france.html.
24. Lisi, *History*, 222–25.
25. Ibid., 254–57.
26. www.independent.co.uk/news/world/medellin-mourns-its-murdered-sports-star-1411489.html.
27. Lisi, *History*, 277–79.
28. Ibid., 296–99.
29. Ibid., 307, 312–13.
30. Ibid., 328–32.
31. Ibid., 383–90.

Afterword

1. www.bbc.com/sport/0/Football/28122263.
2. Simon Kuper and Stefan Szymanski. *Soccernomics* (New York: Nation Books) 2009, 297–298.
3. Ibid, 306.
4. http://m.fifa.com/worldcup/matches/round=255959/match=300186501/quotes.html.

Bibliography

Books and Periodicals

Allaway, Roger. *Rangers, Rovers and Spindles: Soccer, Immigration and Textiles in New England and New Jersey*. Haworth, NJ: St. Johann, 2005.
Andrews, David L. "Contextualizing Suburban Soccer: Consumer Culture, Lifestyle Differentiation, and Suburban America." In *Football Culture: Local Contests, Global Visions*, edited by Gerry P. T. Finn and Richard Giulianotti. Portland, OR: Frank Cass, 2000.
Appalachian State University. *1996 Appalachian Men's Soccer.* Boone, NC: Appalachian State University Sports Information Office.
Appalachian State University. *2007 Appalachian Men's Soccer*. Boone, NC: Appalachian State University Sports Information Office.
Appalachian State University. *Women's Soccer Media Guide*. Boone, NC: Appalachian State University, 2013.
Asian Football Feast. "J. League." http://www.asianfootballfeast.com/?portfolio=j-league-3.
Clark, Matthew. *Playing Away: The A–Z of Soccer Sex Scandals*. Edinburgh: Mainstream, 2004.
Cosgrove, Stuart. *Hampden Babylon: Sex and Scandal in Scottish Football.* Edinburgh: Canongate, 2002.
Cuadros, Paul. *A Home on the Field: How One Championship Team Inspires Hope for the Revival of Small Town America.* New York: Rayo, 2006.
Doyle, John. *The World Is a Ball: The Joy, Madness and Meaning of Soccer*. New York: Rodale, 2010.
Dunmore, Thomas, and Scott Murray. *Soccer for Dummies*. Hoboken, NJ: John Wiley, 2013.
Foer, Franklin. *How Soccer Explains the World: An Unlikely Theory of Globalization*. New York: HarperCollins, 2004.
Frank, Thomas. "Lie Down for America." *Harper's Magazine* (April 2004).
Gould, Jack. "TV: Soccer Makes Its Network Debut." *New York Times*, April 17, 1967.
Gravett, Paul. *Manga: 60 Years of Japanese Comics*. New York: Harper Design, 2004.
Hill, Declan. *The Fix: Soccer and Organized Crime*. Toronto: McClelland and Stewart, 2010.
Hout, Michael. "How Class Works in Popular Conception." Working Paper. Berkeley, CA: Survey Center, 2007.
Jones, Maldwyn. *Destination America*. New York: Holt, Rinehart and Winston, 1976.
Jose, Colin. *American Soccer League, 1921–1931*. Lanham, MD: Scarecrow, 1998.
_____. *North American Soccer League Encyclopedia*. Haworth, NJ: St. Johann, 2003.
Kochhar, Rakesh, Roberto Suro, and Sonya Tafoya. "The New Latino South: The Context and Consequences of Rapid Population Growth." Pew Hispanic Center, 2005.

Kuper, Simon, and Stefan Szymanski. *Soccernomics*. New York: Nation Books, 2009.
La Gasse, Alfred, and Walter E. Cook. *History of Parks and Recreation*. Arlington, VA: National Recreation and Park Association, 1974.
Lange, Dave. *Soccer Made in St. Louis: A History of the Game in America's First Soccer City*. St. Louis: Reedy, 2011.
Le Tissier, Matt. *Taking Le Tiss*. New York: HarperSports, 2010.
Lisi, Clemente A. *A History of the World Cup, 1930–2010*. Lanham, MD: Scarecrow, 2011.
Markovits, Andrei, and Steven Hellerman. *Offside: Soccer and American Exceptionalism* Princeton, NJ: Princeton University Press, 2001.
McWilliams, Mark, ed. *Japanese Visual Culture: Explorations in the World of Manga and Anime*. New York: East Gate, 2008.
Péle and Robert L. Fish. *My Life and the Beautiful Game: The Autobiography of Soccer's Greatest Star.* New York: Doubleday, 1977.
Pescador, Juan Javier. "Soccer (Fútbol) in the Americas." In *Oxford Bibliographies in Latino Studies*, Ilan Stavanas, ed. Spring 2013.
Powell, Robert Andrew. *This Love Is Not for Cowards: Salvation and Soccer in Ciudad Juarez*. New York: Doubleday, 1977.
"President Eliot on Football." *The School Journal*, Vol. 70. New York: United Education, 1905.
Price, Marie, and Courtney Whitworth. "Soccer and Latino Cultural Space: Metropolitan Washington Fútbol Leagues." In *Hispanic Spaces, Latino Places*, edited by Daniel D. Arreola, 167–86. Austin: University of Texas Press, 2004.
The Rhododendron. Boone, NC: Appalachian State University, 1963.
The Rhododendron. Boone, NC: Appalachian State University, 1964.
The Rhododendron. Boone, NC: Appalachian State University, 1966.
The Rhododendron. Boone, NC: Appalachian State University, 1975.
Richards, Ted. *Soccer and Philosophy: Beautiful Thoughts on the Beautiful Game*. Chicago: Open Court, 2010.
Schodt, Frederick. *Manga! Manga! The World of Japanese Comics*. New York: Kodansha USA, 1983.
Toye, Clive. *A Kick in the Grass*. Haworth, NJ: St. Johann Press, 2006.
Wangerin, David. *Distant Corners*. Philadelphia: Temple University Press, 2011.
_____. *Soccer in a Football World*. Philadelphia: Temple University Press, 2006.
Watt, Tom. *A Beautiful Game*. New York: HarperOne, 2010.
Wesson, John. *The Science of Soccer*. London: Institute of Physics, 2002.
Wilson, Brent. "Becoming Japanese: Manga, Children's Drawings, and the Construction of National Character." *Visual Arts Research* 25, no. 2 (1999): 48–60.
Wilson, Steve. *The Boys from Little Mexico*. Boston: Beacon, 2002.
Zwick, D., and David Andrews. "The Suburban Soccer Field: Sport and the Culture of Privilege in Contemporary America." In *Football Cultures and Identity*, edited by G. Armstrong and R. Guilanotti, 211–22. New York: Palgrave Macmillan, 1999.

Interviews and Presentations

Álvarez, Alfredo. Interview by Bruce Allen Dick. Boone, NC, June 25, 2012.
Christian, Vaughn. Interview by Bruce Allen Dick and Gregory G. Reck. Boone, NC, June 6, 2012.
DeGroat, Steve. Telephone interview with Bruce Allen Dick. July 15, 2013.
Jones, Jim. Interview by Bruce Allen Dick and Gregory G. Reck. Boone, North Carolina, June 6, 2012.
Peacock, Ken, and Paul Cuadros. "Soccer's Power to Transform" (presentation). *Appalachian Perspective*, Appalachian State University, Boone, North Carolina. October 2007.

Rex, Art. Interview by Bruce Allen Dick. Boone, North Carolina, July 29, 2013.
Steinbrecher, Hank. Telephone interview with Bruce Allen Dick. July 31, 2013.
Udogu, Emmanuel. Interview by Bruce Allen Dick and Gregory G. Reck. Boone, North Carolina, May 14, 2013.
Usiyan, Thompson. Telephone interview with Bruce Allen Dick and Gregory G. Reck. July 7, 2012.

Online and Media

Baran, Stanley. http://www.museum.tv/eotv/sportsandte.htm.
Baseball-Reference.com. "1929 Major League Baseball Attendance & Miscellaneous." http://www.baseball-reference.com/leagues/MLB/1929-misc.shtml.
Baseball-Reference.com. "1932 Major League Baseball Attendance & Miscellaneous." http://www.baseball-reference.com/leagues/MLB/1932-misc.shtml.
Baseball-Reference.com. "1933 Major League Baseball Attendance & Miscellaneous." http://www.baseball-reference.com/leagues/MLB/1933-misc.shtml.
Baseball-Reference.com. "2013 Major League Baseball Attendance & Miscellaneous." http://www.baseball-reference.com/leagues/MLB/2013-misc.shtml.
BBC.com. "World Cup 2014: USA Coach Jurgen Klinsmann Proud after Exit." July 2, 2014. http://www.bbc.com/sport/0/football/28122263.
"Ben Millers of St. Louis Defeat Fore River for National Soccer Title." http://www.query.nytimes.com/mem/archive-free/pdf?res=9402E6DF103FE432A25753C1A9639C946195D6CF.
Boehm, Charles. "Jurgen Klinsmann Gushes Over Clint Dempsey." July 2, 2013. http://www.mlssoccer.com/news/article/2013/06/02/jurgen-klinsmann-gushes-over-clint-dempsey-one-best-players-usmnt-history.
Borg, Simon. "Was That Cristiano Ronaldo Flirting with MLS?" http://www.mlssoccer.com/blog/post/2012/08/03/was-cristiano-ronaldo-flirting-mls.
Bondy, Filip. "'World' Beats Reunified German Soccer Team." April 1, 1990. http://www.community.seattletimes.nwsource.com/archive/?date=19900401&slug=1064097.
Borden, Sam. "High School Players Forced to Choose in Soccer's New Way/" March 2, 2012. http://www.nytimes.com/2012/03/04/sports/soccer/soccers-all-year-model-forces-high-school-players-to-choose.html.
_____. "A U.S. Soccer Star's Declaration of Independence." April 10, 2013. http://www.nytimes.com/2013/04/11/sports/soccer/megan-rapinoe-does-it-her-way-in-us-and-in-france.html.
Brick, Kate, et al. "Mexican and Central American Immigrants in the United States." http://www.migrationpolicy.org/pubs/MexCentAmimmigrants.pdf.
Briggs, Simon. "England v USA: Fabio Capello's Men Need to Fear Lesson of Belo Horizonte." June 11, 2010. http://www.telegraph.co.uk/sport/football/teams/usa/7821735/England-v-USA-Fabio-Capellos-men-need-to-fear-lesson-of-Belo-Horizonte.html.
Bundesliga. "10 Years of Academies." http://www.static.bundesliga.de/media/native/autosync/dfl_leistungszentren2011_gb.pdf.
Carlisle, Jeff. "U.S. Soccer overhauls its youth programs." January 29, 2009. http://www.soccernet.espn.go.com/columns/story?id=614020&cc=5901.
_____. "USSF models youth development on a mix of foreign concept." February 5, 2009. Soccernet.com. http://www.soccernet.espn.go.com/print?id=616267&type=story&cc=5901.
Chesser, John. "Hispanics in N.C.: Big Numbers in Small Towns." UNC Charlotte Urban Institute (2012). http://www.ui.uncc.edu/story/hispanic-latino-population-north-carolina-cities-census.
CNN. "Best Places to Live: 2012." http://www.money.cnn.com/magazines/moneymag/bestplaces/2012.

Coats and Clark. "200 Years." http://www.coatsandclark200years.com/pdf/timeline.pdf.

Cochrane, Mickey, and Len Oliver. "American College Soccer, 1946–1959: The Postwar Era." 1998. http://www.homepages.sover.net/~spectrum/collegepostwar.html.

"The Comeback: New Poll Shows Concerns of American Middle Class." March 15, 2010. http://www.abcnews.go.com/WN/abc-world-news-poll-us-middle-class-concerns/story?id=10088470.

Davis, Steve. "Klinsmann's Thoughts on U.S. Soccer's Present and Future." July 2, 2010. http://www.sbnation.com/2010/7/2/1549267/klinsmanns-thoughts-on-u-s-soccers.

Davison, Phill. "Medellin Mourns Its Murdered Sports Star." July 4, 1994. http://www.independent.co.uk/news/world/medellin-mourns-its-murdered-sports-star-1411489.html.

Dempsey, Ryan. "Klinsmann Believes Pickup and Playground Soccer Is Key to Early Success—Part 1." May 5, 2012. http://www.goal.com/en-us/news/1679/us-national-team/2012/03/05/2947800/klinsmann-believes-pickup-and-playground-soccer-is-key-to.

Dick, Bruce, Andrés Fisher, and Gregory Reck, dirs. *Offside(s): Soccer in Small-Town America*. Boone, NC, 2009. DVD.

Dorish, Joe, "Average Salaries in the NBA, NFL, MLB and NHL." http://www.sports.yahoo.com/nba/news?slug=ycn-10423863.

Eligon, John. "For M.L.S., the Sport's Future Is in the Eye of the Beholder." November 11, 2005. http://www.nytimes.com/2005/11/11/sports/soccer/11soccer.html.

ESPN. "NBA Attendance Report—2013." http://www.espn.go.com/nba/attendance/_/year/2013.

FIFA. "Germany-Argentina: Quotes." July 14, 2014. http://m.fifa.com/worldcup/matches/round=255959/match=300186501/quotes.html.

_____. "Okudera's Memories and Hopes." http://www.fifa.com/classicfootball/players/do-you-remember/newsid=1080926/index.html.

_____. "Women's World Cup-USA 1999 Overview." 2009. http://www.fifa.com/tournaments/archive/tournament=103/edition=4644/overview.html.

The Football Association. "History of the FA Cup." http://www.thefa.com/Competitions/FACompetitions/TheFACup/History/historyofthefacup.

Gammon, Clive. "The Cosmos Reach Their Goal." September 5, 1977. http://www.si.com/vault/article/magazine/MAG1092771/index.

_____. "The Joint Was Jumping." September 29, 1980. SportsIllustrated.com. http://www.si.com/vault/article/magazine/MAG1123797/index.

Goalwa.net. "Original Sounders: Soccer Bowl '77 Memories Remain in Technicolor." March 27, 2013. http://www.goalwa.wordpress.com/2013/03/27/original-sounders-soccer-bowl-77-memories-remain-in-technicolor.

"Growth of College Varsity Soccer, 1908–1999." March 14, 2000. http://www.homepages.sover.net/~spectrum/collegecount.html.

"Harry Keough: Footballer who helped beat England." February 16, 2012. http://www.independent.co.uk/news/obituaries/harry-keough-footballer-who-helped-beat-England-6945646.html.

Harvey, Randy. "Germany Reunifies—on Field." March 27, 1990. http://articles.latimes.com/1990-03-27/sports/sp-219_1_east-german.

Hersh, Phil. "W. Germany Wins a Wretched Final." July 9, 1990. http://articles.chicagotribune.com/1990-07-09/sports/9002270544_1_edgardo-codesal-argentina-mario-zagalo.

HistoryOrb.com. "Famous Deaths for Year 1951." http://www.historyorb.com/deaths/date/1951.

Holroyd, Steve. "Billy Gonsalves: The Babe Ruth of American Soccer." October 30, 1990. http://www.homepages.sover.net/~spectrum/gonsalves.html.

_____. "The First Professional Soccer League in the United States." September 4, 2000. http://homepages.sover.net/~spectrum/alpf.html.

_____. "The Year in American Soccer—1914." March 4, 2005. http://www.homepages.sover.net/~spectrum/year/1914.html.

_____. "The Year in American Soccer—1923." March 4, 2005. http://www.homepages.sover.net/~spectrum/year/1923.html.

_____. "The Year in American Soccer—1925." October 4, 2005. http://www.homepages.sover.net/~spectrum/year/1925.html.

_____. "The Year in American Soccer—1926." May 19, 2010. http://www.homepages.sover.net/~spectrum/year/1926.html.

_____. "The Year in American Soccer—1927." February 17, 2008. http://www.homepages.sover.net/~spectrum/year/1927.html.

_____. "The Year in American Soccer—1928." May 30, 2008. http://www.homepages.sover.net/~spectrum/year/1928.html.

_____. "The Year in American Soccer—1973." February 8, 2005. http://www.homepages.sover.net/~spectrum/year/1973.html.

Honigstein, Raphael. "How Germany Reinvented Itself." July 1, 2010. http://www.sportsillustrated.cnn.com/2010/soccer/world-cup-2010/writers/raphael_honigstein/07/01/germany.reinvention/index.html.

J.League. "J.League 20th Anniversary." 2013. http://www.j-league.or.jp/aboutj/pdf/2013/aboutj_eng.pdf.

Jorstad, Keith. "NWSL Attendance Watch: Week 19." August 20, 2013. http://www.equalizersoccer.com/2013/08/20/nwsl-attendance-watch-week-19.

Kassouf, Jeff. "A Quick Look at NWSL Salaries." April 11, 2013. http://www.equalizersoccer.com/2013/04/11/nwsl-salaries-national-womens-soccer-league.

Kirby, Gentry. "Pele, King of Futbol." http://www.espn.go.com/classic/biography/s/Pele.html.

Leonardis, Jason." "The McDonaldization of American Soccer." January 19, 2005. http://www.homepages.sover.net/~spectrum/mcdonald.html.

Litterer, David. "North American Soccer League (NASL) 1967–1984." July 15, 2012. http://www.homepages.sover.net/~spectrum/nasl/nasl-standings.html.

_____. "North American Soccer League I (NASL) 1967–1984." March 8, 2008. http://www.homepages.sover.net/~spectrum/naslhist.html.

_____. "Women's Soccer History in the USA: An Overview." August 17, 2011. http://www.homepages.sover.net/~spectrum/womensoverview.html.

_____. "The Year in American Soccer—1930." February 17, 2008. http://www.homepages.sover.net/~spectrum/year/1930.html.

_____. "The Year in American Soccer—1932." May 4, 2005. http://www.homepages.sover.net/~spectrum/year/1932.html.

_____. "The Year in American Soccer—1950." June 6, 2004. http://www.homepages.sover.net/~spectrum/year/1950.html.

Livability.com. "Top 10 Soccer Cities." http://www.livability.com/top-10/top-10-soccer-cities.

Local Media Marketing Solutions. "TV Basics." June 2012. www.tvb.org/media/file/TV_Basics.pdf.

Longman, Jere. "How a 'Band of No-Hopers' Forged U.S. Soccer's Finest Day." December 9, 2009. http://www.nytimes.com/2009/12/10/sports/soccer/10soccer.html.

MacDonald, J. Fred. "Sports and Television." 2009. http://www.jfredmacdonald.com/onutv/sportstv.htm.

Major League Soccer. "All-Star Game History." http://www.mlssoccer.com/history/allstar.

_____. "Players." http://www.mlssoccer.com/players.

Martin, Douglas. "Giorgio Chinaglia, Italian Star and the Cosmos' Leader, Dies at 65." http://www.nytimes.com/2012/04/03/sports/soccer/giorgio-chinaglia-italian-star-and-the-cosmos-leader-dies-at-65.html?_r=0.

MLS Players Union. "Player Salary Information." 2014. "http://www.mlsplayers.org/salary_info.html.

National Park Service. "Theodore Roosevelt Quotes." http://www.nps.gov/thro/historyculture/theodore-roosevelt-quotes.htm.

National Recreation and Park Association. http://www.nrpa.org.

NCAA. "D1 Men's Soccer: Championship History." http://www.ncaa.com/history/soccer-men/d1.

_____. "D1 Women's Soccer: Championship History." http://www.ncaa.com/history/soccer-women/d1.

NCYouthSoccer.com. http://www.ncsoccer.org.

Ng Wai-ming. "The Impact of Japanese Comics and Animation in Asia." *Journal of Japanese Trade & Industry* (July/August 2002) http://www.cuhk.edu.hk/jas/staff/benng/publications/anime1.pdf.

Phillips, David. "Gates in the J.League—a Cause for Concern? (Part 2)." July 9, 2012. http://www.jleague.co.uk/2012/07/09/gates-in-the-j-league-a-cause-for-concern-part-2.

"Population of Watauga County, North Carolina: Census 2010 and 2000 Interactive Map, Demographics, Statistics, Graphs, Quick Facts." 2010. http://www.censusviewer.com/county/NC/Watauga.

Reed, J.D. "It's Happy Days at Appy." *Sports Illustrated*, November 10, 1980. http://www.sportsillustrated.cnn.com/vault/article/magazine/MAG1123938/index.

_____. "Look at Me! I Am Giorgio Chinaglia! I Beat You!" May 21, 1979. http://www.sportsillustrated.cnn.com/vault/article/magazine/MAG1094961/index.

Salisbury, Mark. "American Attitudes Toward Soccer." July 20, 1995. Leonardis, Jason." http://www.homepages.sover.net/~spectrum/hist1.html.

Scarletknights.com. "The First Intercollegiate Game—November 6, 1869." http://www.scarletknights.com/football/history/first-game.asp.

Schultz, Tom. "Week 15 Attendance Update." June 30, 2014. http://www.mlsattendance.blogspot.com.

Segura, Melissa. "A Gringo's Game." May 24, 2010. http://www.si.com/vault/article/magazine/MAG1169764/index.

_____. "Texas Tough: Dempsey's Upbringing in Naco-Nowhere Led to U.S. Dream." June 9, 2010. http://www.sportsillustrated.cnn.com/2010/soccer/world-cup-2010/writers/melissa_segura/06/09/dempsey/1.html.

Shubert, Atika. "Hidetoshi Nakata Talkasia Transcript." Interview with Hidetoshi Nakata. October 18, 2005. http://www.edition.cnn.com/2005/WORLD/asiapcf/10/18/talkasia.nakata.script.

Smith, Chris. "Major League Soccer's Most Valuable Teams." November 20, 2013. http://www.forbes.com/sites/chrissmith/2013/11/20/major-league-soccers-most-valuable-teams.

"Soccer as a Popular Sport: Putting Down Roots in Japan." September 2006. www.tjf.or.jp/eng/content/japaneseculture/32soccer.htm.

The Soccer Mom Manual. "Soccer Salaries: How Much Do Soccer Players?" Make soccer mommanual.com/soccer-salaries-how-much-do-soccer-players-make.

SportsIllustrated.com. "MLS Announces Expansion Team New York City FC." http://www.si.com/soccer/2013/05/21/mls-expansion-team-new-york-city-fc.

Springfield, Tom. "14 Classic Johan Cruyff Quotes Explained." February 25, 2013. http://www.isleofholland.com/read/sports/14-classic-johan-cruyff-quotes-explained.

Taylor, Daniel. "A True Tale of Sorrow as Dempsey Forms His Own Dream Team with Lost Sister." November 23, 2007. http://www.theguardian.com/football/2007/nov/24/newsstory.fulham.

TeachUSHistory.org. "Gottfried Duden Recommends Immigrating to Missouri." http://www.teachushistory.org/nineteenth-century-immigration/resources/duden-recommends-immigrating.

Tomaszewicz, Matthew. "Why Would Clint Dempsey Move from Spurs to the Seattle Sounders?" Augst 7, 2013. www.theguardian.com/football/the-shin-guardian-blog/2013/aug/07/clint-dempsey-tottenham-hotspur-seattle-sounders.

UEFA. "East and West come together in Germany." November 19, 2010. www.uefa.com/memberassociations/association=ger/news/newsid=1564918.html.

Wahl, Grant. "Seattle's Clint Dempsey Opens Up About His Move Back to MLS." April 12, 2013. http://www.sportsillustrated.cnn.com/soccer/news/20130812/clint-dempsey-seattle-sounders-mls-interview.

Watauga County (NC) Parks and Recreation Department." "Watauga County Parks and Recreation Comprehensive Systemwide Plan, 2010-2019." www.wataugacounty.org/main/App_Pages/Dept/ParksRec/Forms/Parks_and_Rec_Master_Plan_2010-2019.pdf.Wikipedia. "List of Major League Soccer Stadiums." http://en.wikipedia.org/wiki/List_of_Major_League_Soccer_stadiums.

Wetzel, Dan. "Clinton Hops on U.S. Soccer Bandwagon." June 23, 2010, http://www.sports.yahoo.com/news/clinton-hops-u-soccer-bandwagon-204400660—spt.html.

Witz, Billy. "Deals Show M.L.S. Is No Longer an Afterthought." January 9, 2014. http://www.nytimes.com/2014/01/10/sports/soccer/deals-show-mls-is-no-longer-an-afterthought.html.

_____. "Most Popular Soccer Team in the U.S.: Mexico?" May 6, 2010. http://www.nytimes.com/2010/05/07/sports/soccer/07soccer.html.

Worldfootball.net. http://www.worldfootball.net.

Index